Kierkegaard's Dialectic of the Imagination

American University Studies

Series V
Philosophy

Vol. 71

PETER LANG
New York • Bern • Frankfurt am Main • Paris

David J. Gouwens

Kierkegaard's
Dialectic of the Imagination

PETER LANG
New York • Bern • Frankfurt am Main • Paris

Library of Congress Cataloging-in-Publication Data

Gouwens, David Jay
   Kierkegaard's dialectic of the imagination / David J.
Gouwens.
     p. cm. – (American university studies. Series V,
Philosophy ; vol. 71)
    Bibliography: p.
    Includes index.
    1. Kierkegaard, Soren, 1813-1855. 2. Imagination –
History – 19th century. 3. Romanticism – Germany.
4. Idealism, German. I. Title. II. Series.
B4377.G68   1989   128'.3 – dc19   88-9354
ISBN 0-8204-0853-0   CIP
ISSN 0739-6392

CIP – Titelaufnahme der Deutschen Bibliothek

Gouwens, David J.:
Kierkegaard's dialectic of the imagination /
David J. Gouwens. – New York; Bern; Frank-
furt am Main; Paris: Lang, 1988.
  (American University Studies: Ser. 5,
Philosophy; Vol. 71)
  ISBN 0-8204-0853-0

NE: American University Studies / 05

Printed by Weihert-Druck GmbH, Darmstadt, West Germany

ACKNOWLEDGMENTS

Many persons have assisted me in this study. Professors Paul L. Holmer and Don E. Saliers first awakened and guided my interest in Kierkegaard's thought. Professors Hans W. Frei and Karsten Harries introduced me to the Romantic and Idealist background to Kierkegaard. Professors Louis Dupré and Gene Outka provided helpful criticism and encouragement. I am also grateful to the following persons for their personal, professional, and technical assistance: Professor Leslie Ellen Moore, Susanna Knoble, Ann Chambers, Robin Mayne, David Mayfield, and my colleagues at Brite Divinity School, Professors Sharon Iverson and Mark G. Toulouse. I am indebted to Brite Divinity School, Texas Christian University, for providing me with a summer research grant.

The Journal of Religious Ethics has kindly granted permission to reprint portions of an earlier version of Chapter V, which appeared as "Kierkegaard on the Ethical Imagination," The Journal of Religious Ethics 10/2 (Fall 1982) 204-20. I also gratefully acknowledge permission to quote from the following translations of Søren Kierkegaard's works protected by copyright: Concluding Unscientific Postscript, trans. David F. Swenson and Walter Lowrie, copyright 1941, © 1969 by Princeton University Press; Either/Or, Vol. 1, trans. David F. Swenson and Lillian Marvin Swenson, copyright 1959 by Princeton University Press; Either/Or, Vol. 2, trans. Walter Lowrie, copyright 1959, © 1972 by Howard A. Johnson, published by Princeton University Press; Fear and Trembling and Repetition, trans. Howard V. Hong and Edna H. Hong, copyright 1983 by Princeton University Press; Philosophical Fragments and Johannes Climacus, trans. Howard V. Hong and Edna H. Hong, copyright 1985 by Princeton University Press; The Sickness Unto Death, trans. Howard V.

TABLE OF CONTENTS

INTRODUCTION

Describing himself in The Point of View for My Work as an Author (1848) as a "poet-dialectician," Søren Kierkegaard looks back on his youth and reflects on his most distinctive intellectual qualities--imagination and dialectic:

> My imagination and my dialectic constantly had material enough to operate with, and time enough, free from all bustle, to be idle. For long periods I have been employed with nothing else but the performance of dialectical exercises with an adjunct of imagination, trying out my mind as one tunes an instrument--but I was not really living.[1]

Evident here is a person of self-confidence, aware of his gifts, but at the time of which he writes, not yet clear on how to use those gifts. The essay later reports how Kierkegaard, under divine Governance as he believed, came to train his imagination and dialectic. The "tuning of the instrument" was the preparation for his entire authorship.[2]

Kierkegaard correctly identified his primary gifts as imagination and dialectic: his literature is a remarkable blend of both imaginative richness and dialectical skill. But the relation between "imagination" and "dialectic" is even more intimate than the Point of View passage suggests. It is not that for Kierkegaard the imagination is simply a gift of genius he happened to possess in abundance. Rather, this study argues that for Kierkegaard the imagination is itself a central human capacity basic to being a person and that Kierkegaard's philosophical and literary analyses of the imagination reveal this capability's conceptual shape; the imagination is not inchoate, but describable in a "dialectical" way. To say that Kierkegaard develops a dialectic of the imagination means that he describes various uses of the imagination, and also, following Plato's definition of dialectic, sees these uses in their interconnection.[3]

Kierkegaard never wrote a treatise on "the concept of the imagination," as he did on the concepts of irony, anxiety, and despair, and perhaps because his comments on the imagination are usually ad hoc and occasional, his understanding of the imagination has not been analyzed at greater length as a concept possessing a dialectic. Nonetheless, because his reflections on the imagination are never accidental, and possess remarkable consistency and detail, Kierkegaard's writings do exhibit a dialectic of the imagination. The aim of this study is to analyze Kierkegaard's dialectic of the imagination by allowing his reflections to stand out clearly in their interconnectedness.

To do this we must avoid two main dangers. First, because Kierkegaard is not only a philosopher but also a poet, psychologist, and religious writer, any treatment of his understanding of the imagination must take these multiple roles seriously and avoid viewing the concept too narrowly, merely as a technical philosophical term. Conversely, we must not suppose that Kierkegaard uses the term in a loose sense without close definition.

Too much of the secondary literature falls into one or the other error, as we will see in more detail throughout this study. We will argue that to appreciate the breadth of Kierkegaard's understanding of the imagination, the various dimensions of the term--philosophical, psychological, religious, and literary-- must be kept in view. We will focus on outlining the structure of the imagination's dialectic in its aesthetic, philosophical, and religious dimensions, yet we will analyze as well some of Kierkegaard's literary prototypes, characters who embody various psychological types of imagination.

We will maintain, too, that because of the religious teleology that emerges in the literature, Kierkegaard always has in view the relation of the imagination to God. On the one hand, he is consistently careful to criticize any claims that the imagination leads to God; on the other, he is convinced that a cultivated, controlled imagination is a condition for possessing an intentional relationship to God.

The imagination is a complex and protean category, not only in its philosophical and literary history, but in common parlance as well. To orient ourselves to the complexities we will encounter, it will be helpful to discriminate certain simple senses of the word.

1. To "imagine" can mean having or entertaining "pictures in the mind." The verbal form "imagining" is common here. Often such imagining is taken to be an intentional activity. If asked to picture Copenhagen, I can do so, whether or not I have been to Copenhagen. But such imagining can be on the mere borderline of intentional activity; in daydreaming, one can have a sense of images flowing before "the mind's eye." There is a kind of passivity to daydreaming that is akin to play and restfulness, and that passivity may lead one (critically or not) to contrast the imagination with active "perception" or "thought." Thus, a contrast emerges between "perception" directed to the "real world" and "imagining" directed to an "unreal" or "possible" world; or if the opposition is between "thought" and "imagining," a contrast develops often between thought's "rationality" and the imagination's "irrationality."

2. From this contrast between the empirical or rational and the imaginative there easily emerges a wider contrast between a "descriptive" language or form of consciousness and an "imaginative" or "poetic" language or form. One may say that language empirically or rationally used is "descriptive," whereas "imaginative" or "poetic" language is "metaphorical," a "stretched" use of language that is often seen either as a corruption of descriptive language or consciousness, or a liberation from empirical or rational restraints.

3. It is not adequate, however, to define the imagination as an activity of "picturing in the mind"; the imagination can be understood as a capacity. Indeed,

since Gilbert Ryle's <u>The Concept of Mind</u>, the notion that the imagination consists in mental picturing has been largely discredited. Instead, Ryle argues, imagination indicates how one does something. In one of Ryle's examples, when children play at being bears, they do not necessarily picture their hairy paws; "imagination" describes rather how they growl and swipe with their "paws."4

Hence, it becomes possible to see many different sorts of activities as imaginative: one can be imaginative not only in creating "pictures in the mind," but in writing, painting, telling a story, planning a day's excursion, or thinking of a person one loves. This does not mean that one must entertain a mental image, but rather that creativity and spontaneity attend the activity.

4. More particularly, having "imagination" can mean possessing a <u>capacity for fiction</u>. This can be simply a capacity to imagine oneself in different circumstances; it can also be a capacity for story, or a sophisticated and cultivated capacity for entertaining "unreal possibilities."

5. "Imagination" may mean, of course, the capacity enabling one to produce or enjoy <u>the arts</u>. But then the question arises, what role does this capacity for the aesthetic play in the wider texture of a person's life? Is imagination simply an adornment, or is it part of one's education? Indeed, is the highest capacity of a person that which elevates him or her above all practical concerns or gives refuge from the pain of life?

6. This leads us to another sense of the term, in which "imagination" denotes more than how one does something, or a capacity for fiction, or a predilection for the arts, but also a <u>capacity of the entire person</u> and the basis of important human qualities. As such, we use the concept in many contexts. In the arts, for example, we may use the term "imaginative" to describe not only what one does, or how one does it, but also who one is; we say not only that

"Rembrandt paints imaginatively" when we describe his technique and style, but we also say that "Rembrandt is an imaginative person." In our moral lives, we rightly say that if a person lacks imagination, he or she will lack sympathy as well. We can say that such a person not only "lacks imagination," but is "an unimaginative person," lacking a basic requirement for being ethical.

Thus, the adjective "imaginative" exists on a continuum; it describes what one does, how one does something, and finally it describes the entire person. In short, "imaginative" can denote a disposition, a long-term propensity in behavior and thought. The "imagination" proves to be an almost insistently expansive concept.

7. But just how expansive is the concept? The imaginative powers of the person--the ability to stand in another age or place by means of the imagination, the ability to recall the past or project into the future--seem at times to push to the limits of human possibility. In the beautiful and the sublime, so urgently investigated by eighteenth-century aestheticians and celebrated by the Romantics, it is especially tempting to say that the imagination gives a final sense of the wholeness of the world and of oneself. A person's imagination can even appear to deliver, in some way, a union with the transcendent. Whether the imagination can do this, or whether the dreams of the imagination's union with the divine are "vain imaginings," is as much a matter of dispute in our own age as in Kierkegaard's.

With these distinctions in mind, we can now survey our investigation of Kierkegaard's own understanding of the imagination. In Part I (Chapters I-III) we will place Kierkegaard in the polemical context in which he attacked so much of the common Romantic and Idealist understanding of the imagination. Chapter I will relate briefly the history of the increasing expansion of the imagination in philosophy and literature from Kant to the early German Romantics. In Chapter

II, we will see how the young Kierkegaard grappled seriously with this Romantic tradition, culminating in his dissertation, The Concept of Irony, in which he attacks Friedrich Schlegel, Ludwig Tieck, and K. W. F. Solger as paradigms of the broader phenomenon of the Romantic imagination. Chapter III will examine the other side of Kierkegaard's two-edged polemic, directed against "the System" for its denigration of the imagination in favor of reason. In Chapters I-III, then, we will see how Kierkegaard polemically defines his own understanding of the imagination against his contemporaries.

In Part II (Chapters IV-VI) we will step back from the polemical definition of the problem to examine Kierkegaard's own corrective. His solution is to attain clarity on both the necessity and limits of the imagination by examining its manifold functions in the stages or spheres of existence. We will argue that the key concept here is Kierkegaard's notion in The Sickness Unto Death that the imagination is "the capacity instar omnium," the capacity for all capacities. In using Kierkegaard's stages to trace the permutations of the imagination, the aim is not to impose a false consistency or structure on Kierkegaard's reflections on the imagination; rather, because the stages exhibit the relations among diverse ways of being imaginative, the aim is to show the overarching dialectical relations within this diversity. From an examination of the stages, Kierkegaard will emerge as a modern figure who appreciates the various contexts in which one is imaginative. In contrast to the Romantics and Idealists who either laud or condemn "the imagination," Kierkegaard presents a nuanced analysis of the different ways one may exercise the imagination: the "imagination" proves to be not a simple capacity, but a dialectically complex concept that can name an activity, a capacity or faculty, a long-term disposition of a person, a medium (especially the poet's medium), and a passion.

Chapter IV will examine the place of the imagination in logic and cognition, as well as in the entire aesthetic sphere of existence. Chapter V will turn to Kierkegaard's understanding of the place of the imagination in the ethical sphere of subjectivity by examining Judge William's reflections on the actual and ideal selves. In Chapter VI we will look at the increasingly complex dialectic of the imagination in the religious spheres, especially Kierkegaard's understanding of the role of the imagination in Christian faith. Throughout this study the aim will be to allow Kierkegaard's voice to stand forth clearly, and to investigate the implications of his suggestive remark that the imagination is "the capacity _instar omnium_."

NOTES TO INTRODUCTION

[1] Søren Kierkegaard, The Point of View for My Work as an Author, trans., introd., and notes Walter Lowrie, ed. and pref. Benjamin Nelson, Cloister Library (New York: Torchbook-Harper, 1962) 80 (hereafter, PV).

[2] Kierkegaard's one-time secretary and companion, Israel Levin, notes the same intense imaginativeness, but describes it as almost pathological. "Generally he lived in a world of imagination and empty reflections which seized upon everything and transformed it in every possible way, examining it from all sides and reflecting upon it. He never understood himself, in his intellectual activity he sought nourishment for his infinite yearning. The idea itself was enough for him, he imagined himself into every sort of existence. . . . That is why he sought release in reveries and poetic images, and, with his gift for languages and his demonic imagination, the effect he achieved was astonishing. . . . His imagination was so vital that it seemed he saw pictures before his very eyes. It was as though he lived in a world of the spirit, and with a remarkable impropriety and eccentricity he could depict the most frightful things in a degree of vividness which was terrifying. . . ." "Remarks concerning S. Kierkegaard 1858 and 1869"--dictated; reproduced from Steen Johansen's Erindringer om Søren Kierkegaard (Recollections of Søren Kierkegaard) (Copenhagen: Reitzel, 1955) 33-38, quoted in Henning Fenger, Kierkegaard, The Myths, and Their Origins: Studies in the Kierkegaardian Papers and Letters, trans. George C. Schoolfield (New Haven: Yale UP, 1980) 15-16. Levin's implication that Kierkegaard's own imagination was somehow pathological is not our concern, since a psychological account of a thinker's imagination is not the same as that thinker's philosophical and literary account of the imagination or even use of the imagination. Our concern is with

Kierkegaard's understanding of the imagination as a human capacity. On the limits of a psychological approach to studying Kierkegaard, see Mark C. Taylor, Kierkegaard's Pseudonymous Authorship: A Study of Time and the Self (Princeton: Princeton UP, 1975) 14-15.

3 Gregor Malantschuk, Kierkegaard's Thought, trans. Howard V. Hong and Edna H. Hong (Princeton: Princeton UP, 1971) vi, 116-17. On "dialectic" in imagination, see also James Engell, The Creative Imagination: Enlightenment to Romanticism (Cambridge: Harvard UP, 1981), and on Kierkegaard's use of dialectic, David F. Swenson, "The Existential Dialectic of Søren Kierkegaard," Something About Kierkegaard, ed. Lillian Marvin Swenson (Minneapolis: Augsburg, 1941) 71-94.

4 Gilbert Ryle, The Concept of Mind (New York: Barnes, 1949) 245ff.

PART ONE: DIALECTIC AGAINST THE AGE

CHAPTER ONE

The Early German Romantics on the Imagination

> The understanding . . . knows only of the Universe;
> let the imagination rule, and you have a God.
> --Friedrich Schlegel, Ideen 8

At the end of the Concluding Unscientific Postscript, Kierkegaard issues his well-known request not to "lay a dialectical hand" upon his authorship.[1] Despite all his protests, Kierkegaard feared that scholars would attempt to "understand" his thought by placing it within an historical account of the network of influences on him. But for Kierkegaard, historical study is not the proper medium for approaching his literature. To begin a study of Kierkegaard by a rehearsal of the intellectual history prior to him therefore immediately raises the question whether such an approach is appropriate to his writings.

Kierkegaard's warning is not simply intellectual pride on his part, a misanthropic unwillingness to avow connections between himself and other thinkers. He acknowledged his intellectual debts to Plato, Aristotle, Lessing, Hamann, and Trendelenburg in particular. He even admitted with appreciation Hegel's influence on his thought. Writing in his journal in 1845, Kierkegaard says:

> I here request the reader's attention for an observation I have often wished to make. Do not misunderstand me, as if I fancied myself to be a devil of a thinker who would remodel everything etc. Such thoughts are as far from my mind as possible. I feel what for me at times is an enigmatical respect for Hegel; I have learned much from him, and I know very well that I can still learn much more from him when I return to him again.[2]

Kierkegaard's warning against an historical approach to his authorship is, rather, a recommendation on how to read his pages, a reminder that an historical approach to the literature can obscure two points. First, Kierkegaard urges that understanding his literature in terms of historical antecedents is an obstacle to true philosophical, subjective understanding. Kierkegaard's conviction is that understanding his literature requires a "primitivity" on the part of the reader. To be a thinker, for Kierkegaard, means not tracing the history of intellectual influences; to be a thinker means possessing a passion for thought and for a congruity between thought and life--passions he found characteristic of Greek philosophy, of whom Socrates was the model. Second, Kierkegaard believed that his intellectual concerns were not those of his contemporaries. His reflections were outside the mainstream of the Western tradition--certainly outside the mainstream of the Hegelian-inspired rise of philosophy of history and historical theology.

Some historians of thought have recognized this clearly. Claude Welch, in his study of nineteenth-century Protestant thought, gives Kierkegaard a place at the end of his book in a separate chapter. Welch says that although "the central problems of mid-nineteenth-century theology were also his problems," Kierkegaard does not fit easily into text-book generalizations:

> To select and organize aspects of Kierkegaard's thought from the standpoint of the mid-nineteenth-century theological scene is of course to give a one-sided interpretation. In other ways, he quite escapes the dominant tendencies of the time and belongs to no age.[3]

There is, however, an historical approach to the Kierkegaard literature that can respect his warning. It can recognize that historical understanding is not the same as primitive understanding, and that Kierkegaard is an independent thinker at once conversant with the intellectual issues of his day and "polemically poised" against the dominant intellectual atmosphere. He wrestles dialectically both with and against the problems of the day, often taking the material of current discussions and creatively reworking it in unexpected ways.

Kierkegaard's simultaneous familiarity with his contemporaries and his polemical stance against them is especially evident in his concept of the imagination. For this reason, it may be useful and even congruent with his thought to begin with an historical account of Kierkegaard's struggle with Romanticism and Idealism. The argument in this and the next two chapters will be that in the course of his polemic against Romanticism and Idealism Kierkegaard works out the basic elements of his own concept of the imagination.

In 1841 the young Kierkegaard appended this footnote to the section of his dissertation, The Concept of Irony, in which he attacked Friedrich Schlegel's novel Lucinde:

> That the imagination alone rules is repeated throughout the whole of Lucinde. Now who is such a monster that he is unable to delight in the free play of imagination? But it does not follow from this that the whole of life should be given over to imagination. When the imagination is allowed to rule in this way it prostrates and anesthetizes the soul, robs it of all moral tension, and makes of life a dream.[4]

This comment goes to the heart of Kierkegaard's understanding of the Romantic imagination. The imagination is the source of the play of spirit and mind, and as such one can delight in it, but one cannot devote one's whole life to the imagination, for it will in the end make of life a dream.

There is nothing remarkable by itself in Kierkegaard's statement of the need for a balanced imagination, one that attempts to give the imagination its due, and yet demands that life not be a dream. But his position takes on added force when one sees it against the background of the resurgent Romantic interest in the imagination that permeated poetic practice, metaphysics, epistemology, psychology, aesthetics, and religion in the early part of his century. "Imagination" in Romantic thought had become a central category, complex and subtle in its permutations. It was not only the heart of poetic creativity, but also the central human faculty and the locus of the Romantic quest for wholeness, a wholeness in which the world is poeticized and redeemed, and in which the individual is even able to find union with the infinite. In criticizing Schlegel's "imagination," therefore, Kierkegaard orients himself against this entire tradition. As we will see further in the next chapter, Kierkegaard's criticism becomes even more interesting when it is seen against the background of his own struggles with the Romantic spirit in his early development as thinker and poet. In attacking the Romantic imagination, Kierkegaard wrestles with a pattern of thought that he finds vivifying and intriguing, and if in the last analysis it is seductive and enervating, he learns much from the Romantics that he incorporates into his own thought and literary activity.

Our task in this chapter is to set the stage for Kierkegaard's attack on the imagination in The Concept of Irony, by gaining a sense of the motives and content of the "Romantic imagination" against which Kierkegaard struggles. We will begin by sketching the rise of the imagination in Kant, J. G. Fichte, and Schelling to a central category of thought. Then we will turn to a more detailed analysis of the full flowering of the imagination in the early German Romantics whom Kierkegaard attacks in his dissertation: Friedrich Schlegel, Ludwig Tieck, and K. W. F. Solger.

The intellectual background of early German Romanticism

The starting point for a study of the intellectual sources of the Romantic imagination can be conveniently located in the thought of Immanuel Kant.[5] This is not to say, of course, that purely poetic developments were not also at work; the interplay of poetic and intellectual influences is complex in German Romanticism. But Romanticism was self-consciously philosophical, drawing inspiration from the critical philosophy's new interest in the powers and capacities of the person. Kant's thought on the imagination was a seedbed for the thinking of both Idealists and Romantics who, going beyond Kant, placed the imagination in the center of their understanding of what it means to be a human being.

Kant, in retrospect, helped effect a revolution in aesthetics, establishing the imagination at the center of epistemological and aesthetic concerns. As Alfred Baeumler has written, eighteenth-century thought prior to Kant saw the imagination as an irrational factor both in the notion of the person and in aesthetics.[6] Neither continental rationalism, with its emphasis on clear and distinct ideas, nor British empiricism, with its stress on the concreteness and vividness of sense-impressions, could adequately account for the faculty of imagination or for aesthetics as a realm of activity. For rationalism, the imagination did not possess the clarity of rational ideas; for empiricism, the imagination seemed to lack the concreteness and vividness of sense-impressions.

Kant's answer to these difficulties is not to dismiss the imagination for this alleged irrationality, but to vindicate the imagination by redefining the criteria of "rationality" in aesthetics, so that one is not tempted to judge the imagination by the standards of either rationalism or empiricism. The brilliance of his approach is that he undercuts both rationalist and empiricist standards. He argues that the judgment of taste is just that--a judgment--universal and binding (in answer to the rationalists) but found in the human subject, not in the object (in answer to the empiricists). In this reevaluation of the imagination, Kant is at once an Enlightenment figure who summarizes the polite aesthetics of his century, yet he also opens the way for nineteenth-century aesthetics. Aesthetics may not be a realm of cognitive truth, but it is a discrete and ordered realm of human experience. Yet Kant turns the interest of philosopher and artist both to the subjective aspects of aesthetic judgment.

The Critique of Pure Reason (1781 and 1787) and the Critique of Judgment (1790) exhibit a careful but ever increasing role for the imagination. In the first critique, Kant links the imagination to the control of the understanding, but, importantly, defines the functions of the imagination as productive as well as reproductive.[7] The imagination operates in a receptive, "reproductive" way, for example, connecting particular sense-impressions into a series in an empirical "association of ideas." But as a logical condition for this reproductive imagination, there is also an actively "productive" imagination possessing a higher transcendental function necessary for empirical experience and the association of ideas. To simplify Kant's argument, it is the productive imagination, linked with understanding, that helps render sensation into unified, ordered experience. The imagination in understanding applies the categories to the manifold of sensation, "synthesizing" the manifold into an unambiguous structure of space and time. It at once orders appearance as the self's experience and also applies to appearance the categories of space and time; appearances can thereby be experienced not simply in a raw diversity, but in unity and relation. The imagination's particular function in understanding is to fit sensation into the categories of space and time. For example, in perceiving a sequence in time, the imagination retains the first event in the sequence when it has past, and thus enables the mind to connect it with the next event in the sequence. While Kant sometimes treats the imagination as an aspect of understanding, at other times he can see it more expansively, as a faculty in its own right, linking understanding and sensibility, self-consciousness and consciousness. Kant even suggests in places that the imagination is the common root of understanding and sensibility.[8] In any event, "pure imagination, which conditions all <u>a priori</u> knowledge, is . . . one of the fundamental faculties of the human soul."[9]

But it is in the <u>Critique of Judgment</u> that the imagination takes on monumental importance in Kant's philosophy. Kant increases the role of the imagination so that in addition to its close relation with understanding in the first critique, it also becomes in the <u>Critique of Judgment</u> a key to accounting for teleological and aesthetic judgments. Even more important, the imagination comes very close indeed to healing the breach between two Kantian accounts of the person: the first, that the person is an element in mechanistic nature, and the second, that the person is seen in terms of freedom. The question remains, however, as to how these two accounts can be united. Should such a healing be effected by the imagination in aesthetic judgments, nature and freedom, the finite and the infinite, would be reconciled: the imagination would grasp reality in an apprehension of a "positive Infinite." While Kant himself refuses to make such a claim for the imagination, there are elements in the <u>Critique of Judgment</u> that contribute to a vision of the imagination as an organ for the divine, and the pre-eminent faculty for attaining wholeness.

The elements for this vision are found in Kant's discussion of the imagination's place in the judgments of the beautiful and the sublime. In the judgment of the beautiful, the understanding and the imagination engage in free play; the necessity of the understanding and the freedom of the imagination are united in the judgment of beauty so that one experiences an endless, reposeful infinitude that releases the individual, momentarily, from the demands of duty.

There is here a positive infinitude, but one in which there is no content--only the play of faculties.

The second realm for the expansion of the imagination is in the judgment of the sublime; here, one can argue, Kant comes closest to asserting an infinitude of the self that succeeds in grasping reality. In the analytic of the sublime, Kant points out that the experience of the sublime, whether mathematical or dynamical, exhibits a strange trait. Unlike the experience of the beautiful, where the imagination and the understanding are together in play, in the sublime the understanding is overwhelmed. For example, if one contemplates the infinite vault of heaven or the raging ocean, this entails ideas that the imagination cannot present to the understanding, and so the imagination struggles with reason as the faculty of ideas, the "faculty expressing the independence of absolute totality."[10] In one sense the imagination fails here too, for it is unable "to make the representation of the sense adequate to these (ideas)."[11] Yet in another sense the imagination is not overwhelmed, but is confirmed in its dignity and freedom. Kant writes:

> The satisfaction in the sublime of nature is then only negative (while that in the beautiful is positive), viz. a feeling that the imagination is depriving itself of its freedom, while it is purposively determined according to a different law from that of its empirical employment. It thus acquires an extension and a might greater than it sacrifices--the ground of which, however, is concealed from itself--while yet it feels the sacrifice or the deprivation and, at the same time, the cause to which it is subjected.[12]

Important to note here is that "the imagination acquires an extension and a might greater than it sacrifices." Despite the fact that the understanding reaches its limit and is overwhelmed in attempting to comprehend the sublime, Kant may be hinting here that our ability to apprehend the limitless in the imagination is undefeated.[13] We experience our human dignity in that we are confirmed in our capacity as moral beings to match both the internal and external natures,

> for the imagination, although it finds nothing beyond the sensible to which it can attach itself, yet feels itself unbounded by this removal of its limitations; and thus that very abstraction is a presentation of the Infinite, which can be nothing but a mere negative presentation, but which yet expands the soul.[14]

The imagination in the sublime is now truly itself in experiencing freedom unbounded, expanding the soul, yet this sense of the unbounded is finally only a negative infinite. It does not achieve the repose belonging to the beautiful, but strives without success for a positive representation, since the imagination and the reason, in the experience of the sublime, are in conflict. There is no "what" in the imagination's experience, but only the sense of the apeiron, the boundless, "the ground of which . . . is concealed from itself." Thus, Kant refuses to conclude that the imagination delivers an epiphany. The imagination does not give access to the positive Infinite, but only a sense of the powers and dignity of the self. For Kant an aesthetic religion is finally impossible; the highest goals of the self remain in the ethical, where the powers and dignity of the self can be truly exercised. The hope of aesthetic repose in union with the Infinite, effected by the imagination, is finally but a dream, "yet expands the soul."

Those who followed Kant--such as J. G. Fichte, Schelling, and the Romantics--saw his reflections on the imagination as a challenge and a possibility. The challenge was to resolve the problem, as they saw it, of the continuing split between nature and freedom; the possibility was to extend even further Kant's expansion of imagination as an answer to that challenge. In Fichte and Schelling, in different ways, the imagination comes to the center; their epistemology, anthropology, and metaphysics find in the imagination the clue to a unified, total philosophy.[15]

Fichte's and Schelling's extrapolations from the Kantian imagination, however, differ remarkably. For both, the imagination plays a central role in cognition and metaphysics, but while for Fichte the passion behind this is primarily ethical, for Schelling it is aesthetic. Fichte is the philosopher of the striving moralist, Schelling of the striving artistic genius.

In his reflections on cognition, Fichte places the imagination at the basis of the formation of the categories. Extending Kant's discussion of the place of the imagination in the application of the unity of apperception to the manifold, he argues that the imagination operates in the very formation of the categories.[16] In Ray Hart's words, Fichte believed that Kant rightly saw the

> regulative character [Gesetzmässigkeit] of the categories, i.e., their universal applicability to objects through the schematism of the synthetic imagination. In Fichte's lights, however, Kant left out of view the origin of the categories. If they are to be indisputably applicable to objects, on Fichte's view, they must originate with objects and so from an identical source.[17]

Because of this union of the categories with objects, Fichte goes beyond a phenomenology of consciousness to a metaphysics of the ego, in which the ego is the source of the whole sphere of the objective, including nature. The imagination is productive not only in a cognitive sense, as with Kant, but in a metaphysical sense as well. Furthermore, Fichte interprets the ego as a supraindividual absolute, never the finite individual self. The imagination, then, for Fichte is the absolute ego's power producing the idea of an independently existing non-ego, although this non-ego is actually dependent on the ego. Imagination is not a third force independent of the ego and the non-ego in this process, but is the activity of the ego itself, foundational to categories and objects alike.

Furthermore, and most important to the Romantics who read Fichte, the imagination reveals itself in the striving of the absolute ego. As Fichte puts it in his Basis of the Entire Theory of Science (Grundlage der gesamten Wissenschaftslehre) (1794), there is

> an impulse toward something entirely unknown which reveals itself only in a sense of need, in a feeling of dissatisfaction or emptiness which though craving to be satisfied does not indicate how it possibly might obtain satisfaction.[18]

It is this craving of the imagination that is the presupposition of all knowledge and all morality.

While Fichte expands the role of the imagination, his essential orientation is nonetheless to an ethical rather than to an aesthetic understanding of the imagination. The striving of the absolute ego in positing the non-ego is for Fichte an image of the ethical life rather than of an aesthetic striving for the infinite. The freedom of the creative "I" is a freedom based on Kant's second rather than third critique.

Schelling, like Fichte, affirms the attainment of a positive Infinite with content. But whereas Fichte makes the metaphysical imagination the basis for ethical striving, Schelling sees it as significant for art, for in art one finds the manifestation of the absolute world unity.[19] In aesthetic intuition the identity of the ideal and real, the conscious and the unconscious, occurs objectively and concretely; indeed, the aesthetic intuition is the objective and universally valid form of intellectual intuition and knowledge. Hence, it is art that shows the way to the philosopher. In a famous passage of the System of Transcendental Idealism (System des transcendentales Idealismus) (1800), Schelling writes:

> If aesthetic intuition is merely transcendental intuition become objective, it is self-evident that art is at once the only true and eternal organ and document of philosophy, which ever and again continues to speak to us of what philosophy cannot depict in external form, namely the unconscious element in acting and producing, and its original identity with the conscious. Art is paramount to the philosopher, precisely because it opens to him, as it were, the holy of holies, where burns in eternal and original unity, as if in a single flame, that which in nature and history is rent asunder, and in life and action, no less than in thought, must forever fly apart.[20]

Schelling, then, claims an advance upon Kant's analysis of artistic genius in the Critique of Judgment. Kant had noted in the third critique that the creative genius in presenting "intellectual ideas" such as creation, eternity and even love and fame, "tries, by means of imagination, which emulates the play of reason in its quest after a maximum, to go beyond the limits of experience and to present them to sense with a completeness of which there is no example in nature."[21] For Schelling the imagination does not simply emulate the play of reason in going beyond nature, but actually attains the secret of nature that is beyond unaided philosophic reason. The imagination has such power because, as Rudolf Hablützel argues, the imagination stands at the beginning and the end of Schelling's system of transcendental idealism. Experience begins before consciousness with the individual's primitive productive perception, progresses to the act of coming to consciousness with reflection and reproductive perception, and moves then to the aesthetic perception as productivity with consciousness. The importance of the imagination is that it is the subject of the whole development of the "I" from the beginning to the end, and can be spoken of as the true fundamental capacity of the self.[22]

Not surprisingly, the imagination has for Schelling a profound religious aspect as well. In his later thought, for example in Philosophical Inquiries into the Nature of Human Freedom (Philosophischen Untersuchungen über das

<u>Wesen der menschlichen Freiheit</u>) (1809), Schelling, reflecting Boehme's influence, holds that the imagination operates in the inner life of the divine. As Robert Brown writes:

> The first stage in the process whereby the being of God is produced from the ground corresponds to the point in Boehme's thought at which the <u>Ungrund</u> produces from itself a mirror in which it foresees what it might become. But, for Schelling there is born in God himself an inward, imaginative response, corresponding to this longing, which is the first stirring of divine being in its still dark depths. Through this response, God sees himself in his own image, since his imagination can have no other object than himself.[23]

Imagination becomes not only the organ of aesthetic intuition, but also the primal movement of the inner life of God. Hence, beyond the Kantian negative infinite given in the sublime, Schelling, like Fichte, affirms the attainment of a positive Infinite with content, reached, however, in aesthetic intuition. The imagination, as the sense of art, the organ of philosophy and the highest example of human freedom, is the instrument of its attainment.

In Kant, Fichte, and Schelling the imagination becomes a protean category. In this Idealist development, so stimulating to the early German Romantics, the imagination emerges as the central capacity of the person, seen not only in Kantian freedom, but in cognitive, metaphysical, and aesthetic intuition. The imagination yields the sovereign wholeness that Kant thought unattainable, a unity of the self with the world, and even a positive union with the Infinite. For Schelling, the artist is the prophet of this union, no longer the mere imitator of nature, but the genius as creator who produces a microcosm apart from the world of nature. In the Idealists' hands, the imagination is the center of an expansive, stimulating vision of human freedom, wholeness, and creativity. It is this vision of the imagination that becomes crucial to the Romantic movement.

The imagination in the early German Romantics

The aim in this section is not to investigate in detail the intricacies of Romantic art or theory, but to clarify the content of the Romantic apotheosis of the imagination against which Kierkegaard would polemicize. For the Romantics the imagination has not simply literary and literary critical uses, but also expands, partly under the influence of Idealist philosophy, partly independently, to a metaphysical, cultural-historical, and religious concept. We can now trace out that expansion, first, by describing the Romantic vision of the imagination's powers, both in the literary product as a microcosm and also in the poet's own person as a genius, possessed by both "passive" and "active" imagination. Second, we will see how the Romantics (Novalis, Friedrich Schlegel, and Schleiermacher in particular) linked the imagination to their yearning for the Infinite, and how this resulted in two distinct religious visions. Third, we will examine irony in its "subjective" and "objective" forms as particular uses of imagination integral to the Romantic religious vision. We will conclude by examining briefly Ludwig Tieck's practice of irony and K. W. F. Solger's theory of irony, both of whom, along with Friedrich Schlegel, Kierkegaard critically analyzes in The Concept of Irony.

Turning first to the imagination's powers, the Romantics used the terms "imagination," "fantasy," and the "fantastic" to describe both the form of the literary product and the powers of the poet. With regard to the work of art, Friedrich Schlegel after his early "classical" stage, reevaluated the role of the fantastic in literature, arguing that the work of art should exhibit three "poetic ideas": the "absolute fantastic," the "absolute sentimental" (the poet's emotional involvement), and the "absolute mimetic" (the realistic). The "absolute fantastic" signifies not just the imaginative content of the work, or only the imagination's role in the production of the work, but also the complex structure of Romantic poetry, its "fantastic form."[24] "Fantastic form" exhibits the fictitious, the strange, and the miraculous as typical not only of folk-literature, myth, and the literature of the revered Middle Ages, but also as a desideratum of modern poetry.[25]

The Romantics' interest in the art object's fantastic form leads them insistently to consider the origin of that imaginative form: the poet's personal creativity. While retaining interest in the art object, the Romantics locate the very essence of poetry in the psychological and spiritual state of the poet; thus, the artist's imagination becomes the focus of their reflections on poetry.

The artist is a creative genius, and the imagination is the unique faculty of that genius. Although Fichte disapproved of much of the Romantic concentration on artistic imagination rather than ethical imaginative striving, the Romantics celebrate Fichte's freedom as the essential drive of the absolute ego. For Novalis and others, the Fichtean "cult of the Ich," as Charles Taylor puts it, resounds through their work.[26] Coupled with Schelling's understanding of art as the organon for metaphysical understanding of the structure of the world itself, the Romantics conclude that it is the imagination's creativity that distinguishes the poetic genius above all others and enables one to unite the unconscious with the conscious, the subject with the object, the ideal with the real.

The power of the Romantic conception of imagination becomes more clear when one sees how for Novalis the imagination is both a passive and active capability, uniting receptivity and creativity. As passive, the productive imagination of the poet opens one to the richness of the world. But the productive imagination is also active; it is a power, subject to the will. Novalis writes: "Feeling, understanding, and reason are, so to speak, passive--just as their names signify--on the contrary, only the power of imagination [Einbildungskraft] is power--it alone is active--moving."[27]

This brings us to the second point, the infinity of Romantic longing and striving that seeks union with the Infinite. It is this combination of passive and active imagination that makes Sehnsucht, yearning, the essential mood of the Romantic poet, a yearning at once receptive and active. As Arthur Lovejoy notes, Kant's ethical ideal in the second critique makes the categorical imperative an object not of actual realization, but of endlessly progressive approximation; and Fichte incorporates this into his moral vision of the striving of the Absolute Ego.[28] The Romantics translate this striving into a Sehnsucht that stresses less Kant's and Fichte's moral imperative than the artist's endless striving in freedom. The boundlessness of the imagination in creating art, the utilization of new subjects for art that formerly were denied it by classical standards, and the sense of the freedom or Willkür of the artist, liberated from classical canons of art, lead to a new appreciation of the openness of human possibility. Just as the creative artist breaks the bonds of classical standards in the production of art, so too the artist's striving breaks all bonds: the artist's striving is itself limitless.

Just as the striving is limitless, so the object of this striving is limitless: it is the Infinite. Seeking to communicate this sense of yearning for the Infinite, Friedrich Schlegel, elaborating on Novalis' notion, formulates a pseudo-mathematical formula in which the unification of the poetic ideal (absolute fantasy, absolute sentiment, and absolute mimetic) in turn equals "God."[29] For the Romantics, the blend of active and passive imagination gives a sense of one's own inner infinity joined with the Infinite. In the passive contemplation of nature, in active poetic production, in music, and especially in the beloved--one thinks of Novalis' Hymns to the Night (Hymnen an die Nacht) in which Sophie von Kühn symbolizes the poet's yearning--the Romantic poet idealizes experience and so recovers the self.[30] This recovery of self amounts to no less than the divinization of the self. For Novalis, the poet's aim is to become deified by way of the passive-active imagination.[31]

Yet, as Jack Forstman argues, not all Romantic poets shared Novalis' boldness. The Romantic religious vision, focussed on imagination, took two different forms, depending on how they conceived this meeting of infinite striving with the Infinite. The first form of the Romantic religious vision is a religion of "transcendent" striving for the Infinite that sees the finite world as a veil hiding true reality. A second, very different religious vision holds that the Infinite is given in the experience of the finite, as its ground. The imaginative intuition in this case seeks the Infinite within the world, and does not attempt to transcend the world in the struggle to merge with the Infinite. Novalis and, increasingly, Friedrich Schlegel represent the first form, the infinite yearning that is in tension with the world and seeks to strive for the Infinite beyond the finite world. Friedrich Schleiermacher (and the early F. Schlegel) represent the second tendency.

The best symbol of the first form of Romantic religious yearning, that of striving for the Infinite beyond the finite, is the symbol of the veil of Isis, which has an interesting history during this period. Kant refers to the veil of Isis in the Critique of Judgment, and Schiller writes to Novalis in 1790 of the inscription on the pyramid at Sais: "I am everything, what was, what is, and what shall be. No mortal has lifted my veil."[32] In Schiller's poem, "The Veiled Statue of Sais" ("Das verschleierte Bild zu Sais") (1795), a student's attempt to lift the veil of

Isis, to behold ultimate reality, ends tragically: he lifts the veil, but in the morning is found unconscious, and soon dies.[33]

Yet the Romantics, with their confidence in the imagination's infinite striving, and the Infinite's openness to this striving, reconsider the possibility of lifting the veil. In <u>Ideen 1</u> Friedrich Schlegel exclaims confidently, "It's time to tear away the veil of Isis and reveal the mystery. Whoever can't endure the sight of the goddess, let him flee or perish."[34] In Novalis' uncompleted symbolic novel, <u>The Disciples at Sais</u> (<u>Die Lehrlinge zu Sais</u>) (1800), Hyacinth, the melancholic poet who travels in search of rest, courage, and love, does lift the veil, this world of partial vision and polarities. But, significantly, the active imagination finds its fulfillment in passivity; it is in a dream that Hyacinth is transported beyond space and time. In that dream world, he lifts the veil and there stands Roseblossom, his beloved, who sinks into his arms. The veil is lifted.[35]

What does Novalis mean by lifting the veil? Forstman argues that it is not quite that this world is to be left behind, but rather that the world is a tissue that obscures the vision of a higher reality, preventing the union of the infinities of beauty and the sublime that would allow the poet to become divine. For Novalis, the dream of lifting the veil means that the poet does indeed grasp the Infinite, but passively. He becomes a god, but through poetic activity united with a "heavenly quietism." In Forstman's words, for Novalis, "The deification of man takes place through the imagination. As such it is both a gift and a task."[36]

The alternative Romantic religious vision, that of Schleiermacher and the early Friedrich Schlegel, is to find in the finite world itself the revelation of the Infinite. In this view, the imagination brings the poet, not beyond the world to a merger of the self with the Infinite, but to a perception of the world itself as infused by the Infinite. The world is not so much a veil to be lifted in a transcendent vision as it is the visible symbol of the Infinite. For Friedrich Schlegel, the poetic task, then, is not to rise above the world but to create in the ideal poem a microcosm of the universe, exhibiting these same signs of the Infinite. In the Romantic aesthetic, the old notion of art as imitation or mimesis is retained to this extent: the poem is a microcosm imitating the world as macrocosm. In terms of Schlegel's formula for the poem, cited above, the poem's fantastic form reflects the world's infinite plenitude (unendliche Fülle), while the poem's sentimental content reflects the world's infinite unity (unendliche Einheit) in the embrace of eternal eros. The poem, like the world, is a "diversified chaos" united by imaginative sentiment, just as plenitude and unity are merged in the universe. So too, in the poem as in the world, the divine manifests itself; in Schlegel's words, "The universe is the poem of the Godhead."[37] In the Ideen of 1800, he sums up this faith in the imagination's power to perceive the divine in the world. Praising the young Schleiermacher, Schlegel says, "The understanding, says the author of the Speeches on Religion, knows only of the universe; let the imagination rule, and you have a God. Quite right. The imagination is man's organ for the Godhead."[38]

The irony of the Romantics, our third area of concern, is directly related to their religious vision. At first sight, the two conceptions of the imagination's role--whether as key to the self's transcendence beyond the finite world or to the Infinite within the finite world--appear contradictory. But both forms of imagination entail irony, a distancing of the self from the given world of human experience. For the "transcendent" form of Romantic religion, such as in Novalis and the later Schlegel, the finite world must be ironized in order to grasp the Infinite beyond the finite. But there is an irony too in the second, immanent form of Romantic religion, for in order to render the finite revelatory, it must be imaginatively perceived as "infinite plenitude" and "infinite unity." Within this immanent Romantic religion, irony resolves the tension between the given world and the vision of that world as infused by the Infinite.

In both forms of Romantic religion, then, irony is the poet's proper attitude to the finite world, to one's work, and to oneself. As "subjective irony" it is especially characteristic of the transcendent form of Romantic religion (although not absent from the immanent form). In subjective irony the artist hovers over his art, perhaps even consciously destroying its effect, aware of the tenuousness of human achievement, the gap between the ideal and the real, and the frequency of poetic failure.[39] Early in his career, Friedrich Schlegel points to Socrates as the figure who embodies this attitude, for Socrates "links that which is most holy with the frivolous and joyous."[40] Such irony can be frivolous and joyous because there is still exhilaration in the task of discerning the holy; seriousness and jest are united. Yet in seeking to lift the veil, subjective irony can easily turn against the poet. One can descend into madness, despairing over whether one can "name the gods" anew (Hölderlin); one can come to doubt whether one's feelings do indeed come from God (Wackenroder) or whether one's transcendent vision is any more than a mere aesthetic achievement (Novalis).[41] Ominously, the infinity of desire can encounter frustration rather than fulfillment.

Yet Romantic irony can become "objective" as well, aimed not at oneself but at the world. This objective irony can be held not only by Romantics like Novalis who seek to transcend the world, but by those who seek the Infinite within the finite world. For both, the bourgeois philistine world that fails to appreciate the imaginative ideal comes under bitingly satiric criticism. Yet here, too, there is danger, since satire can turn back on the Romantic poet, destroying Romantic feeling itself.

Ludwig Tieck's works exhibit in a complex manner this conflict between ideality and satire. Ideality can function as a goal of creative activity, seeing the phenomenal world as a clue to the divine. In the words of Oskar Walzel, Tieck's experiments with poetic form (e.g., the interchangeability of sight and sound impressions) "sought to penetrate through the mass of sense impressions to the ultimate secret which lay buried behind these myriad perceptions and . . . to grasp the truth not in the trite and obvious every-day things but in the realm of the supersensual."[42] But Tieck shifts often to another quite different mood, one of ironic detachment, critical of the world and even of Romantic sentiment. In his dramatic works, for example "Puss in Boots" ("Der gestiefelte Kater") (1797), Tieck experiments with the ironization of the work, directed at creating and then destroying illusion. As a play-within-a play, the "audience" on the stage are philistines who comment on the action before them, revealing to the true audience its own smugness and self-complacency, giving them a series of mirrors in which illusion is destroyed in an endless romantic-ironic reflection and re-reflection. The Romantic ideal leads not only to the satire of world-irony, but to a blasé suspension of the sentimental ideal itself.[43]

It is, however, Tieck's friend, K. W. F. Solger, who gives a full theoretical account of Romantic irony in both its objective and subjective forms. Solger is not a typical Romantic ironist; he disapproves, for example, of Friedrich Schlegel's irony as frivolous.[44] Nonetheless, Solger does appreciate subjective irony--not as a cavalier breaking of illusion, but as a means of understanding how ephemeral artistic accomplishment is. So too, Solger sees the importance of objective irony not only in its relativizing of the world, but in its preserving the world in artistic creativity. In an elaborate dialectic he attempts to merge subjective and objective irony in a positive form; irony is finally a creative process in which the poem, the world, and the artist are at once suspended yet retained.

Most important, Solger arrives at this union of subjective and objective irony by analyzing the creative imagination's role in art. For Solger, not only satire and comedy, but all art is ironic because it is all symbolic, reflecting a gap between the loftiness of the act of its creation and the transitoriness of the unity it achieves out of opposites. In the act of creativity, the imagination symbolizes the divine creativity in which act and achievement are unified. At the same time the poet's imagination, with subjective irony, sees the nothingness of one's own efforts.[45] Objective irony, however, represents the imagination's triumph, for in "world-irony" the art object is created. The imagination is the key to this entire dynamic, artistic process.

Solger has a complex, obscure philosophical vocabulary by which he seeks to illuminate art as symbolic creative activity, merging achievement and ironic detachment. With regard to the imagination, the essence of the matter is that Solger, like Schelling, distinguishes between Einbildungskraft (fancy) and Phantasie (imagination), but further, within the latter is the Phantasie der Phantasie (imagination of the imagination), the creative power of the artist analogous to divine creativity. It is this spontaneity of the artist as creator in the Phantasie der Phantasie that, starting with the whole as Idea, merges with the perceptive faculty of Phantasie, on its side beginning with empirical reality. These two functions of Phantasie come together in the "artistic dialectic" in such a way that Idea and reality pass into each other. With the addition of Sinnlichkeit (defined not as a system of sense perceptions, but rather as the absorption of the artist's consciousness in existence) the artistic act becomes symbolical; the artist, absorbed in the multiplicity of appearance, develops this multiplicity into universality, colored by feeling. Finally, with the addition of Verstand (understanding) the whole process is seen to be more than the general determining the particular; rather, the antitheses of general and particular enfold one another as the Idea merges with the artistic product.

For Solger, this merging of the Idea with the empirical means a dissolution of the Ideal into empirical reality. At this point, the essence of art is attained: an artistic irony is achieved that unites and relativizes Idea and reality. Irony is the final effect of art, mirrored in inspiration (Begeisterung). In irony, the Idea is dissolved into empirical reality eliciting from us a sense of our own nothingness; in inspiration, the artist nonetheless feels the divine Idea reveal itself within artistic activity.[46]

Solger's aesthetic involves also a religious vision, one that with its interaction of finite and infinite is more akin to Schleiermacher's immanent religion than to Novalis' transcendent religion. Philosophy and religion too trace the self-destruction and self-revelation of the infinite divine being in the finite--an ironic relation to the finite, to be sure, since the divine and the finite are both transformed in the process. The self-revelation of the divine is a self-sacrifice, for it is an immersion of the divine in the world. So, too, the phenomenal world is at once the arena for this divine self-sacrificing revelation, and is also itself ironically rendered into "nothingness" in face of the divine. Finite and infinite merge, coalesce, and intermingle. Not surprisingly, art, philosophy, and religion are in essence identical apprehensions of the divine, for in each of them the divine is the ultimate that confronts and destroys the world, at the same time sacrificing itself and merging with appearance. Viewed as God's self-revelation and self-sacrifice, this is religion; viewed as a revelation of the divine in appearance, it is art; viewed self-consciously, it is philosophy.[47]

In this elaborate metaphysical justification of Romantic irony, Solger gives an extensive and systematic place to the imagination. The imagination refers not only to the ambiguous striving of the poet to achieve reality, but becomes the principle for a system of thought that attempts an expansive understanding of irony as the locus for the interplay of the finite and infinite. Art, philosophy, and religion are all functions of the imagination, ironic and symbolic; yet it is preeminently in the activity of the poetic imagination that the finite world and the Ideal are united.

In his famous Athenaeumsfragment 116, sometimes called the manifesto of the young German Romantics, Friedrich Schlegel writes that Romantic poetry's

> aim and mission is, now to mingle, now to fuse poetry and prose, genius and criticism, the poetry of the educated and the poetry of the people, to make life and society poetic, to poeticize wit, to fill and saturate the forms of art with matters of genuine cultural value and to quicken them with the vibrations of humor; it embraces everything that is poetic, from the most comprehensive system of art . . . to the sigh or kiss which the poetic child expresses in artless song.[48]

Whatever their fears of the dangers of irony, the Romantics were sustained by faith in their mission to restore wholeness. Their aim was not only literary wholeness, whether in the merger of sentimental content with fantastic form, or in overcoming the Kantian conflict between genius and taste, or in unifying the finite and the Infinite in creativity. They also sought a wholeness in the lofty goal of making "life and society poetic," whether this meant transcending the finite in a vision of the Infinite, infusing the finite world with imagination, or suspending self and world in creative irony. In any case, the tendency of Romanticism was to "poeticize the world," to make everything an object of aesthetic, imaginative apprehension. As Erich Heller has written, early German Romanticism advocates an absolute poetic imperialism: poetry must conquer the world, the world must become poetry. Every aspect of the community of men--religion, science, politics--must, by direct attack or peaceful infiltration, become infused with the poetic spirit and in the end be transformed into a work of art. . . . The world will be the body of poetry, and poetry will be the body of the world.[49]

"Poetry" expands to enfold within it religion, philosophy, society, politics--the entire realm of human activity and aspiration. René Wellek rightly comments that "one must recognize how influential this cosmic extension of the meaning of poetry (with its antecedents and parallels in Plato and Shelley) became during the nineteenth century."[50]

The Romantics hope, moreover, that poetry would, in one sense or another, redeem the world.[51] Romantic aesthetics is not content to remain simply an aesthetics in the technical sense, but becomes a "theory of life" (Theorie des Lebens).[52] The Romantics reverse the restraints Kant placed on the imagination in the interests of ethics; in direct contrast, for them the aesthetic becomes the foundation of the ethical. It is not that art is didactic; Tieck especially opposed such a "philistine" understanding. Art is not the servant of moral instruction, but its foundation. The ideal is the "beautiful soul"--later analyzed so critically by Hegel in his Phenomenology of Spirit--a state of mind and heart in which the person of feeling generates a moral standard from the dictates of his or her own sensitive, individual conscience. The new ethics advocated by Friedrich Schlegel aims at an "aesthetic morality" (ästhetische Sittlichkeit) and an "aesthetic imperative" (ästhetische Imperativ) achieved through the Medium der Poesie.[53] The productive imagination is recruited not only for poetry, but for the purpose of grasping the meaning of life, history, and ethics. In this sense, the imagination is salvific and even eschatological. If imagination, writes Friedrich Schlegel, gains victory over reflection, then will arrive the fulfillment of humankind, the virtual appearance of the "messiah."[54]

Romanticism effects an apotheosis of the imagination as the foundation for a complete life-view. The promise of the imagination in Kant and Fichte is a promise of freedom. In Schelling it becomes the basis for the development of the world, and in aesthetic creativity the source of truth in philosophy. In the Romantics, the imagination is the hope of freedom and the victory of human wholeness, the vehicle of yearning for the Infinite, and the instrument of an irony that in complete sovereignty can raise one above the world--even to the point of turning against feeling itself. It was this complex elevation of the imagination that Kierkegaard, himself a young poet, later confronted in the years before he wrote his dissertation.

[1] Søren Kierkegaard, Concluding Unscientific Postscript, trans. David F. Swenson, trans. completed, introd. and notes Walter Lowrie (Princeton: Princeton UP, 1941) 554 (hereafter, CUP).

[2] Søren Kierkegaard, Søren Kierkegaard's Journals and Papers, trans. and ed. Howard V. Hong and Edna H. Hong, 7 vols. (Bloomington: Indiana UP, 1967-78), entry 1608 (VI B 54:12). Hereafter this will be cited as JP, followed by volume and entry numbers; in parentheses will follow the standard international references to Søren Kierkegaard, Søren Kierkegaards Papirer, ed. P. A. Heiberg, V. Kuhr, and E. Torsting, 20 vols., I-XI[3] (Copenhagen: Gyldendal, 1909-48), and date of the entry, if known. In the entry just quoted, Kierkegaard continues by noting that Hegel leaves one in the lurch, and that "some one who is really tested in life . . . will find Hegel comical despite all his greatness." But the admiration for Hegel was there. For an elegant account of Hegel's influence on Kierkegaard's aesthetic categories, see Stephen Crites, "Introduction," Crisis in the Life of an Actress and Other Essays in Drama, by Søren Kierkegaard, trans. with introd. and notes Stephen Crites (New York: Torchbook-Harper, 1967) 19. Three studies dealing very differently with the relation of Kierkegaard and Hegel are Niels Thulstrup, Kierkegaard's Relation to Hegel, trans. George L. Stengren (Princeton: Princeton UP, 1980), Mark C. Taylor, Journeys to Selfhood: Hegel and Kierkegaard (Berkeley: U of California P, 1980), and Stephen N. Dunning, Kierkegaard's Dialectic of Inwardness: A Structural Analysis of the Theory of Stages (Princeton: Princeton UP, 1985).

[3] Claude Welch, Protestant Thought in the Nineteenth Century, 2 vols. (New Haven: Yale UP, 1972-85) 1: 292 and n2.

4 Søren Kierkegaard, <u>The Concept of Irony, with Constant Reference to Socrates</u>, trans., introd. and notes Lee M. Capel (Bloomington: Indiana UP, 1965) 308n (hereafter, <u>CI</u>).

5 The background, of course, precedes Kant. For a comprehensive study of the developments in the concept of the imagination extending from Hobbes to Coleridge, and analyzing both British and Continental figures, see James Engell. A useful anthology of translations of Kant, Fichte, Schelling as well as Hegel and Schopenhauer is to be found in David Simpson, ed., <u>German Aesthetic and Literary Criticism: Kant to Hegel</u> (Cambridge: Cambridge UP, 1984).

6 Alfred Baeumler, <u>Kants Kritik der Urteilskraft: ihre Geschichte und Systematik</u> (Halle: Niemeyer, 1923).

7 Immanuel Kant, <u>Critique of Pure Reason</u>, trans. Norman Kemp Smith (1929; New York: St. Martin's, 1965) 142ff (A 118ff); cf. Engell 128-33.

8 Kant, <u>Pure Reason</u> 182-83 (A 141); cf. Immanuel Kant, <u>Critique of Judgment</u>, trans. and introd. J. H. Bernard, Hafner Library of Classics 14 (New York: Hafner, 1972) 184-91 (sec. 57).

9 Kant, <u>Pure Reason</u> 146 (A 124); cf.. 61-62 (A 15=B 29) and 165 (B 151-52).

10 Kant, <u>Judgment</u> 108.

11 Kant, <u>Judgment</u> 109.

12 Kant, <u>Judgment</u> 109.

13 I am indebted to Professor Karsten Harries for insights on the "triumph" of imagination in the judgment of the sublime.

14 Kant, <u>Judgment</u> 115.

15 Hegel, as we shall see in the next two chapters, sees such hopes as groundless, and turns instead to the powers of reason for a solution to the problem.

[16] Johann Gottlieb Fichte, Grundriss des Eigentümlichen der Wissenschaftslehre in Rücksicht auf das theoretische Vermögen (1795) 3, VIII, in Werke, ed. and introd. Fritz Medicus, 7 vols. (Leipzig: Eckardt, 1909-25) 1: 578ff.

[17] Ray L. Hart, Unfinished Man and the Imagination (New York: Herder, 1968) 358.

[18] Johann Gottlieb Fichte, Grundlage der gesamtem Wissenschaftslehre, I, 303, in Fichte 1: 494; see Oskar Walzel, German Romanticism, trans. Alma Elise Lussky (New York: Putnam's, 1932) 29.

[19] Walzel 54.

[20] F. W. J. Schelling, System of Transcendental Idealism (1800), trans. Peter Heath, introd. Michael Vater (Charlottesville: UP of Virginia, 1978) 231.

[21] Kant, Judgment 158.

[22] Rudolf Hablützel, Dialektik und Einbildungskraft: F. W. J. Schellings Lehre von der menschlichen Erkenntnis (Basel: Verlag für Recht und Gesellschaft, 1954) 81.

[23] Robert F. Brown, The Later Philosophy of Schelling: The Influence of Boehme on the Works of 1809-1815 (London: Assoc. U Presses, 1977) 127-28.

[24] Hans Eichner, Friedrich Schlegel, Twayne's World Authors Series 98 (New York: Twayne, 1970) 65-67.

[25] Eichner, Friedrich Schlegel 65. It should be noted, however, that F. Schlegel did not advocate a mixing of genres. See René Wellek, The Romantic Age, vol. 2 of A History of Modern Criticism, 1750-1950 (New Haven: Yale UP, 1955-86) 2l: "On the whole, Schlegel obviously holds to the doctrine of the distinction and even purity of genres." Nevertheless, as Wellek notes, while Schlegel maintains the purity of genres, he also stresses that the

"essence of poetry itself" is the "ceaselessly inventive and creative, eternal imagination."

26 Charles Taylor, Hegel (Cambridge: Cambridge UP, 1975) 532.

27 Quoted in Jack Forstman, A Romantic Triangle: Schleiermacher and Early German Romanticism, American Acad. of Religion Studies in Religion 13, ed. Stephen Crites (Missoula, MT: Scholars, 1977) 41-42. Novalis uses Einbildungskraft for the power of the poet. Other Romantics follow Schelling in speaking of this power as Phantasie rather than Einbildungskraft. A. W. Schlegel, for example, distinguishes between primary and secondary imagination, that is, mere Einbildungskraft (fancy), in contrast to artistic Phantasie (imagination). Solger too follows the distinction, in which Einbildungskraft is a function of ordinary cognition and human consciousness, whereas Phantasie is the creative imagination in the proper sense. This is an important distinction for readers who are used to Coleridge's distinction (also inspired by Schelling) between the primary and secondary imagination, plus the third category of fancy (Biographia Literaria, ch. 13). The confusion can arise in that Coleridge uses "imagination" for both primary (ordinary consciousness) and secondary (artistic) uses, and "fancy" for the lower capacity as "a mode of memory," working according to the law of association; see Samuel Taylor Coleridge, Biographia Literaria, or Biographical Sketches of My Literary Life and Opinions, ed. and introd. George Watson, 2nd ed. (1965; London: Everyman's Library, 1971) 167. On German and English Romanticism as a literary, social, philosophical and religious phenomenon, see M. H. Abrams, Natural Supernaturalism: Tradition and Revolution in Romantic Literature (New York: Norton, 1971). A useful anthology of translations of the Schlegels, Novalis, Tieck, Solger, Richter, and Goethe is Kathleen M. Wheeler, ed.,

German Aesthetic and Literary Criticism: The Romantic Ironists and Goethe (Cambridge: Cambridge UP, 1984).

[28] Arthur O. Lovejoy, "Schiller and the Genesis of German Romanticism," Essays in the History of Ideas (Baltimore: Johns Hopkins UP, 1948) 211.

[29] Hans Eichner, "Friedrich Schlegel's Theory of Romantic Poetry," Proceedings of the MLA 71 (1959): 1024.

[30] Wilhelm Anz, Kierkegaard und der deutsche Idealismus (Tübingen: Mohr, 1956) 16.

[31] Forstman 38.

[32] Kant, Judgment 160n; Schiller's report is quoted in Forstman 38.

[33] Friedrich Schiller, "Das verschleierte Bild zu Sais," Werke, ed. Alfred Brandstetter, 6 vols. (Zürich: Stauffacher, 1967) 1: 227-30.

[34] Friedrich Schlegel, Friedrich Schlegel's Lucinde and the Fragments, trans. and introd. Peter Firchow (Minneapolis: U of Minnesota P, 1971) 241.

[35] Or, in a variant reading, Hyacinth beholds himself; Forstman 48; Novalis [Friedrich von Hardenberg], Werke, ed. with commentary Gerhard Schulz (München: Beck, 1969) 95-128; see esp. 108-112; Abrams 248.

[36] Forstman 39.

[37] Eichner, Friedrich Schlegel 68-69; quoted in Forstman 65.

[38] Ideen 8, quoted in Forstman 79. For Schleiermacher, however, the divine is immediately intuited not in activity, but in "passivity."

[39] Some poets, like Heine, could capriciously and gleefully destroy the effect of their own work (Walzel 236). Friedrich Schlegel was accused of a similar frivolity, but as Raymond Immerwahr argues, Schlegel's subjective irony does not destroy his art, but asserts in a subtle way the artist's sovereignty over

the work. Raymond Immerwahr, "The Subjectivity or Objectivity of Friedrich Schlegel's Poetic Irony," Germanic Review 26 (1951): 190-91.

40 In Geschichte der Poesie der Griechen und Roemer, cited in Walzel 42.

41 Wellek 89.

42 Walzel 243.

43 Ludwig Tieck, "Der gestiefelte Kater," in Werke, ed. with concluding remarks and notes, Marianne Thalmann (Munich: Winkler, 1963-66) 2: 205ff. See also Walzel 201 and 226, and Ralph Tymms, German Romantic Literature (London: Methuen, 1955) 63-68.

44 Solger's disapproval, however, ignores the "objective" side of Friedrich Schlegel's irony, Wellek 300.

45 Wellek 299.

46 K. W. F. Solger, Vorlesungen über Aesthetik, ed. K. W. L. Heyse (Leipzig: Brockhaus, 1829) 183-256; Percy Matenko, Tieck and Solger: The Complete Correspondence (New York: Westermann, 1933) 41-63, gives a detailed account of Solger's analysis of imagination and irony.

47 Matenko 62-63.

48 Quoted in Eichner, Friedrich Schlegel 57-58.

49 Erich Heller, "The Realistic Fallacy," The Artist's Journey into the Interior and Other Essays (New York: Vintage-Random, 1968) 92.

50 Wellek 18.

51 Gerhard vom Hofe, Die Romantikkritik Sören Kierkegaards (Frankfurt am Main: Athenäum, 1972) 178.

52 Friedrich Schlegel's phrase, quoted in Hofe 180.

53 Hofe 177.

54 Quoted in Hofe 177-78.

CHAPTER TWO

Kierkegaard and the Romantic Imagination:

The Concept of Irony

> When the imagination is allowed to rule . . . it
> prostrates and anaesthetizes the soul, robs it of all
> moral tension, and makes of life a dream.
> --Kierkegaard, The Concept of Irony

Early in his studies, before the beginning of his formal authorship, Kierkegaard began a critical analysis of the Romantic tradition, a tradition that intrigued him, but against which he assumed a polemical stance almost at once. In this chapter we will trace Kierkegaard's investigations of the Romantic imagination, beginning in the journal entries where he quickly formulates his judgment of Romanticism. We will turn then to the culmination of these reflections in the attack launched against the Romantic imagination in his dissertation The Concept of Irony (1841).[1]

The young Kierkegaard and the Romantic imagination

Kierkegaard's journals reveal that, beginning about 1835, he turned his attention to Romanticism in a sustained way, showing his lively interest in German Romanticism as well as the Danish Romantic interest in literature and folklore. Kierkegaard immersed himself in the Romantic spirit.

Romanticism made an important literary impact on Denmark in the early nineteenth-century. In 1802 Henrik Steffens, a student of Schelling, delivered his popular Copenhagen lectures on Romanticism, attended by such current and future Danish luminaries as Adam Oehlenschläger, Steffens' cousin N. F. S. Grundtvig, J. P. Mynster, and the brothers H. C. and A. S. Ørsted. In his lectures Steffens vigorously presented a manifesto of Romantic ideals. He attacked scientific empiricism in favor of the unity of spirit and nature, and described the "presentiment" (Ahnelse) of the presence of the eternal in the finite. Denigrating the values and culture of the eighteenth-century, Steffens elevated poetic imagination above understanding. Mythology, he argued, is the purest poetry, in which the religion and life of a people are most manifest. Even before Steffens' 1802 lectures, the young Oehlenschläger had published his important Poems 1803 (Digte 1803), influenced strongly by A. W. Schlegel and Tieck. The book exhibits the Romantic love of mixed styles, including narrative and lyric poems, a drama, and a satirical comedy in the style of Tieck.[2]

Romanticism, however, never became a dominant literary movement in Denmark, but was absorbed as a powerful element into the wider Danish literary and cultural milieu. Many in Steffens' audience kept their distance; even Grundtvig, who with his passion for mythology soon was a catalyst for the later nationalist romanticism of the mid-1820's, remained ambivalent about Steffens and in 1806 broke publicly from Oehlenschläger's romantic religion. Steffens and Oehlenschläger themselves both soon turned to Weimar classicism, to Schiller and Goethe.[3] The future of Danish literature lay not in the undiluted Romanticism of the early Steffens and Oehlenschläger, but in the absorption of it in the eighteenth-century traditions that were powerful until around 1825. And in the period that followed, Denmark's "Golden Age" (1825-48), J. L. Heiberg--poet, critic, Copenhagen's arbiter of taste, and eventually managing director of the Royal Theater, a man who dominated Denmark's artistic-intellectual life for over twenty-five years--synthesized Romanticism with French classicism, Goethean humanism, and Hegelian speculation.[4]

Nonetheless, the Romantic impact on Denmark was fruitful. With their sense of the unity of spirit and nature, the truth of poetic inspiration, and the growing passion for Danish folk literature, the Romanticism of Steffens and Oehlenschläger left a strong heritage to Danish intellectual life in the following decades.

Kierkegaard's journal entries of 1835-37 reveal his sustained effort to come to terms with the concept of the "Romantic," and also to investigate the Romantic imagination in his own moods and experience. One of his early entries questions whether the Romantic can be defined at all, "for the romantic lies essentially in flowing over all boundaries."[5] But in an entry dated March 24, 1836, Kierkegaard transcribes passages on "Romanticism" from Christian K. F. Molbech's Lectures on Recent Danish Poetry (Forelaesninger over den nyere danske Poesie) (1832), remarking that "some of it is not new."[6] Included in Kierkegaard's transcriptions are comments by Molbech on the typically Romantic imagination. Imagination is "the foundation of the whole world of the fabulous." Reminiscent of Steffens, Molbech sees in the Romantic the "tendency to draw the eternal and the infinite . . . down into the world of phenomena." It is "the mystical and the profound in thought, which simultaneously seeks to be identified with feeling and imagination." It is not essentially the sentimental, the chivalrous, or the marvelous, but "it is rather the infinitude, the freedom without physical barriers in the working of the imagination, in the intuiting of the ideal, in the fullness and depth of feeling, in the idea-oriented power of reflection." Molbech cites Jean Paul's remark that the Romantic "is the beautiful without boundaries or the beautiful infinite, just as there is a sublime infinite," and that "all poetry writing is a kind of truth-saying art, and romantic poetry is a presentiment of a greater future."[7] Molbech claims that Romanticism seeks by means of this infinitude and freedom "to fill in the broad chasm between idea and essence, between the eternal . . . and these forms [of art] themselves," an attempt Molbech himself believes to be "eternally unattainable, even for the most powerful imagination." The Romantic "must not be confused with an exclusively spiritual or mystical striving for a union with the higher, the extrasensory." The Romantic is also "oriented to the sense-world," and delights in the "combination of the most motley, marvelous, fabulous, and imaginative forms and images, a comprehensible whole to the assimilating imaginative power."[8]

What strikes Kierkegaard particularly is the unsatisfied yearning characteristic of the Romantics. In an entry from the same month he too distinguishes between the yearning and the plenitude of Romantic activity: "The romantic depends upon whether it is primarily a longing gazing into an eternity (the more sentimental) or a diversity conditioned by vigorous action."[9] Yet striving is of the essence of the Romantic spirit: "Does the romantic lie in variety, multiplicity? No, for the classical does indeed have nymphs, nereids, etc., but the romantic in variety consists in this, that an unsatisfied need has evoked it, yet without finding any satisfaction in it."[10] So too he comments: "The romantic was also expressed in a distinctive way in the Middle Ages by all the wandering about that went on: wandering knights, traveling scholars, itinerant singers, musicians, monks, etc.--"fliegendes Blatt."[11]

Kierkegaard reads much in the Romantic authors: not only the Danes like Oehlenschläger, but the German authors like E. T. A. Hoffmann, Eichendorff, Jean Paul, Tieck, Brentano, Schleiermacher's Vertraute Briefe über die Lucinde, G. H. Schubert, and especially Novalis and Friedrich Schlegel.[12] Kierkegaard evidently appreciates much about the Romantic imagination. He approves Schiller's distinction between naive and sentimental poetry,[13] and he quotes a

comment of Tieck's on the importance of imagination in allegorical literature.
Tieck says:

> There is perhaps no invention of the imagination which, even
> if unconsciously, does not have the allegory as the very
> ground of its character. . . . Novalis says: only the story
> that can also be a fable is truly a story. But there is also
> much sick and feeble literature of this type which only drags
> us about in concepts without engaging our imagination
> [Phantasie], and that is the most irksome kind of
> entertainment.[14]

Kierkegaard also knew the Romantic spirit at first hand, exploring in
himself the moods and affections of the Romantic sensibility. At the end of 1837
he records his enjoyment of fairy tales, wherein "all earthly finite cares vanish;
joy, yes, even sorrow, are infinite (and for this reason are so enlarging and
beneficial)."[15] Four days later he reports that

> I was in a strange mood the other day, collapsed within (as
> an old ruin must feel), abstracted from myself and my I in a
> pantheistic state of dissolution, and I read an old folk song
> (published by Sneedorf-Birch), which tells of a girl who
> waited for her lover one Saturday evening, but he did not
> come--and she went to bed "and wept so bitterly"; she got up
> again "and wept so bitterly." Suddenly the scene expanded
> before my eyes--I saw the Jutland heath with its
> indescribable solitude and its lonely lark--and now one
> generation after another rose before me, and the girls all sang
> for me and wept so bitterly and sank into their graves again,
> and I wept with them.

Characteristically, Kierkegaard immediately shifts from reporting the experience
to analyzing how his imagination operates; he couples his reveries with an
equally Romantic self-analysis:

> Strangely enough my imagination [Phantasie] works best
> when I am sitting alone in a large assemblage, when the
> tumult and noise require a substratum of will if the
> imagination is to hold on to its object; without this

environment it bleeds to death in the exhausting embrace of an indefinite idea.[16]

Kierkegaard appreciates not only the Romantic imagination but also the Romantic irony. He trained himself as a "master-thief," one with the insight to probe the psychological states of others (in particular, his father), a skill, Gregor Malantschuk notes, that he made the basis of his entire experimental psychology.[17] But he also knew the inner split that the practice of observation could create in the observer, especially when he turned to an examination of his own states of mind and feeling. His intellectual life was marked to a high degree by this combination of imagination and reflection. Kierkegaard knew the kind of inner infinity that irony could give, a self-reflection turning over endless possibilities in the imagination, in a wealth of impressions and thoughts, all of which, however, remained simply possibilities. In the preface to his first published book, From the Papers of One Still Living (1838), he presents an author with a double personality, "like two souls in one body." The author stands removed from the world and converses with his alter ego, his "friend" who acts as mediator with the world, the author's confidant, and sharp observer of the author's frame of mind.[18]

It is typical of Kierkegaard that he early forms a conviction on an intellectual issue or movement, and his subsequent reflection elaborates that judgment. So in this instance Kierkegaard's psychological analysis of the Romantic state of mind--the infinity of imagination and irony--early leads him to a settled judgment on the inadequacy of the Romantic life stance. Already in March, 1836, he notes that Christianity and Romanticism should not be too closely identified; Romanticism is a phenomenon not of Christianity but of northern paganism:

> it has been said that Christianity really developed the
> romantic, but if it was Christianity that did that (which, after

all, is doubtful, for Christianity admittedly lures thought out beyond the earthly to something on the far side and to that extent is romantic, but that far side is a judgment or a sleep-like dormant state prior to judgment), it was only through contact with the northern culture, which precisely by the conception of life and death so characteristic of northerners, a conception of life as a battle, here as well as beyond, and of death as downfall in this life parallel to downfall in the other life as a transition to standing again--gave rise to the genuinely romantic.[19]

In 1836 Kierkegaard elaborates on this distinction, concluding that the assimilation of Romanticism to Christianity is impossible. Kierkegaard develops his dialectical evaluation of the Romantic spirit through a study of, first, mythology, in which he begins to formulate the notion of stages, and second, the relation of medieval "Romantic" figures to Christianity (Don Juan, Faust, and Ahasuerus). Kierkegaard's interest in these studies of the Romantic is not simply literary, historical, or aesthetic, but is also a quest for a precise grasp of these literary figures as existence possibilities in relation to Christianity and classicism (the latter represented by Goethe, Hegel, and the later Schleiermacher).[20] As such they represent both historical phases in the development of the human spirit and also continuing possibilities for any person in any age.

Reflecting on mythology, Kierkegaard defines it in an 1836 journal entry as "the compacting (suppressed being) of the idea of eternity (the eternal idea) in the categories of time and space."[21] In a flurry of journal entries from January 1837, including entries on Mozart, Kierkegaard develops from these reflections on mythology his first formulation of the stages: "Something About Life's Four Stages, also Concerning Mythology."[22] The first stage, Oriental mythology, in which only the possibility of self-consciousness is given, is followed by Greek mythology, which holds to equilibrium and youth's well-being in family and school (state and church) as its ideal. The Romantic stage follows in which "a question arises about a satisfaction lying beyond the world and which therefore cannot be found in the world."[23] The fourth stage, definitely set apart from the other three, is Christianity, which is not properly a mythology, but "certainly has the greatest historical significance regarding the solution of this issue," i.e., the issue of a satisfaction lying beyond the world, and "has answered it."[24]

During this same period, 1835-37, Kierkegaard analyzes mythical figures of the Middle Ages--Don Juan, Faust, and Ahasuerus--culminating in an abortive plan for a series of Faustian letters.[25] Kierkegaard investigates these figures, as he investigates mythology, not only for their literary-aesthetic significance, but as representatives of different aspects of the Romantic spirit. Again, Kierkegaard is clear that all three of these figures stand dialectically related to one another as stages prior to Christianity. He studies them for their typological meaning and their interrelationships, as representing life outside of religion in three forms.[26] Don Juan represents enjoyment, the "incarnation of the flesh" as a stance of sensuous reaction to the spiritualization introduced by Christianity; Faust is "doubt personified," and "expresses the individual after the abrogation of the Church, severed from its guidance and abandoned to himself."[27] Finally, Ahasuerus, the Wandering Jew, is the representative of despair. Most important, these three figures represent an intensification of the Romantic standpoint, one that Kierkegaard maintains must be "mediated and embraced in life by the single individual," and "not until then do the moral and religious appear."[28]

In summary, during 1835-37 Kierkegaard formulates a thoroughly dialectical position with respect to Romanticism. On the one hand, he appreciates its liveliness and its wealth of ideas, and he does not dispute Romanticism's claim to be more than a poetic theory; he accepts their claim (recalling Wellek's phrase) to a "cosmic extension of the meaning of poetry."[29] On the other hand, from his own experience in reflection, imagination, and psychological experimentation, Kierkegaard comes to see Romanticism's inadequacy. He finds that inadequacy typified in the failure of the "Romantic representatives" to embody more than negative qualifications of spirit. The tireless sensuousness of Don Juan, the ceaseless doubt of the medieval Faust, and the endless wandering despair of Ahasuerus do reach infinity, but only a negative infinite. Kierkegaard in these years is in quest of a position that can yield more than the Romantic negativity embodied in these three representative ideas, one that gives a unified view of life. In his Gilleleje letter of 1835 he wrote, "The crucial thing is to find a truth which is truth for me, to find the idea for which I am willing to live and die."[30] Yet Kierkegaard's confrontation with Romanticism is not over, for he continues to develop a dialectical response to Romanticism that can surpass their position, and in this he turns increasingly to Socrates.[31] In the entry cited earlier on Faust as the figure who represents "the individual after the abrogation of the Church," Kierkegaard compares Faust and Socrates, for Socrates represents not only "the individual's emancipation from the state," but also the paradigm of irony.[32]

Kierkegaard focusses, then, on the Romantic irony as the heart of concern. His aim is to "mediate and embrace" the figures of Don Juan, Faust, and Ahasuerus within a larger moral and religious understanding that reveals the limited validity and also weakness of Romantic irony. The questions before us will be: what is Kierkegaard's case against Romantic irony, and what does this reveal about Kierkegaard's attitude to the imagination?

The Concept of Irony: The dilemma of the Romantic imagination

Kierkegaard's dissertation for the master's degree, The Concept of Irony, is sometimes unduly ignored by scholars, partly because of Kierkegaard's own not entirely favorable attitude toward it in later years.[33] Published and defended in September 1841, The Concept of Irony is however central in exhibiting Kierkegaard's first mature criticism of the Romantic imagination, a critique he never abandons, but elaborates in his subsequent thought. The Concept of Irony launches a thorough attack against the pretensions of the Romantic claim that the imagination alone provides an adequate life-stance.

In the course of this critique of irony, Kierkegaard indirectly judges the Romantic notion of imagination as well. Just as he claims that the term "irony" is equivalent to the term "Romantic,"[34] so too, from our analysis of the shape of the Romantic movement, in which "irony" and "imagination" are so closely intertwined, any critique of "Romantic irony" is also a critique of the Romantic imagination. Furthermore, Kierkegaard's references to the imagination in The Concept of Irony exhibit his clear awareness that irony is a form of imaginative life.

Kierkegaard's negative argument against the Romantic imagination is twofold. 1) The Romantics are guilty of expanding the functions of the imagination to such an extent that they "fantastically" lose contact with finite "actuality," and thus lose themselves in imagination. The entire vision of a human freedom achieved through the imagination--whether Fichtean or Romantic--comes under attack. But Kierkegaard is more subtle, for, as we have seen, the Romantics in every case, even Novalis, seek to "redeem" the finite through a transcendent vision, and Kierkegaard is aware of this. His strategy, thus, is to exploit the Romantics' own doubts about the possibility of this redemption, showing that their alleged redemption of the finite fails. Contrary to the Romantics' hopes, their failure means that their imagination is not anchored to the finite and actual world, but diffuses the self in a world of endless "possibility."

2) Because the redemption of actuality fails, the actual takes its revenge on the Romantic ironic imagination, rendering it self-contradictory as a life-stance. As Kierkegaard noted in his reflections on Molbech, there are two poles of Romanticism--Sehnsucht and the manifold sensuous world--and the second pole in the Romantic imagination is not cancelled but remains in an unresolved, destructive relationship to Romantic expansiveness. And, as we have seen, Kierkegaard remarks on the Romantics' striving that disturbs the classical equilibrium, seeking a supramundane satisfaction. Kierkegaard agrees that such a satisfaction is to be sought, since Christianity too seeks this satisfaction. But because in Romanticism the two "poles" are unsatisfactorily related, striving can become not only fiercely active, but passively dreamlike: the manifold sensual world takes its revenge on the Romantic in an endless proliferation of images and moods, exemplified best, as we will see, in Friedrich Schlegel's "vegetative" ideal in Lucinde. The striving of the imagination does end in passivity; in this Novalis' novel on the veil of Isis was right. Yet the passivity is mere lassitude rather than transcendence. Thus, because these two poles are unrelated, the ironist becomes the victim of irony. The result is that the Romantic imagination is self-defeating: Romantic irony is not true irony, its feeling is not true feeling, its freedom is not true freedom, its ethics is not ethical, its poetry is unpoetic, and its philosophico-religious speculation ends in confusion. Tieck's fear of irony's curvatus in se is, in Kierkegaard's lights, all too true.

Before investigating these criticisms of the Romantic imagination in more detail, it is necessary to see how Kierkegaard employs Socrates' irony against both the Romantics and Hegel. Ironically, it is Socrates, one of the Romantics' favorite models, who reveals for Kierkegaard the weakness of Romantic irony. The essence of the historical Socrates is irony, a fact that is shown only by critical analysis of the portrayals of Socrates in the works of Xenophon, Aristophanes, and Plato. Socrates' irony consumes and relativizes his given historical actuality, and the whole of existence becomes alien to him. He emerges from an "infinite absolute negativity" to the giddy height of infinite possibility. As such, "irony is itself the first and most abstract determination of subjectivity."[35] It is the first movement of the self into its freedom. So far this seems akin to Romanticism, but Kierkegaard argues that whereas Friedrich Schlegel takes Socrates as a prefigurement of Romantic irony, Socrates' irony has the qualification of being in the direction of spirit. By contrast, Romantic irony is an antiquated and spiritually inadequate form of irony.[36] In saying that Socrates' irony is in "the direction of spirit," Kierkegaard means that Socrates' irony is ethically oriented. Socrates was "not the apparent but the actual zenith of irony, because Socrates was the first to arrive at the Idea of the good, the beautiful, and the true as a limit, that is, to arrive at ideal infinity in the form of possibility."[37] The question concerning Romantic irony is whether it recovers this ethically-oriented Socratic irony, or whether Romantic irony fails to be ethically oriented, losing itself in sheer negativity. In Kierkegaard's judgment, it is the latter.

But Socrates is also enlisted against Hegel's dismissal of irony. In many ways Kierkegaard's critique of Romantic irony is informed by Hegel's criticisms. But Kierkegaard also uses Socrates' irony as a standard against Hegel's disavowal of the ironic. He charges that Hegel distorts Socrates by discounting the latter's irony, seeing him simply as the founder of morality. For Hegel, Socrates' virtue was to have attained consciousness of his subjective freedom, necessary to ethics, in which he orients himself to the good as the universal, in contrast to the Sophists, who see the good as merely the useful or advantageous.[38] That is, Socrates relativizes the concrete ethic of Hellenism and understands that in order for a person to be truly ethical, one must possess a moral conscience that acts from knowledge rather than custom. Socrates thus universalizes subjectivity and the good as the requirement for morality.[39] According to Hegel, Socrates' defect is that this principle remains for him abstract and is not given concrete expression in the idea of the state as the realm for exercising ethical virtues.[40]

Kierkegaard counters that Hegel has failed to understand the infinity of Socrates' irony and, therefore, has failed to see the importance of irony both in the historical development of spirit and as a continuing element in the development of each person's ethical subjectivity. Kierkegaard agrees that the significance of Socrates' irony lies in his orienting the person ethically. He adds, however, that Hegel has completely ignored Socrates' ironic stance as being the means by which one is oriented in the direction of the good as an infinite goal. Socrates was, says Kierkegaard, a "divine missionary." With all those he encountered he was a Charon who "ferried the individual from reality over to ideality, and ideal infinity, as infinite negativity, became the nothingness into which he made the whole manifold of reality disappear."[41] Socrates' irony is an infinite absolute negativity, and it is this that Hegel consistently ignores in his treatment of Socrates. That infinite negativity resides in the fact that the moral person must ironically oppose the world of actuality in grasping life as a task; further, one can never fully realize the good as task, never reach the goal that remains an infinite absolute negative over one's life, prompting continual striving.[42] By contrast, Hegel, confident of the embodied possibility of the ethical in the idea of the state, identifies Socrates' irony with Plato's irony, and irony becomes "'more a manner of conversation, a social pleasantness, and not pure negation, not the negative attitude.'"[43] Kierkegaard replies that Socrates' irony endeavored to move his contemporaries from the concrete to the abstract, from the confusing limits of custom to the true idea of the good as an object of ethical passion. For Kierkegaard, Socrates establishes the validity of ironic negativity in a way that Hegel cannot allow, and opens the way to a continuing non-Hegelian role for irony in the life of the individual person, in the shape of "mastered irony." For Kierkegaard, irony is not a surpassed moment on the way to objectivity, but is a continuous factor in each individual's ethical subjectivity. Irony is, indeed, the beginning of subjectivity, and mastered irony, not the death of irony, is the goal.

We will return to Kierkegaard's concept of mastered irony later in the chapter, but having seen Socrates' role as a standard of irony over against both the Romantics and Hegel, we can now better grasp Kierkegaard's critique of the Romantic irony. Again, while agreeing that Romantic irony is a limited position, Kierkegaard argues that irony still has its uses for a person oriented to the ethical. The error of the Romantics is not that they are ironic, but that they misuse irony.

Kierkegaard grants that the Romantics performed an important service in protesting against "an age in which men had become ossified . . . within the finite social situation":[44]

> Everything took place on the stroke of the hour. One was inspired by nature on Midsummer Day. One was full of contrition on the fourth Friday after Easter. One fell in love when he reached his twentieth year. One went to bed at ten o'clock. One married, one lived for domesticity, one filled his position in the state. One had children and family cares.[45]

In reaction against this, Romanticism was "a chilling wind" that "rejuvenated the world."[46] The trouble, though, is that the Romantics rejuvenated the world by sheer negativity: the world awoke, but, as Heine observed, it became a little child again.[47] The awakening that Romanticism promised was bought at the price of a complete denial of actuality: "Poetry awakens, forceful longings, mysterious presentiments, exciting emotions all awaken, nature awakens, the enchanted princess awakens--the romanticist falls asleep."[48]

The Romantics' problem is, as we have already seen, that their position is a regression back behind the irony of Socrates. Whereas the Socratic irony is a negativity oriented to the true, the beautiful, and the good, the Romantic irony is negativity pure and simple, a negativity that loses both the ideal and the actual.

Kierkegaard follows Hegel in placing the historical blame for the development of this Romantic negative infinite in the elder Fichte's "transcendental ego," a negative infinity that sacrificed utterly any relation to actuality.[49] The Romantics then applied this to the striving of the empirical ego, but misapplied it, for,

> first, it was to confound the empirical and finite ego with the eternal ego; and secondly, it was to confuse metaphysical actuality with historical actuality. Thus it was to apply an abortive metaphysical standpoint directly to actuality. Fichte would construct the world, but what he meant was a systematic construction; Schlegel and Tieck, on the other hand, would dispose of a world.[50]

The result is that irony is not used to negate the actual for the sake of a new "self-created actuality," as in Socrates, but is simply an eccentric subjectivity, "a subjectivity raised to the second power." It is this "subjectivity raised to the second power" that Kierkegaard critically analyzes, adding that "Hegel's efforts to oppose it were quite in order."[51]

As we have seen, Kierkegaard has two basic theses to argue against the Romantics' imagination, first, that they are guilty of losing actuality and themselves by fleeing into imagination, and, second, that the actual world takes its revenge on the Romantics, rendering their position self-contradictory. Turning to the first thesis, Kierkegaard maintains that, unlike Socrates, for whom a negative infinity was oriented to the idea, the Romantic negative infinity imaginatively expands the ideal so that the actual is caricatured and lost rather than redeemed.[52] The very strategy of celebrating the plenitude and unity of the finite world renders that world imaginative. The Romantic sees the given actuality as a limit to the self's autonomy and so imaginatively lifts all reality into possibility, as the negation of the necessary: "Its actuality is sheer possibility."[53] Moreover, for Kierkegaard this objective world irony leads inevitably to a self-destructive subjective irony. Not only the finite world but the self is volatilized. The Romantic irony dispenses with both the world and the ethical, losing both the finite world and the self. Socrates' "world-irony," on the other hand, is saved from this result by focussing on an ideal that prompts ethical action and so redeems both the actual and the self. The Romantic hope that the imagination can attain a positive Infinite, a union with the Infinite either beyond or within the world, is a vain hope--as the Romantics themselves feared.

It is essential here to note Kierkegaard's basic ethical conviction that "actuality," as the given in human experience, is retained and redeemed only in action, not in dreaming. For Novalis, it will be recalled, the imagination is both gift and task. In Kierkegaard's mind "actuality," not imagination, is gift and task.[54] The Romantics negate actuality as a gift by denying the past, both the past of the individual and of the race. Kierkegaard sees here too the influence of Fichte's eternal ego on the Romantics, the metaphysical impulse to sacrifice the given historical actuality for the sake of an atemporal metaphysical view of the actual. The Romantic propensity to myth reflects this de-historicizing, for a myth, or a mythologizing of an historical event, is for the Romantics a means of retaining one's freedom over actuality: "All history became myth, poetry, saga, fairy-tale--irony was free once more."[55] Like Hercules lifting Antaeus into the air in order to wrestle him to the ground, irony mythologized the historical in order to bring it low.

Actuality is more than gift, however; it is task as well, since a person's actuality, those given abilities and characteristics, requires one to realize those gifts by relating to them ethically in responsibility. Socrates totally negated the given situation, but always with his eye on actuality as an ethical task. The Romantics, however, despite their celebration of life as a task of imaginative striving, have no task in the true sense, but only grandiose plans and possibilities. They do not understand life in the ethical or religious sense as an education in responsibility, but as a poetic production of the self.[56] All things being possible to their imaginations, they live in a fantastic, imaginative world, regarding with equanimity both their endless entertainment of possibilities and the fact that nothing comes of that self-entertainment. In words reminiscent of his earlier "Faustian letters," Kierkegaard describes how the Romantic ironist "has most often traversed a multitude of determinations in the form of possibility, poetically lived through them, before he ends in nothingness."[57] His ironic state of mind allows him to entertain even his remorse as an interesting aesthetic fact, "examining whether it be poetically correct."[58] The Romantic tendency is to see everything as an aesthetic object. Their final inadequacy is an ethical inadequacy, more amoral than immoral, since the Romantic lives too abstractly "ever to arrive at the concretion formed by ethics and morals."[59]

This brings us to Kierkegaard's second thesis against the Romantic imagination: ironically, the actual takes its revenge on the Romantics, rendering their imagination into self-delusion. Unsatisfactorily related to the actual, the imagination degenerates into either fruitless striving or lassitude. The Romantic imagination claims to achieve feeling, freedom, a true ethic, an invigorated poetry, and a philosophically-based religious vision. But precisely because the self is volatilized in imagination, Kierkegaard argues, these endeavors are impossible. The ironist, in sacrificing the actual and the ethical as gift and as task, loses too the basis for feeling, freedom, ethics, poetry, and religion. We can analyze this by following Kierkegaard's diagnosis of each of these Romantic claims in turn.

1) The Romantic's purported depth of <u>feeling</u> is only moodiness. The imagination gives each mood ultimate validity for that moment, only to cancel it ironically in the next: "As the ironist has no continuity, so the most contrary feelings are allowed to displace each other. Now he is a god, now a grain of sand."[60] The Romantic hovers over feeling: "He poetizes that it is he who evokes the feeling, he keeps on poetizing until he becomes so spiritually palsied that he must cease."[61] One's emotions become mixed, unattached to any object; jest conceals grief, and joy is hidden in lament.

2) The Romantic ironist sees this sovereignty of mood as a positive <u>freedom</u>, but since the Romantic's emotions are so fitful, freedom has nothing to direct; as a mere negative freedom, with no task at which to aim, it wastes away to nothing.[62] This is the height of irony's deception of the ironist, in that "irony lapses into the very thing it most opposes, for the ironist acquires a certain similarity to a thoroughly prosaic person, except that he retains the negative freedom whereby he stands poetically creating above himself."[63] The ironist, at the mercy of moods, becomes, like the prosaic person, whatever "happens" to one. The imagination remains active, but it results, ironically, in passivity. The only continuity the Romantic imagination finds is the same as that of the prosaic person: boredom, the cancellation of both feeling and freedom:

> Yes, boredom: this eternity void of content, this bliss
> without enjoyment, this superficial profundity, this hungry

satiety. . . . Boredom is the negative unity assimilated into personal consciousness, the negative unity in which opposites disappear.[64]

Kierkegaard's case for actuality is that it provides a ground for feeling and freedom. The gift and task of actuality allow feeling and freedom the proper atmosphere in which to flourish. Imagination by itself cannot provide this atmosphere.[65]

3) In his criticisms of Romantic ethics Kierkegaard is more explicit about the imagination's role in the volatilization of the ironist's capacities. Schlegel, in by far the most important analysis, represents irony's uneasy relation to actuality, in which the imagination lapses into passivity, and Romantic ethics reveals itself as non-ethical.

Friedrich Schlegel's Lucinde, although written in 1799, was of current interest in Kierkegaard's youth, thanks in part to Karl Gutzkow's republication of Schleiermacher's Confidential Letters on Lucinde (Vertraute Briefe über die Lucinde) in 1835, following Schleiermacher's death.[66] Lucinde was, in Kierkegaard's phrase, "the gospel of the Young Germany," the progressive literary and philosophical movement of which Gutzkow was a founder, and which revived Romantic irony--especially Schlegel's--in Germany and France.[67] While Lucinde was, in Hegel's eyes, the epitome of the early Romantics' life-stance, Kierkegaard returns to Lucinde, not only in its own right, but also as the source of the new Romanticism in the Young Germany movement.[68]

The novel was notorious in its own day, although hardly "obscene" as Kierkegaard calls it, even by the standards of 1799 or 1841.[69] Yet as a novel in which the Romantic creed is most explicit, Kierkegaard chooses his target well. Lucinde exhibits the variety of genres and the self-conscious suspension of chronology that were the marks of ironic form. Kierkegaard comments on the form of the book that Schlegel "renounces all understanding and allows the phantasy alone to rule, it may well be possible to let the imagination maintain this confusion in a single perpetually moving image."[70]

Yet it is the ethical content of Lucinde, not the form, that elicits Kierkegaard's harshest attack. The heart of Lucinde's ethic is not a simple anti-philistinism or a denunciation of ethical rules. Rather, Lucinde's ethic is Schlegel's "ästhetische Imperativ": marriage, for example, is sacred, but only insofar as marriage reflects true love.[71] Hence, marriage can be dissolved for an aesthetically superior love, a love that is also ethically superior because it unifies the sensual and the spiritual. Schlegel's ideal of love unifies the sensual and spiritual in the form of passive receptivity to the unconscious, the spontaneous, the sensual, and the imaginative. As such, Lucinde is opposed to the understanding, the conscious, the active, and the higher ethical.[72] Kierkegaard, borrowing Heine's phrase, calls it the "Rehabilitation des Fleisches."[73]

Kierkegaard does not at all object to Lucinde's anti-philistinism, but he does object to the novel's elevation of the imagination over against ethical actuality. The irony in the novel, he says, aims "to cancel all actuality and to set in its place an actuality that is no actuality." The central characters, Lucinde and Julius, live in an erotically self-contained world. "It is one of Julian's [i.e., Julius'] great tasks," observes Kierkegaard, "to bring before his imagination an eternal embrace--presumably as the only true actuality."[74]

Julius' imagination is a mirror in which he sees his fragmentation, his lack of emotional continuity. Schlegel writes:

> In his imagination his whole existence was a mass of unrelated fragments. Each fragment was single and complete, and whatever else stood next to it in reality and was joined to it was a matter of indifference to him and might just as well not have existed at all.[75]

But Schlegel's answer to this fragmentation is an increase in the passive imagination, epitomized in the natural growth of the plant. Idleness is the secret of artistic activity, of life, and of religion. Julius says:

> Really, we shouldn't neglect the study of idleness so criminally, but make it into an art and science, even into a religion! In a word: the more divine a man or a work of man is, the more it resembles a plant; of all the forms of nature, this form is the most moral and the most beautiful. And so the highest, most perfect mode of life would actually be nothing more than pure vegetating.[76]

Personality is not the reward for ethical striving, but occurs through an organic process; Julius' "life now came to be a work of art for him, imperceptibly, without his knowing how it happened."[77] In one of the book's fantasies, Prometheus suffers because of the bad example his striving set the human race. Bound in chains and whipped into haste by monstrous creatures, Prometheus is condemned to the labor of creating human beings out of fire and "glue and other material"; the finished products are cast into the audience who behold the scene, and become indistinguishable from the audience. A young devil points out the moral of this tableau of ceaseless activity:

> you foolishly feel compelled to aspire to having a personality, or else you're eager to observe and plumb each other's depths. That's a bad beginning. . . . Prometheus, because he seduced mankind into working, now has to work himself.[78]

The vegetative ideal leads the lovers, Julius and Lucinde, to yearn for an utter restfulness in which the distinctions, not only of traditional sexual roles, but of personality are lost. Lucinde bids Julius see her as an object of his yearning and finally simply as a projection of his soul. She says to him: "When the turmoil has died down and nothing mean or common distracts your noble soul, then you see reflected in me--in me who am forever yours--the marvelous flower of your imagination."[79] In a chapter called "The Dalliance of the Imagination," Lucinde advocates the smothering of intention, to be replaced by an inner stream of eternally flowing images: "The acme of intelligence is choosing to keep silent, restoring the soul to the imagination [Phantasie], and not disturbing the sweet dalliance of the young mother and her baby."[80]

Kierkegaard's response is that ethics implies "a relation of mind to mind," a development of intention and a distinction of personality that Lucinde seeks to dissolve in imagination.[81] The imagination in Lucinde is a gauze enveloping everything, resulting in what Kierkegaard calls "an aesthetic stupor."[82] Commenting on the "dalliance" passage, Kierkegaard speaks directly of the negative and disastrous role of the imagination in Schlegel's view of life:

> That the imagination [Phantasien] alone rules is repeated throughout the whole of Lucinde. Now who is such a monster that he is unable to delight in the free play of the imagination? But it does not follow from this that the whole of life should be given over to imagination [Phantasie-Anskuelse]. When the imagination [Phantasien] is allowed to rule in this way it prostrates and anaesthetizes the soul, robs it of all moral tension, and makes of life a dream. Yet this is exactly what Lucinde seeks to accomplish.[83]

Lucinde's ethic presents an irony that indeed cancels Kierkegaard's understanding of the ethical and proposes imaginative idealization in its place. Kierkegaard argues that this ethic is self-defeating, since the imagination so diffuses itself that the ideal collapses into its opposite, a sensuality unleavened by reflection or resignation. The ideal becomes a "vegetative ideal" in which the actual takes its revenge on the ideal: "The [Romantic] ego seeks a higher freedom, seeks to negate ethical mind, but it thereby succumbs to the law of the flesh and the appetites."[84] The result is not, however, sheer unconsciousness or sensuality. Because the relation of ideal and real, infinite and finite, is so unstable, because feeling and freedom are so enervated, there is nothing to prevent an eccentric return from the sensual to the mock-spiritual and abstract.[85] The Romantic ethic of imagination destroys itself in a restless vacillation between imagination and the sensual, the ideal and the real.

4) Whereas Schlegel's ideal of poetic imagination is Kierkegaard's main target in The Concept of Irony, Ludwig Tieck's work is the occasion for a literary-critical analysis of the futility of Romantic poetry. Tieck's error is more subtle, for unlike Schlegel, who ends in "the pantheistic infinity of poetry," Tieck's purpose is not to attack actuality directly; rather, he "abandons himself to a poetical exuberance while preserving its indifference towards actuality."[86] Kierkegaard has in mind not the Tieck of the first novels, nor of the last works, but the Tieck of the lyrics and satirical dramas, where he most extravagantly displays an unbridled poetic fantasy.[87]

Whereas Schlegel's imagination ends in lassitude, Tieck's imagination is ceaselessly active in ironic sentiment and the suspension of sentiment. Kierkegaard argues that Tieck is caught between the one pole of attacking philistinism and the second pole of the ideal. But this ideal has no stability, for "the more caricatured actuality becomes, the higher gushes the ideal--except the fountain which here gushes forth does not flow unto everlasting life." Caricature endlessly pursues and overtakes the ideal. The resulting vacillation destroys the unity of Tieck's poetry: "the whole design fails to order itself into a poetic totality."[88] Because of this, Tieck lacks a truly poetic relation with the reader, for Tieck's disordered style defeats the reader's effort to follow the poet's caprices. Poetic freedom requires a poetic unity as the background for caprice, and this unity Tieck lacks.

Tieck, says Kierkegaard, begins in imagination and ends in imagination. His productivity has no governing factor, and so simply revels in the fantastic.

Kierkegaard quotes the Hegelian critic H. G. Hotho approvingly; in Tieck's poetry:

> the adventurous license of the imagination [Phantasie] retained unlimited room for every species of image: daring episodes swirl forth at will, arabesque-like curiosities twist themselves into teasing laughter through the loose, spangled fabric, allegory expands the otherwise constricted shapes until nebulous, here and there the parodic jest hovers in topsy-turvy abandonment. And this genial pleasure is wedded to a feeble indulgence unable to refuse any idle invention which springs from its own bosom.[89]

The boundlessness of Tieck's imagination is a symptom of a deeper spiritual malady.[90] The imagination as the power of envisioning possibilities in endless play needs to be governed, in the poetic realm just as much as in the personal realm, by a true relationship to the ideal. Tieck attains an imaginary eternity, a vanishing point that is always external to his existence as a poet and hence never controls the proliferation of his creative images.[91] Just as Romantic feeling, freedom, and ethics are evanescent, Tieck's poetry is evanescent, ending in a lyricism approaching the musical, the ideal becoming "fainter and fainter until it vanishes like the distant soundings of a fainting echo."[92] True poetry, however, is a victory over the actual world, but unlike Tieck's poetry, a victory opening up a higher actuality in the idea, with the idea unifying the work.[93]

5) Turning finally to the inadequacy of Romantic religion, Kierkegaard analyzes Solger. Like Hegel, Kierkegaard is more respectful of Solger than of the other Romantics; Solger holds an important place in Kierkegaard's discourse on irony's proper uses. But Solger, too, has difficulty, and it is a difficulty in his uses of the imagination. Kierkegaard cites the section in Solger's lectures on aesthetics, "The Organism of the Artistic Spirit," in which Solger formulates his detailed concept of the imagination that we analyzed in the last chapter.[94]

Kierkegaard never explicitly discusses Solger's concept of the imagination but he does analyze Solger's discussion of the metaphysical and religious implications of irony centered on the creative imagination of the artist, which Kierkegaard finds to be metaphysically inadequate and essentially irreligious.[95]

The heart of Solger's metaphysics, it will be recalled, is that in irony the empirical and the ideal merge in the artistic moment, negating them both but, paradoxically, incorporating the ideal within the empirical in symbol. Kierkegaard argues that Solger, while not denying the place of the finite and actual as does Schlegel, finally is in the same dilemma, for "Solger has got himself lost in the negative."[96] Because he claims that true actuality is only given in the moment of imaginative intuition in which the finite and infinite abrogate each other, he is unable to grant the finite its true validity; the finite is finally nothingness (das Nichtige), the eternally vanishing moment of negation, through which the ideal appears. Kierkegaard then analyzes some of the theological aspects of Solger's thought, particularly his notions of the atonement and the doctrine of sin. Here Kierkegaard's attitude has a certain ambivalence, for he still seems at this time to be intrigued by the metaphysical contribution that Solger's dialectic can give to theology; as Capel notes, Kierkegaard offers a guardedly sympathetic view of Solger's elliptical theological language. But Kierkegaard concurs with Hegel that Solger finally fails.[97]

For Kierkegaard, Solger's attempt to make irony a philosophical key to the understanding of ethics, theology, and art is abortive. It is not difficult to see why this would be, for Solger, despite his contrast to other Romantics, still cannot give an adequate account of the importance and place of actuality as gift and as task. Solger's ethics predictably identifies evil with phenomenal appearance, and his theology ends in a theocentric pantheism; he lacks a doctrine of creation that would separate the infinite and the finite, instead of constantly collapsing them together in "divine self-sacrifice."[98] Solger's aesthetics ends in an irony that destroys the false finite without establishing a new finitude. Although Kierkegaard does not analyze Solger's concept of the imagination, it is clear that Kierkegaard's judgment on it would be largely negative. The imagination in conjunction with irony negates actuality, not so much in the infinite realm of possibility, but in the metaphysical interaction of the finite and the infinite. In Solger the imagination becomes an active force that excludes actuality as gift and as task.

We can now summarize Kierkegaard's opposition to the Romantic imagination. To live in imagination is to live in possibility, the very opposite of the actuality that gives the self an historical situation (as gift) and an ethical definition (as task). The imagination may attempt to incorporate the actual and finite, but as long as the imagination is itself the medium of that attempt, it is doomed to failure. Schlegel, Tieck, and Solger in different ways represent the same unsuccessful incorporation of actuality into possibility. Schlegel most clearly denies actuality and flees into an imaginary life that falsely claims to attain infinity in an ideal life; but the finite takes its revenge, and the imaginative idealization dissolves into sensuality. Tieck's denial of actuality produces formlessness in his poetic production. His imagination, opposed to the static forms of the philistine world, makes his artistic work arbitrary and empty. Lacking a definite relation to an ideal, his imagination vitiates both the infinite, ever-vanishing ideal and the finite world. Solger's attempt to give a philosophical and religious account of the place of irony that retains the finite fails, since his understanding of the artistic moment dissolves the finite into an imagined nothingness.

Central to Kierkegaard's diagnosis of the Romantic imagination's self-contradictions is his conviction that they lack a consistent principle of form by which to order experience, an organic "life-view" (Livsanskuelse) necessary to both personal and artistic self-integration. In possessing a life-view an author acquires a depth of outlook that unifies a work of art, delivering it from arbitrariness. Without a life-view, feeling, freedom, ethics, poetry, and religion become formless 'and imaginary, and in this inchoate state dissolve into self-contradiction, having at best the negative coherence of a recurring idea.99

For Kierkegaard the concept of Livanskuelse is already oriented in an ethical and Christian direction, as suggested in his earlier polemic against Hans Christian Andersen in From the Papers of One Still Living (1838).100 Andersen's difficulty is that although he has the qualifications of a lyric poet and short-story writer, he does not possess the maturity of a reflective Livsanskuelse necessary for the higher art of "epic poetry," in this instance, the novel. The principle character in Andersen's Only a Fiddler (Kun en Spillemand) turns from the harsh vicissitudes of life that frustrate genius and dwells in an imaginative world in which he can brood over his resentment, finally dying in poverty. As Frithiof Brandt observes, for Kierkegaard

> the genesis of Andersen's novels seems to have resulted from the fact that his poetic desires, ousted from the world, take refuge in his imagination, but his personal resentment at the real world is then transferred to his imaginary figures; in this way a double light falls on his novels. The cause is the absence of a view of life which is actually Providence in the novel, the deeper unity.101

Only a Fiddler lacks a Livsanskuelse that would give it unity; instead the author and characters alike find refuge in a flight into imagination. Andersen lacks a self-consciousness that has gained an inner understanding of experience, illuminated by reflection.102

While Kierkegaard does not employ the term Livsanskuelse in his argument against the Romantics in The Concept of Irony, he makes the same point by using the term "fantasy-intuition" (Phantasie-Anskuelse) to describe the Romantic imagination. Kierkegaard first uses this term, which comes to have great importance for him, in his criticism of Friedrich Schlegel in The Concept of Irony. In a passage we have already cited Kierkegaard says: "Now who is such a monster that he is unable to delight in the free play of the imagination [Phantasien]? But it does not follow from this that the whole of life should be given over to imagination [Phantasie-Anskuelse]."[103] In Kierkegaard's analysis of the Romantics in The Concept of Irony, to live in Phantasie-Anskuelse is to lack a Livsanskuelse. In using the term Phantasie-Anskuelse, Kierkegaard extends his earlier critique of Andersen's lack of a coherent life-view, focussing now on the Romantics for their aesthetic disintegration and ironic opposition to actuality. In this way the imagination, as well as irony, becomes the concept Kierkegaard contrasts to Livsanskuelse in both life and art.

At this point two questions arise about Kierkegaard's understanding of the imagination in The Concept of Irony. First, if Kierkegaard associates the imagination so strongly with a negative infinity diagnosed as Phantasie-Anskuelse, is there a positive infinity available that can reconcile one with actuality? Second, if so, is there an explicit positive role for the imagination in this? The first question can be answered with certainty from The Concept of Irony, but the second is more difficult to judge.

Kierkegaard gives two avenues for answering the first question on the availability of a positive Infinite that can be reconciled with the finite. One avenue is religion as the only possible means of reconciling the ideal and the actual, the infinite and the finite. The other avenue is that of "mastered irony," with which Kierkegaard closes his dissertation.

Religion is the first means for a positive reconciliation of the infinite and the finite. The problem of the finite and the infinite for the Romantics,

Kierkegaard claims, is that they self-evasively keep the infinite outside of themselves as an external goal, stifling their relation to the actual in their search for a poetic reconciliation beyond the given world. Echoing the common post-Kantian sentiment, Kierkegaard grants that poetry is a victory over the world and does provide "a kind of reconciliation," since it gives one "another actuality," in contrast to the imperfect actuality in which we live.[104] But, again with Kant, Kierkegaard says that poetry cannot give true reconciliation. This is because in poetry a person seeks an infinite, never-ending enjoyment, and in enjoyment one is "outside" oneself, contemplating an object that pleases. This external infinite is self-defeating, however, since life becomes an endless proliferation of images, moods, and stimuli that prevent one from examining oneself concretely. The Romantic enjoys the world, but escapes the self.

In religion, however, infinity is internal. Religion, too, "renders actuality infinite for me," but, as "internal," the source of joy is not a dream outside the self, but simply one's actual self in all of its concrete determination.[105] When this finite actual life is brought before God, infinite and internal enjoyment arises. Religion is the reconciliation for which the Romantics yearn, but the reconciliation comes only from a religion cognizant of finitude, not from the false infinite of poetic imagination.[106] This may appear similar to Schleiermacher's understanding of the Romantic religious vision that we described in the last chapter, in which the infinite is found within the finite, yet Kierkegaard's emphasis is quite different, for the source of religion is ethical and religious action rather than a feeling of absolute dependence implicit in all experience. It is only through action that the finite and the infinite are reconciled. The Romantic's hope for salvation through imaginative intuition and a religion of poetic vision is vain.

This leads to the second avenue Kierkegaard takes in discussing the means by which the finite and the infinite are reconciled: the concept of "mastered irony." Kierkegaard's use of Socrates as his model of irony means that irony is not excluded by religion, but is redeemed. Irony's negation of the finite is the first step in the development of subjectivity. In this sense the Romantic irony, although abortive, is correct. In mastered irony, the ironic stance is not left behind, but is raised to a higher power and becomes integrated into a positive relation with actuality. The truth of irony is that it makes one aware of how unsatisfying the actual is for a person; irony is justified in its yearnings and in the criticism of society that results.[107] The difference, however, is that the "wild infinity" of the Romantic irony is tamed, and irony discovers its validity, no longer as unmastered, but in itself both mastered and also a master:

> Irony now limits, renders finite, defines, and thereby yields truth, actuality, and content; it chastens and punishes and thereby imparts stability, character and consistency. Irony is a disciplinarian feared only by those who do not know it, but cherished by those who do.[108]

Irony can now function to return one to actuality, that is, to permeate the finite with the sense of the infinite in contrast to the Romantic flight into imagination. Criticism and yearning remain, but no longer as a rejection of the actual, "a cowardly, effeminate ruse for sneaking oneself out of the world."[109] By means of mastered irony, yearning becomes a healthy love in which one returns to the world in ethical action: "Actuality acquires its validity through action."[110] It is only through action that the finite and the infinite are balanced.

Mastered irony has important consequences for the artist too. Kierkegaard praises Goethe, as well as Shakespeare, as poets whose works exhibit such mastery: Goethe "succeeded in making his existence as a poet [Digter-Tilvaerelse] congrue with his actuality."[111] Although Kierkegaard does not use the term Livsanskuelse in discussing mastered irony, we return here to the theme of Kierkegaard's critique of Andersen, that a poet must have a mature life-view. In this maturity, the poet becomes "in some measure a philosopher," the artistic work has an internal rather than an accidental relation to the poet, as a moment in the poet's own life-history.[112] The work of art does not exhibit the capriciousness of Romantic poetry, nor does it awaken in the poet the ironic disgust that destroys the work.[113] The poet has a self-relation in an inward infinity, analogous but not identical to the inward infinity of the religious.[114] This restores the true freedom of the poet over the work, in contrast to Romantic caprice.[115]

Religious inwardness and mastered irony, therefore, are the arenas for a positive union of finite and infinite. But this brings us to the second question: does Kierkegaard allow in The Concept of Irony a positive evaluation of the imagination? It appears at first glance that Kierkegaard must evaluate the imagination positively. Irony is a necessary step in the development of one's spirit, and it could be argued that the imagination, like irony, has a mastered moment in a life that balances the finite and infinite in action. The productive imagination that secures for Kant the autonomy of the self could here become central.[116] Just as Kierkegaard states that the poet who masters irony regains freedom, and just as he seems to imply that the Romantic self-contradictions are overcome in mastered irony, so too the imagination could be redeemed in mastered irony. And Kierkegaard does say, as we have seen, "Now who is such a monster that he is unable to delight in the free play of the imagination?"[117]

All of these are plausible conclusions one could draw from The Concept of Irony. But Kierkegaard himself does not directly advance them in the dissertation, and he finally gives no clear positive function for the imagination beyond a blessing on its enthusiasm. The reasons for this are not difficult to find. Kierkegaard concentrates in the dissertation on the negative uses of the imagination; his references to it are almost entirely in the polemic against the Romantic ironists. Furthermore, the imagination as Phantasie-Anskuelse has a thoroughly negative connotation, opposed as it is to Livsanskuelse. Religious inwardness and its analogue, mastered irony, are presented as the only means of raising actuality to the infinite without volatilizing oneself and the infinite in the realms of fantasy.[118] While it is true that the poetic work of a master of irony incorporates the poetic, such a work avoids the imaginative capriciousness that characterizes the Romantics. Kierkegaard grants that poets are imaginative, to be sure, but he uses the imagination as a summary term for much that he attacks in the dissertation.

There are two passages in The Concept of Irony where Kierkegaard could give, or at least imply, a positive account of the imagination, but both are ambiguous. The first, and most likely, is in the discussion of Solger in the section on mastered irony. The second is in Kierkegaard's discussion of the role of imagination and myth in Plato's dialogues.

In the section on mastered irony, Kierkegaard indirectly indicates a positive role for the imagination, but he does not develop it, and it is finally unclear how Kierkegaard would judge the specifics of Solger's understanding of imagination. As we noted earlier, Kierkegaard directly cites Solger's discussion of irony, dominated by the concept of the imagination. In that section Kierkegaard says that "irony and enthusiasm are . . . set forth as the two factors necessary for the artist. What is to be understood by this will be discussed in its proper place."[119] The "proper place" is a favored place, the next section of Kierkegaard's dissertation, that on mastered irony. Kierkegaard begins his discussion by noting that "Solger in his lectures on aesthetics makes irony a condition for every artistic production."[120] Solger's virtue is his recognition that irony, as in Shakespeare, preserves the "objectivity" of the depiction, rather than allowing "the substantial content to evaporate in an ever more volatile sublimation."[121] Even in Shakespeare's depictions of madness there is objectivity. Kierkegaard praises Solger, in short, for his refusal to be drawn into a nihilistic irony. The discussion of Solger is muted, however, for Solger's metaphysic, as we have seen, is inadequate to the task of establishing the concrete finite pole necessary to a fruitful relation of finite and infinite. Indeed, one could argue that Kierkegaard favors Solger's limitations on irony and imagination rather than Solger's positive account of the imagination, since it is the imagination that makes Solger's metaphysics untenable. Given Kierkegaard's qualified support of Solger, yet his criticism of Solger's metaphysical religious views, it simply is unclear what Kierkegaard's evaluation would be of Solger's understanding of the imagination. Capel suggests that Kierkegaard intends, slyly and indirectly, to support Solger's metaphors as "elliptical compressions of the imagination" against Hegel's discursive reasoning; this may be the case, but is somewhat speculative. At most Kierkegaard would appear to approve the imagination's "enthusiasm" as an ingredient in mastered irony.

The second passage that may describe a positive role for the imagination treats the role of myth in Plato's dialogues. This is the most extended discussion of the imagination in the dissertation, but it, too, is extremely ambiguous, and unhelpful in attempting to find a more positive view of the imagination.

In this passage, Kierkegaard discusses the imagination in relation to myth and dialectic. Kierkegaard asks what the role of the mythical is in the Platonic dialogues, and he argues, against Ast and Baur, that it is not merely an accommodation to the listener or a vestige of traditional forms of thought.[122]

Rather, the mythical has an internal significance, and indeed an internal history, in the development of the dialogues. Whereas in the earlier dialogues the mythical has an external relation to dialectic--in fact is the opposite of dialectic--in the later dialogues the mythical has an internal, "more amiable" relation to the dialectic: myth becomes image in the later Plato.

In the earlier dialogues, the result of the dialectic is negative, and, Kierkegaard argues, the mythical comes in to provide a satisfaction that is beyond the dialectical. For example, in the Phaedrus, the enormous span of time the soul traverses is a mythical representation of the existence of the soul after death. What happens, claims Kierkegaard, is this:

> The dialectical first clears the terrain of everything extraneous and now attempts to climb up to the Idea; when this attempt fails, however, the imagination [Phantasien] reacts. Fatigued by these dialectical exertions the imagination lays itself down to dream, and from this is derived the mythical.[123]

The mythical is, thus, "the Idea in a condition of estrangement," representing the Idea in temporal and spatial terms.[124] The mythical is imagination's enthusiasm "in the service of speculation, and, to a certain extent, what Hegel calls the pantheism of the imagination [Phantasien]."[125] Kierkegaard's point is that mythology is the product of the imagination when it comes into contact with reflective consciousness. The imagination attempts to conceive what the reflective consciousness fails to conceive. The myth is not believed to be true, for then it would not be myth, but reflection, yet at this stage of the process reflective consciousness "is not yet permitted to destroy" the myth.[126]

A later stage in the development of the Platonic dialogues occurs when myth is transformed into the image:

> As soon as consciousness appears, however, it becomes evident that these mirages were not the Idea. If, after consciousness awakens, the imagination [Phantasien] again

> desires to return to these dreams, the mythical exhibits itself
> in a new form, that is, as image. . . . The mythical is there
> for the first time assimilated into the dialectical, is no longer
> in conflict with it.[127]

In short, the stage of the image shows a greater sophistication with regard to the

mythological, since it perceives the inadequacy of myth. But Kierkegaard adds

two comments to this. First, the mythological and imagistic are both Platonic

rather than Socratic elements. The young Plato, Kierkegaard speculates, resisted

the "hungry dialectic" of Socrates; the result is the unassimilated mythology of

the early dialogues.[128] Second, even in the stage of the image, Plato never really

moved past representative thought (Forestillingen): "Because Plato never arrived

at the speculative movement of thought, the mythical, or more precisely, the

image, may still be a moment in the representation of the Idea. Plato's element is

not thought but representation."[129] The mythical-imagistic is "the unripened

fruit of speculation" that ferments into the late dialectic, but "never fully ripens in

Plato" because the dialectic never completely replaces the imagistic.[130]

What are we to make of this analysis of the imagination in relation to

dialectical and to speculative thought? Is Kierkegaard championing, in an ironic

way, the representative form of thought, and hence the imagination, or is he

serious in his presumably negative judgment that Plato never attains to

speculation beyond imagistic thought? Scholars disagree on this, and it is related

to the question of just how Hegelian Kierkegaard was when he wrote the

dissertation. The consensus is that Kierkegaard was not Hegelian, and that there

is throughout the dissertation an ironic polemic against Hegelianism.[131] But it is

often very difficult in particular instances to discern when Kierkegaard is or is

not being ironic. The translator of The Concept of Irony, Lee Capel, believes

Kierkegaard ironically implies that Plato's imagistic thinking is actually superior

to speculative (Hegelian) thought, that the reference to the ripening of speculation and the process of fermentation is parallel to an early journal entry "where the end product is ambiguously represented both as maturation and putrefaction." Thus, Capel concludes, "one simply cannot do without the possibility of irony."[132]

Gregor Malantschuk, by contrast, takes seriously Kierkegaard's implied negative comparison of Plato's imagistic and representative thinking to speculation, seeing this passage as the fullest explication of Kierkegaard's ordering of the steps of cognitive thought: 1) mythological reflection; 2) metaphorical reflection; 3) representative or abstract reflection, which includes Plato; 4) scientific reflection; and 5) reflection on the category of the absurd. Malantschuk notes that the judgment on Plato--that he never goes beyond representative thought--is possible not only from an Hegelian position, but also agrees with Aristotle's assessment of Plato. Malantschuk concludes that Kierkegaard intends this ordering of the cognitive activities seriously, and the only reason Kierkegaard does not discuss this ordering again in his writings is that he is henceforth exclusively concerned with the fifth category, reflection on the absurd. One can infer, therefore, that Malantschuk does not see Kierkegaard's comparison of imaginative and speculative thought as ironic.[133]

Hermann Diem sees the matter more dialectically. For Diem, Socrates' dialectic attains the ideal by way of thought alone, leaving will and feeling behind. Platonic thought is justified in reacting to this abstraction by engaging in imagistic thought, "but this happens as a later reaction to the one-sidedness of the abstracting dialectic of Socrates and hence in a certain neutralizing opposition to the latter."[134] Kierkegaard leaves the conflict unresolved in The Concept of Irony, and he need not be identified with either the Platonic position (as Capel argues) or the Hegelian (as Malantschuk implies).

One can, it is true, note that Kierkegaard speaks of Plato becoming the "master" of the mythical, which immediately calls to mind comparison with Goethe as the master of irony.[135] Just as irony requires a master to supersede and yet incorporate it, so too the mythical could require its own master. But is imaginative, representative thought then higher than the speculative, or not? Irony is at once inferior to speculation as a purely negative moment, and yet can become a "mastered irony" in a way that Hegelian speculation does not recognize. The same may be true of imaginative and representative thought, but this possibility is left completely undeveloped in The Concept of Irony. Diem's judgment is, therefore, the most to be trusted; Kierkegaard reaches in The Concept of Irony a dialectical impasse between imagination and thought that, in the terms of the dissertation, he does not or cannot resolve. This would also help explain why Kierkegaard does not elaborate a more positive role for the imagination in The Concept of Irony.

Despite the hints of a more positive role for the imagination, Kierkegaard views it, by and large, in a negative fashion in The Concept of Irony. The imagination, perhaps even more than irony, is the object of a sustained polemic. His primary interest is to restrain the claims of the imagination to be either the key to the infinite or in any way adequate for a truly human life. And his discussions of mastered irony and of representative thought's relation to speculation are extremely ambiguous. The possible positive senses of the imagination are not developed, and one should avoid undue speculation about implications of his thought that Kierkegaard himself chooses not to develop in the dissertation.

So we are left with a question. Does Kierkegaard, in the interests of his polemic against Romanticism, and his affirmation of the primacy of the ethical, eliminate any positive role for the imagination in human life? To answer this

question, we must turn to other works, now from the formal authorship, in order
to see what positive role the imagination can have for him.

1 Kierkegaard, of course, continues this attack in Either/Or (1843), but The Concept of Irony focusses more directly on Kierkegaard's assessment of Romanticism itself. The broader significance of aestheticism in The Concept of Irony, including wider areas of experience than Romanticism represents, will be discussed in Chapter IV.

2 For accounts in English of Romanticism in Denmark, see P. M. Mitchell, A History of Danish Literature, with introductory ch. by Mogens Haugsted (Copenhagen: Gyldendal, 1975) ch. 6; Henning Fenger and Frederick J. Marker, The Heibergs, Twayne's World Authors Series 105 (New York: Twayne, 1971) ch. 2. See also Robert L. Horn, "Positivity and Dialectic: A Study of the Theological Method of Hans Lassen Martensen," diss., Union Theological Seminary, New York, 1969, 7-12. Horn links Steffens' notion of "presentiment" (Ahnelse) to Martensen's religious intuitionism. Kierkegaard, of course, was familiar with Steffens and Oehlenschläger. He was intrigued by Steffens' later Caricaturen des Heiligsten, I-II (Leipzig: 1819-21) (see, for example, Kierkegaard, JP 3: 2304 and 2305), and he heard Steffens lecture in Berlin in 1841-42. Although Kierkegaard initially found Steffens' lectures interesting, they were finally a disappointment to him; in a letter to P. J. Spang he writes, "The streets [in Berlin] are too broad for my liking and so are Steffens' lectures," Søren Kierkegaard, Letters and Documents, trans. Henrik Rosenmeier, Kierkegaard's Writings 25 (Princeton: Princeton UP, 1978) 97 (Letter 51) (hereafter, LD); cf. 106-07 (Letter 55 to F. C. Sibbern).

3 Horn 15-18; Fenger and Marker 46.

4 Fenger and Marker 46-47.

[5] Kierkegaard, JP 3: 3796 (I A 130), n.d., 1836.

[6] Kierkegaard, JP 5: 5135 (I C 88), March 24, 1836. Molbech (1783-1859) was professor of literary history at the University of Copenhagen.

[7] Molbech notes also that music is the art with the greatest "affinity to the romantic and the capacity to assume the character of the spiritually unlimited . . . for it exceeds all other art in dealing with the infinite, the inexhaustible, the unfathomable in the soul, but here only through feeling, immediately intuited"; cf. Søren Kierkegaard, "The Immediate Stages of the Erotic, or the Musical Erotic," Either/Or, vol. 1, trans. David F. Swenson and Lillian Marvin Swenson, rev. and fwd. Howard A. Johnson (Princeton: Princeton UP, 1959) 43-134 (hereafter, EO1).

[8] All quotations in this paragraph are from Kierkegaard, JP 5: 5135 (I C 88), March 24, 1836.

[9] Kierkegaard, JP 3: 3802 (I A 142), March, 1836.

[10] Kierkegaard, JP 3: 3803 (I A 155), April, 1836.

[11] Kierkegaard, JP 3: 3814 (I A 262), n.d., 1836. On the phrase "fliegendes Blatt," see Lee M. Capel's note in CI 396n16: the term refers to the "broadsheet, the form in which poetry was circulated in the sixteenth century."

[12] Hofe 79ff; Anna Paulsen, Sören Kierkegaard: Deuter unserer Existenz (Hamburg: Wittig, 1955) 27; Kierkegaard, JP 5, p. 477n171; Hofe notes Hirsch's opinion that Kierkegaard studied Novalis late in 1835; it is uncertain if Kierkegaard knew Friedrich Schlegel's works in 1836, but he certainly did by 1837, and possessed the Wiener Ausgabe of Schlegel's works.

[13] Kierkegaard, JP 1: 123 (I A 219), n.d., 1836.

[14] Kierkegaard, JP 5: 5138 (I C 95), n.d., 1836, and p. 478n187; the quotation is from Tieck's Phantasus.

[15] Kierkegaard JP 5: 5287 (II A 207), ll:30, December 26, 1837.

[16] Kierkegaard JP 5: 5288 (II A 679), December 30, 1837.

[17] Malantschuk 29.

[18] Arild Christensen, "Der junge Kierkegaard als Schriftstellerpersön-lichkeit und die Persönlichkeitsauffassung in den Frühwerken," Orbis Litterarum 18 (1963): 31-32.

[19] Kierkegaard, JP 5: 5131 (I C 85), March, 1836; cf. Malantschuk 56; Thulstrup, Kierkegaard's Relation to Hegel 85f.

[20] Hofe 81-82.

[21] Kierkegaard, JP 3: 2799 (I A 300), n.d., 1836.

[22] Kierkegaard, JP 4: 4398 (I C 126), January 27, 1837.

[23] Malantschuk (148) argues that "Romantic" in this entry eventually evolves into the "ethical" stage, since the ethical too is concerned about a more than earthly satisfaction. This is questionable, given Kierkegaard's early separation of Romanticism and Christianity in JP 5: 5131 (I C 85), March, 1836. Hofe is closer to the truth in seeing the Romantic as a precursor to the aesthetic stage. Eventually Kierkegaard--and here Malantschuk would agree--unites the first three stages under the category of the aesthetic. Hofe 90-91, 96.

[24] Kierkegaard, JP 4: 4398 (I C 126), January 27, 1837.

[25] See Kierkegaard JP 5, p. 481n245, where Malantschuk, in agreement with Emanuel Hirsch, notes that the Faustian letters are pseudonymous and poetic, and should not necessarily be taken as autobiographical, a point on which many biographers of Kierkegaard have been misled. See Emanuel Hirsch, Kierkegaard Studien (Gütersloh: Bertelsmann, 1933) 2: 490-92, serial pagination. Kierkegaard abruptly abandoned this plan when H. L. Martensen published his study of Lenau's "Faust"; see Lee M. Capel, "Historical Introduction," The Concept of Irony, with Constant Reference to Socrates, by

Søren Kierkegaard, trans., introd. and notes Lee M. Capel (Bloomington: Indiana UP, 1968) 16-28.

26 Paulsen 30.

27 Kierkegaard, JP 5: 5092 (I A 72), June 1, 1835; JP 2: 1968 (II A 53), n.d., 1837.

28 Kierkegaard, JP 1: 795 (I A 150), March, 1836; Hofe 111.

29 Wellek 18.

30 Kierkegaard, JP 5: 5100 (I A 75), August 1, 1835.

31 Capel 15-29.

32 Kierkegaard, JP 2: 1968 (II A 53), n.d., 1837.

33 See, e.g., Kierkegaard, CUP 449.

34 Kierkegaard, CI 292n.

35 Kierkegaard, CI 278, 281.

36 Vincent A. McCarthy, The Phenomenology of Moods in Kierkegaard (The Hague: Nijhoff, 1978) 11-12.

37 Kierkegaard, CI 221.

38 Kierkegaard, CI 251.

39 Kierkegaard, CI 248-49.

40 Kierkegaard, CI 249, 251, and 253.

41 Kierkegaard, CI 255.

42 Kierkegaard, CI 253.

43 Quoted by Kierkegaard in CI 284, from G. W. F. Hegel, Lectures on the History of Philosophy, trans. E. S. Haldane and Frances H. Simson, 3 vols. (London: Routledge, 1955) 1: 402.

44 Kierkegaard, CI 318.

45 Kierkegaard, CI 318.

46 Kierkegaard, CI 319.

[47] Kierkegaard, CI 319.

[48] Kierkegaard, CI 319.

[49] Kierkegaard, CI 290.

[50] Kierkegaard, CI 292. On Fichte, compare an early journal entry from 1836: "In despair Fichte threw the empirical ballast overboard and foundered," Kierkegaard, JP 2:1189 (I A 302), n.d., 1836.

[51] Kierkegaard, CI 292.

[52] Kierkegaard, CI 319-20.

[53] Kierkegaard, CI 296; cf. Hofe 138-39.

[54] Kierkegaard, CI 293. We will investigate Kierkegaard's mature understanding of the relation between the actual and the ideal in Chapter V on ethical imagination.

[55] Kierkegaard, CI 294.

[56] Kierkegaard, CI 297.

[57] Kierkegaard, CI 298.

[58] Kierkegaard, CI 300.

[59] Kierkegaard, CI 300.

[60] Kierkegaard, CI 301.

[61] Kierkegaard, CI 301.

[62] Kierkegaard, CI 301; cf. 316.

[63] Kierkegaard, CI 298.

[64] Kierkegaard, CI 302.

[65] Kierkegaard's debt to Hegel in the negative analysis of Romantic irony and its self-contradictory nature is evident, for example, in Hegel's The Philosophy of Fine Art: "The proximate form of this negativity [irony] is . . . the illusory nature of all that is matter of fact, or moral, or of substantive content, the nothingness of all that is objective and of essential and independent worth."

And on the self-contradiction of irony, Hegel says, "Irony contradicts and annihilates itself as manifested in individuals, characters, and actions, and consequently is an irony which overreaches itself." G. W. F. Hegel, The Philosophy of Fine Art, trans. and notes F. P. B. Osmaston, 4 vols. (London: Bell, 1920) 1: 90-91, 92.

[66] Kierkegaard, CI 260.

[67] Kierkegaard, CI 292n, 302; cf. Capel's notes, 418n14 and 420n1. Kierkegaard's criticisms of irony are thus indirectly aimed at the current "Young Germany" movement, and so his redemption of irony should be seen in contrast to this movement too.

[68] For Hegel's judgment on Lucinde see, for example, Hegel, Fine Art 2: 269: "We have few traces of the wanton disregard of things that are sacred and of the highest excellence such as marks the period of Frederik von Schlegel's 'Lucinde.'" Kierkegaard's concern with the novel does not end with The Concept of Irony. It has been persuasively argued that "The Diary of the Seducer" in the first volume of Either/Or is in some ways modeled on Lucinde; see Jean Wahl, "Kierkegaard et le romantisme," Orbis Litterarum 10 (1955): 297. Gregor Malantschuk argues that Kierkegaard only finally refutes Lucinde in Either/Or by the tactic of showing the Seducer as the logical consequence of the ironic standpoint of Schlegel's hero, Julius; Malantschuk 219. Cf. John D. Mullen, "The German Romantic Background of Kierkegaard's Psychology," Southern Journal of Philosophy 16 (Spring 1978): 658. We will return to this comparison between Julius and Johannes the Seducer in Chapter IV.

[69] Kierkegaard, CI 303; cf. Eichner, Friedrich Schlegel 88-89.

[70] Kierkegaard, CI 308.

[71] Walzel 78-79.

[72] Peter Firchow, "Introduction," Friedrich Schlegel's Lucinde and the Fragments, by Friedrich Schlegel, trans. and introd. Peter Firchow (Minneapolis: U of Minnesota P, 1971) 25.

[73] Kierkegaard, CI 303; Hofe argues from this for the influence of Heine on Kierkegaard's understanding of Friedrich Schlegel, Hofe 158n731.

[74] Kierkegaard, CI 306-07.

[75] Schlegel 78.

[76] Schlegel 66.

[77] Schlegel 102.

[78] Schlegel 68.

[79] Schlegel 126.

[80] Schlegel 128; cited in Kierkegaard, CI 308n.

[81] Kierkegaard, CI 316.

[82] Kierkegaard, CI 311.

[83] Kierkegaard, CI 308n.

[84] Kierkegaard, CI 316.

[85] Kierkegaard, CI 316.

[86] Kierkegaard, CI 317.

[87] Pierre Mesnard, Le Vrai Visage de Kierkegaard (Paris: Beauchesne, 1948) 161.

[88] Kierkegaard, CI 320.

[89] Kierkegaard, CI 320n; the quotation is from H. G. Hotho, Vorstudien für Leben und Kunst (Stuttgart and Tübingen, 1835) 412.

[90] Cf. this to Kierkegaard's own reflection, in PV 68, that, looking back on his authorship from the perspective of 1848, he thanks Governance for restraining his own genius, keeping his poetic productivity within strict bounds: "I have needed God every day to shield me from too great a wealth of thought."

[91] Hofe 165.

[92] Kierkegaard, CI 322; cf. Kierkegaard's journal entries from Molbech, cited above, on music as the essence of the Romantic. This, of course, is a theme Kierkegaard returns to in "The Immediate Stages of the Erotic," Either/Or, Volume I.

[93] Kierkegaard, CI 312.

[94] Kierkegaard, CI 332.

[95] Kierkegaard, CI 312, 323.

[96] Kierkegaard, CI 323.

[97] Kierkegaard, CI 424; Kierkegaard, CI 328, cites especially Solger's letters to Tieck and Abeken, in K. W. F. Solger, Nachgelassene Schriften und Briefwechsel, ed. Ludwig Tieck and Friedrich von Raumer, 2 vols. (Leipzig: Brockhaus, 1826) 1: 502-514 (to Tieck) and 596-607 (to Abeken). In analyzing this material Kierkegaard follows Hegel's 1828 review, in G. W. F. Hegel, Sämtliche Werke, ed. Hermann Glockner, 20 vols. (Stuttgart: Frommann, 1961-71) 20: 132-202, esp. 165ff, 182f; see CI 323 and 328. Malantschuk 220-21, observes that Kierkegaard is intrigued with Solger's attempt to see irony as an organizing principle, but that Kierkegaard believes Solger is unequal to the task.

[98] Kierkegaard, CI 327-29.

[99] McCarthy 142ff; 135-59 offers a fine extended analysis of Livsanskuelse, without, however, indicating directly the contrast with the term Phantasie-Anskuelse in The Concept of Irony.

[100] McCarthy 144. On the implicit "ethical critique" of the artist's need for personal and artistic unity in From the Papers of One Still Living, see George Connell, To Be One Thing: Personal Unity in Kierkegaard's Thought (Macon, GA: Mercer UP, 1985) 21-37.

[101] Aage Henricksen, Methods and Results of Kierkegaard Studies in Scandinavia (Copenhagen: Munskgaard, 1951) 104, summarizing Frithiof Brandt's position.

[102] McCarthy 145f.

[103] Kierkegaard, CI 308n.

[104] Kierkegaard, CI 312.

[105] Kierkegaard, CI 312-13.

[106] Kierkegaard, CI 312-13.

[107] McCarthy 30.

[108] Kierkegaard, CI 338-39; my emphasis.

[109] Kierkegaard, CI 341.

[110] Kierkegaard, CI 341.

[111] Kierkegaard, CI 337.

[112] Kierkegaard, CI 337.

[113] Kierkegaard, CI 337.

[114] Kierkegaard, CI 338. Anz is correct in criticizing Hirsch for seeing the role of poetry in the dissertation as being "the revealer of the natural God-relationship," Hirsch 58. As Anz observes, while there is a formal similarity between poetry and religion, the material difference between them is great. Whereas they both speak of the reconciliation of the finite and the infinite, it is clear from The Concept of Irony that Kierkegaard wins his religious understanding of the person in large part from a critique of the Romantic, poetic spirit (Anz 12n10).

[115] Kierkegaard, CI 336.

[116] Hofe 101-02.

[117] Kierkegaard, CI 308n.

[118] McCarthy 24.

[119] Kierkegaard, CI 332.

[120] Kierkegaard, CI 336.

[121] Kierkegaard, CI 336.

[122] Kierkegaard, CI 131.

[123] Kierkegaard, CI 132.

[124] Kierkegaard, CI 132. Cf. this to Kierkegaard's early definition of myth as "the compacting (suppressed being) of eternity (the eternal idea) in the categories of time and space," Kierkegaard, JP 3: 2799 (I A 300), n.d., 1836.

[125] Kierkegaard, CI 132-33. Thulstrup, Kierkegaard's Relation to Hegel 225 and Hirsch, there cited, claim that the reference is to Hegel's The Philosophy of History, trans. and pref. J. Sibree, pref. Charles Hegel, introd. C. J. Friedrich (New York: Dover, 1956) 141: "The Indian view is a total, universal pantheism, and is, however, a pantheism of imagination, not of thought."

[126] Kierkegaard, CI 133n.

[127] Kierkegaard, CI 134.

[128] Kierkegaard, CI 136.

[129] Kierkegaard, CI 143n.

[130] Kierkegaard, CI 136.

[131] See, e.g., Hirsch 228-29n3; Anz 29n; Thulstrup, Kierkegaard's Relation to Hegel 242ff; beyond Kierkegaard's parodies of Hegel, Dunning (ch. 1) identifies in CI (and throughout Kierkegaard's literature) probably unconscious Hegelian structures of thought.

[132] Kierkegaard, CI 383n18 (Capel's note); Capel does not give a closer citation of the journal passage, but it may refer to JP 4: 1568 (II A 48), n.d., 1837.

[133] Malantschuk 195-96. Niels Thulstrup regards Malantschuk's suggestion as having "a certain tendency to draw quite far-reaching conclusions from isolated expressions and suggestions in Kierkegaard (e.g., in On the Concept of Irony)," yet Thulstrup agrees with Malantschuk's view of "degrees of knowledge" in Kierkegaard; see Thulstrup, Kierkegaard's Relation to Hegel 360n37. Another "isolated expression and suggestion" is in JP 2: 2262 (II A 390), April 3, 1839.

[134] Hermann Diem, Kierkegaard's Dialectic of Existence, trans. Harold Knight (Edinburgh and London: Oliver, 1959) 23.

[135] Kierkegaard, CI 132.

CHAPTER THREE

Imagination and the Subjective Thinker: Kierkegaard's Response to

Idealist Rationalism in the Concluding Unscientific Postscript

> Existing is an art. The subjective thinker is aesthetic
> enough to give his life aesthetic content, ethical
> enough to regulate it, and dialectical enough to
> interpenetrate it with thought.
> --Kierkegaard, Concluding Unscientific Postscript

Kierkegaard's dialectic of the imagination is won in the midst of a polemic

against the Idealists as well as the Romantics. In order to approach the place of

the imagination in his thought, it is necessary to examine both sides of that

polemic. In the second chapter we have seen Kierkegaard's attack on a fantastic

Romantic expansion of the claims of the imagination in human life, in which he

seems ready to grant the imagination, at most, its realm of play and delight.

Kierkegaard does develop, however, a positive role for the imagination, most

evident in his attack on Hegelianism ("the System"). Although The Concept of

Irony voiced for the most part an Hegelian critique of the Romantics' elevation of

the imagination, Kierkegaard is equally critical of the Hegelians' marked

dismissal of the imagination. The muted, ironic critique of Hegel in The Concept

of Irony now expands in the Climacean writings into a central issue: the hatred

of the System for feeling and imagination.

In order to highlight the background of this side of Kierkegaard's two-

front polemic on the question of the imagination, we will first briefly review

Hegel's understanding of the imagination, and then turn to Kierkegaard's

Johannes Climacus (1842-43) for an introduction to the pseudonymous author of

the Postscript, Johannes Climacus. We will then concentrate on Kierkegaard's full attack on the Hegelian denigration of the imagination, as he formulates it in the Concluding Unscientific Postscript (1846).

Hegel on the imagination

Engaged as he was by the Romantic spirit, the young Hegel yearned for the wholeness of the individual and society. He envisioned a revitalized religion of the people, for which there were two requirements:

> I. Its doctrines must be grounded on universal reason.

> II. Fancy, heart and sensibility [Phantasie, Herz und Sinnlichkeit] must not thereby go empty away.[1]

For such a religion "it is of the greatest importance that fantasy and heart not be left unsatisfied, that the former be filled with pure images and that the more altruistic feelings be aroused in the latter."[2] But in his quest for the wholeness of the person, which he shared with the Romantics, Hegel takes a far different approach. As we have already seen, he becomes extremely critical of the Romantics for what he considers to be their uncontrolled indulgence in dreaming, a self-reflexive activity that loses itself in unhappy consciousness, aware of its infinitude, but lapsing into a "bad infinite." Hegel remarks of the Romantic spirit:

> Its activity is a yearning which merely loses itself as consciousness becomes an object devoid of substance, and, rising above this loss, and falling on itself, finds itself only as a lost soul. In this transparent purity of its moments, an unhappy, so-called 'beautiful soul', its light dies away within it, and it vanishes like a shapeless vapour.[3]

Out of this critique of the Romantic spirit, Hegel devises an understanding of the imagination that at once gives it a place, but also strongly curbs its scope.

We can see this in Hegel's remarks on the imagination in regard, first, to subjective spirit, and, second, to aesthetics.

In The Philosophy of Subjective Spirit (Philosophie des Subjektiven Geistes), Hegel analyzes youth and its imaginativeness as the stage of natural life (der natürliche Verlauf der Lebensalter) prior to adulthood:[4]

> In the youth there is the developed opposition of the tension between the ideals, imaginings [Einbildungen], reformings, hopes etc. of a universality which is itself still subjective, and immediate singularity; on the one side there is the world which is inadequate to the yearnings, on the other the attitude to this world of an individual whose existence is still lacking in independence and inner maturity.[5]

Consistent with Hegel's stress on the realization of an objective moral order, he maintains that such a youth will eventually attain maturity and see the "objective necessity and rationality of the implemented world with which he is confronted," and move to find a place within this objective order.[6] Hegel gives the imagination its proper place, however, not in this remark in the section on "anthropology," but in the "psychology." The treatment is not remarkable, but is nevertheless crucial in understanding Hegel's priorities, for while the imagination is important in representation (Vorstellung) as the capacity of the mind to create images, the imagination is subordinate to reason (Vernunft) even in subjective mind. Representation stands between intuition (Anschauung) and thought (Denken), forming an image from the material of intuition, one not yet possessing the freedom of thought.[7] Hegel subdivides representation into recollection (Erinnerung), imagination (Einbildungskraft), and memory (Gedächtnis). He discusses Einbildungskraft in standard terms, as reproductive and associative, distinguishing it from creative or productive Phantasie. Phantasie in true post-Kantian fashion is a great power, for in it "intelligence ceases to be the vague mine and the universal, and becomes an individuality, a concrete subjectivity [concrete Subjectivität], in which the self-reference is defined both to being and to universality."8 But while Phantasie is the organ of the concrete, it does not deal with truth, which is the province of reason:

> Imagination [Phantasie], when regarded as the agency of this unification, is reason [Vernunft], but only a nominal reason [die nur formelle Vernunft], because the matter or theme [der Gehalt der Phantasie] it embodies is to imagination qua imagination a matter of indifference; whilst reason qua reason also insists upon the truth of its content [Inhalt].9

In Hegel's aesthetics, this anti-Romantic subordination of Phantasie to Vernunft in subjective spirit has important results at the dialectically higher level of Absolute Spirit. In the posthumously published lectures on aesthetics, translated as The Philosophy of Fine Art, the imagination has an important but at the same time limited role to play in the philosophy of spirit. Like Schelling, the creative imagination (Phantasie) is first considered as "the most conspicuous faculty of the artist," an instinct-like gift.10 "The free activity of the imagination is the source of the fair works of art, which in this world of the mind are even more free than Nature is herself." Because of this, art makes its appeal to sense, feeling, perception, and imagination.11

Hegel confronts the old question of the supposed "irrationality" of the aesthetic that would preclude a philosophical discussion of it. Hegel, in true Idealist fashion, answers that art is a revelation of the rational and spiritual. Sensuous art is amenable to philosophical reflection because in its highest form it is one mode, along with religion and philosophy, in which "the Divine, the profoundest interests of mankind, and spiritual truth of widest range, art [sic] brought home to consciousness and expressed."12 The content (Gehalt) of art is Truth, the Absolute, the Idea, the Divine.13 The sensuous material is not a problem, because thought can think the sensuous (the opposite of thought) insofar as it is "impregnated" with the Idea.[14] The imagination (Phantasie), therefore, has tremendous capabilities. It is not mere passive, visionary fancy; rather, as creative, it grasps reality, and "manifests the essential truth and reason of the real itself."[15]

But art is also limited, since the imagination exhibits the Idea in a sensuous material, in "the concrete form of actual existence and individuality."[16] The imagination's virtue is that it renders the sensuous material a true vehicle, and in art the necessary vehicle, for the apprehension of the Idea.[17] But the sensuous material is at the same time a limiting principle for Hegel, one in which the sensuous becomes more and more transparent as art progresses spiritually. Thus Hegel can laud Romantic art (in the broad sense of Christian art) because it has language as its medium, which is most transparent to spirit. With the increasing transparency of the sensuous medium, art is better able to depict the particular, and can therefore give free rein to the "adventures of fantasy" (Abenteuern der Phantasie).[18] With this movement, the imagination becomes more important. In poetry, the highest level of art,

> the true medium of poetical representation is the poetical imagination and the intellectual presentation itself. . . . Poetry is, in short, the universal art of mind, which has become essentially free, and which is not fettered in its realization to an externally sensuous material, but which is creatively active in the space and time belonging to the inner world of ideas and emotion.[19]

Yet despite this greater role for the imagination in poetry, it too like the sensuous medium is limited and ultimately surpassed in the history of spirit, for Hegel goes on immediately to add:

> it is precisely in this its highest phase, that art terminates, by transcending itself; it is just here that it deserts the medium of a harmonious presentation of mind in sensuous shape and

passes from the poetry of the imaginative idea into the prose of thought.[20]

This is Hegel's response to the Romantic and Schellingian elevation of the imagination, and his own answer to their common concern with the split in the post-Kantian conception of the person. In contrast to Schelling, Hegel believes that art, although present with us yet, is essentially an outmoded form of consciousness. The advance of the unfolding of Absolute Spirit has gone beyond the stage of aesthetic intuition. Art is finally surpassed for Hegel, both by the representation (Vorstellung) found in religion and by the direct, non-representational statement of the Idea in the form of concept (Begriff), in which the Idea comes to itself in thought.[21] Art, he says, "is and remains for us, on the side of its highest possibilities, a thing of the past."[22] As René Wellek has put it, Hegel is a Janus-head in the history of aesthetics, for whereas on the one hand he looks with longing to the Greek ideal, with its fusion of form and content, on the other hand he looks with equanimity to the future death of art.[23] And the imagination, as central to the mode of consciousness which is art, is also surpassed. The final Hegelian solution to the Romantic elevation of the imagination is the calm judgment that the "poetry of imaginative idea" yields to "the prose of thought."

We can summarize Hegel's understanding of the imagination by saying that he regards it first as a capacity, especially a capacity to create (or enjoy) art, but also as a level or form of consciousness, typified by representation, and finally as a medium, the medium of poetry--all of which are surpassed by thought. In what senses Kierkegaard agrees or disagrees with Hegel's evaluation of the imagination is the aim of the rest of this chapter.

Imagination and the thinker in Johannes Climacus, or De Omnibus Dubitandum Est

It is in the "Climacean" writings, especially the Concluding Unscientific Postscript, and the unpublished book, Johannes Climacus, or De Omnibus Dubitandum Est (written in 1842 or 1843), that Kierkegaard attacks the Hegelian understanding of the imagination. The bulk of this attack is in the Postscript, but Johannes Climacus, not least because of its autobiographical reference, sets the tone for Kierkegaard's understanding of the positive value of the imagination.

In the "Introduction" to Johannes Climacus, Kierkegaard reflects on the importance of the imagination in childhood by depicting in a charming, almost wistful, vignette Johannes Climacus' upbringing by his father, especially the training of the capacities that prepared Johannes for philosophical reflection: dialectic and imagination.[24] The father, to all outward appearances "dry and prosaic," "underneath this rough homespun cloak . . . concealed a glowing imagination that not even his advanced age managed to dim."[25] In lieu of playtime outdoors, the old man would take the young Johannes on walks up and down the room of their home. Anything the boy wanted, whether to take an imaginary walk to Frederiksborg Castle or ramble the streets of Copenhagen, it was all at the boy's pleasure. And the father was equal to the task:

> While they walked up and down the floor, his father would tell about everything they saw. They greeted the passers-by; the carriages rumbled past, drowning out his father's voice; the pastry-woman's fruits were more tempting than ever. Whatever was familiar to Johannes, his father delineated so exactly, so vividly, so directly and on the spot, down to the most trifling detail, and so minutely and graphically whatever was unfamiliar to him, that after a half hour's walk with his father, he was as overwhelmed and weary as if he had been out for a whole day.

The father did not simply dazzle the boy, for

> Johannes quickly learned his father's magic art . . . ; they
> carried on a dialogue on their tour. . . . If the path was
> unfamiliar to Johannes, he made associations, while his
> father's omnipotent imagination was able to fashion
> everything, to use every childish wish as an ingredient in the
> drama that was taking place. For Johannes, it was as if the
> world came into existence during the conversation, as if his
> father were Our Lord and he himself his favored one who
> had permission to insert his own foolish whims as
> hilariously as he wished.[26]

Even Johannes' formal education, including the study of grammar, developed his imagination. The walks with his father encouraged his imagination to depict filled space, "into which he could not fit snugly enough."[27] But his grammar teacher, a man with a philosophical bent, argued that in Greek the accusative implies extension in time and space, and this led Johannes' imagination to take in empty space, the notion of expansion. In an alternative passage in the draft, Kierkegaard contrasts this "imagination of filled space" and "imagination of open space" by depicting a walk in a landscape covered with waterplants; he could at will fix his imagination on the denseness of the growth, the "filled space," or he could exercise his imagination of open space by making the tall grasses into a huge forest in which he shrank to a small creature.[28]

Yet in this upbringing, imagination was quickly united with dialectic. Johannes' "almost vegetative dozing in imagination--at times more esthetic, at times more intellectual," was jolted and enlivened by his father's example, for the old man, "who combined an irresistible dialectic with an omnipotent imagination," delighted in argument.[29] Johannes was astounded at how his father would allow an opponent to state his side of the argument before responding. When the old man did respond, "in an instant everything was turned upside down; the explicable was made inexplicable, the certain doubtful, the opposite was made obvious."[30] Johannes learned the joys of dialectic; and dialectic weaned his soul away from "the enchantment of poetry and the surprise of fairy tales."[31] Imagination and dialectic merged in the child and determined his intellectual habits. If, as Diem suggests, Kierkegaard faces an impasse in The Concept of Irony between Socrates' dialectic and Plato's imagination, in Johannes Climacus he resolves it. Johannes becomes a mature thinker for whom imagination and dialectic are the highest intellectual virtues, prompting his disillusionment with speculation, and equipping him to deal with the peculiar pathetic and dialectic demands of his philosophical concerns. To understand more clearly the place of imagination and dialectic in the "true philosopher," we must turn now to Climacus' own arguments, in the Concluding Unscientific Postscript.

The Postscript on the Romantic and the speculative philosopher: the three levels of analysis

For Hegel, as we have seen, the imagination has a strangely ambiguous role. It can present the Absolute in a sensuous medium, and in this respect Hegel resembles the Romantic quest for union with the infinite. But against Schelling and the Romantics, Hegel maintains that this union with the infinite must be grounded finally in the rational and conceptual, rather than in the imagination, for the Romantics' "'beautiful soul' vanishes like a shapeless vapour that dissolves into thin air."[32] Despite the claims of the imagination, it remains for Hegel a limited mode of consciousness, one that is surpassed in pure conceptual thinking. Kierkegaard, as we saw in the last chapter, goes a long way with Hegel in this critical appraisal of the Romantic imagination. But now Kierkegaard's task is to argue that Hegel's solution, a quest for the infinite by way of reason, is as misguided as the Romantic quest for the infinite by way of the imagination, not least because it dismisses too hastily the place of the imagination.

At first glance, therefore, it would appear as if Kierkegaard could set up a simple opposition in which the Romantics champion the imagination while the Hegelian philosophy limits it severely. This is, indeed, Kierkegaard's appraisal, but his actual procedure is more complex, for he has three levels to his critique, resulting in a deep analysis of both Romantic and Idealist, showing their hidden affinities and common errors.

In the first level of analysis, Kierkegaard's main point, he attacks the Idealist devaluation of imagination and feeling, which stands in such contrast to the Romantics' elevation of imagination. The second level of analysis, however, reveals how the Idealists, despite their critique of the Romantic imagination, are themselves just as "fantastic" as the Romantics they condemn; the Idealists are fantastic intellectually, the Romantics aesthetically. Having dialectically linked his opponents, Kierkegaard argues in the third level of analysis that, by being lost in the imaginative fantastic, the Romantics and Idealists thereby share a profoundly limited understanding of the true scope of the imagination in human life. Kierkegaard will propose, by contrast, uses of the imagination undreamt of in Romantic and speculative thought. The final section of this chapter will examine those uses as Kierkegaard describes them in "the simultaneity of factors" in the subjective thinker.

Kierkegaard's first level of analysis in the Postscript is to examine the opposition between the speculative philosophers as denigrators of the imagination and the Romantics as champions of the imagination. Kierkegaard makes clear that he is just as opposed to the Idealists as he is to the Romantics. In criticizing the Idealists, Kierkegaard notes that

> in the [Hegelian] interpretation of the historical process there
> is . . . a movement from lower to higher; the stages of
> imagination and feeling [Phantasiens og Følelsens Stadier]
> have been left behind, and thought as the highest stage is also
> the last. Everywhere it is decisively concluded that thought
> is the highest stage of human development; philosophy
> moves farther and farther away from contact with primitive
> existential impressions, and there is nothing left to explore,
> nothing to experience.[33]

The Hegelian progression from the aesthetic to the rational is inadequate, since this progression, in effect if not in intent, loses feeling and imagination--the Romantic virtues--in the greyness of speculative comprehension. One of the central aims of the Postscript is to recover "contact with primitive existential impressions" in a responsible way, without falling back into the Romantic excesses of the imagination.

Kierkegaard's attempt to achieve such a responsible contact leads to the second level of analysis. Whereas in the first level the Romantics and the Idealists are opposed on the imagination, Kierkegaard maintains in the second level that both are equally guilty of a "fantastic" (phantastiske) mode of life and thought.[34] While the Romantics may champion the imagination, the Idealists, inadvertently and despite their critique of the Romantic "beautiful soul," lose themselves in the "outmoded form of consciousness," imagination, they themselves condemn. However much the Romantics and Idealists may appear to disagree on the place of the imagination, they are part of an identical spiritual movement.[35]

One reason Kierkegaard can link speculation and Romanticism as "fantastic" is that the version of Hegelianism introduced into Denmark by J. L. Heiberg and H. L. Martensen is so highly aesthetical. Heiberg self-consciously adapted Hegel's speculative philosophy for poetic and artistic causes, incorporating Romanticism and Goethe in the process. For Heiberg poetry is not a surpassed mode of consciousness, but is the medium of a speculative religious vision. Far from being mere representation, poetry can conceptually grasp, not the Infinite in itself, but the infinite in the finite. Heiberg's ideal is that of comic drama and speculative poetry that possess a visionary character, uniting, in Martensen's words, the striving of the Romantics for the infinite with Goethe's concern for form, all interfused with the calm of speculative comprehension and balance.[36]

Kierkegaard, thus, has several targets in his analysis of the "fantastic." His primary concern is to extend his analysis of the Romantics, first fully developed in The Concept of Irony, to speculative philosophy in general, including its most rationalist, anti-Romantic strains. Danish Hegelianism is also in his sights, of course. In its self-conscious attempt to "go beyond" Hegel in combining poetic fantasy, intuition, and speculation in a new synthesis, it demonstrates the underlying kinship between Hegelianism in its pure form and Romanticism.[37]

Kierkegaard's task in this second level of the analysis is to describe the characteristics shared by the Romantic and Idealist; central to that analysis is his understanding of "possibility" as a contrast to ethical "reality." What links Romanticism and Idealism is their tendency to live in possibility rather than in reality. The Romantics lose their reality by living in poetic possibility; the Idealists lose their reality by living in intellectual possibility; the "advance" of Danish Hegelianism is that it manages to do both. As Kierkegaard puts it: "From the poetic and intellectual standpoint, possibility is higher than reality."[38] But for Kierkegaard there is a still higher position, that of the ethical, in which reality is defined as an ethical "interest" or actualization, rooted in decisiveness higher than possibility.[39] With this definition of ethical reality, Kierkegaard can then see that living in "possibility" defines the aesthetic and intellectual alike, uniting them despite all their real, and significant, incompatibilities. Even where the two schools take opposing positions, the possibility-reality distinction is Kierkegaard's ironic tool for understanding their kinship.

The concept of "possibility" allows Kierkegaard to diagnose other ways that the Romantics and Idealists are similar. This can be seen especially in how he redefines the ideas of "disinterestedness" and "aestheticism," so that they both apply to Romantics and Idealists alike. While the Romantics claim that in their aesthetic passion they are supremely "interested," they are actually objective and "disinterested"; conversely, while the Idealists claim to be supremely reflective and disinterested, they are actually just as "aesthetic" as the Romantics they claim to have surpassed. This is, again, because "from the poetic and intellectual standpoint possibility is higher than reality, the aesthetic and intellectual being disinterested."[40]

In contrast to Kant, for whom the aesthetic was disinterested, the Romantics, especially Friedrich Schlegel, regarded the aesthetic as highly "interested," signifying the spiritual power of art. But from the standpoint of ethical passion, Romantic "interest" is clearly just as disinterested as the speculative philosopher's more obvious--because objective--disinterest. The Romantic's passion concerning life is rather an abstraction from self and actuality. In short, Kierkegaard limits the term "interest" to the ethical sphere, so that "disinterest" applies to the aesthetic as well as the intellectual realms:

> Ethically the highest pathos is interested pathos, expressed through the active transformation of the individual's entire mode of existence in conformity with the object of his interest; aesthetically the highest pathos is disinterested. When an individual abandons himself to lay hold of something great outside him, his enthusiasm is aesthetic; when he forsakes everything to save himself, his enthusiasm is ethical.[41]

This passage points also to Kierkegaard's redefinition of the term "aesthetic." In limiting "interest" to the ethical sphere, Kierkegaard also expands the term "aesthetic" to include the Idealist as well as the Romantic. In reflective disinterest, the rationalist may believe that objectivity saves one from Romantic subjective vapidity. So too the rationalist may think that, unlike the Romantic, one is able to reclaim the "actual," as the finite and the ethical, beyond the alienation of the Romantic "beautiful soul." But Kierkegaard argues that the Idealists are indeed "aesthetic," for the term "aesthetic" now covers any form of living in possibility without ethical decisiveness; the Idealist may shun imagination and feeling for rational reflection, but still lives in aesthetic possibility rather than reality. As Wilhelm Anz notes, for Hegel and Goethe, as well as the Romantics, such ideal concepts as "nature," "soul," and "history" possess reality as visible presentations of the Idea, a visible unity of the finite and infinite.[42] But for Kierkegaard such an external presentation of the Idea is still in possibility. The true union of the finite and infinite occurs neither in Romantic intuition nor in Idealist speculation, nor, for that matter, in Danish Hegelianism's attempt to merge them; the union of finite and infinite occurs only in ethical existence.[43] Any position that does not acknowledge the "internal," ethical quality of the union of finite and infinite is by definition in the realm of possibility, and hence aesthetic.

Romantics and Idealists then, both live in possibility, disinterestedly and aesthetically. But what precisely is the imagination's role in these "fantastic" modes of living in possibility? Poetry and thought deal with possibility and cannot in themselves render possibility into ethical reality: "The aesthetic and intellectual principle is that no [concrete] reality is thought or understood until its esse has been resolved into its posse."[44]

Poetry and thought rightly use imagination to discover in the concrete a "possibility," that is, an aesthetic type (e.g., Don Juan as a type of the fleetingly amorous) or, intellectually, a general concept applicable to many diverse instances. But the danger always lies near at hand for the poet or thinker of mistaking reflections on possibility for reality itself. Such a confusion means that the Idealistic thinker, for example, falls into a "fantastic" way of thinking: "From the ethical point of view pure being is a fantastic medium [Phantasterier] and . . . it is forbidden to an existing individual to forget that he exists."[45]

If a philosopher falls into this error, the result is not that one has become pure thought; rather, one fantastically forgets that one is an existing human being. In imagining an identity between thought and being, one is self-deceived. The "fantastic" is for Kierkegaard a diagnostic term. One does not intend to be fantastic, as one can self-consciously and intentionally imagine, say, an absent friend or a golden mountain. Rather, Kierkegaard uses "fantastic" to diagnose the unintended self-deception and forgetfulness arising from thinking only in possibility. The power of the self-deception is so great that, in a sense, the thinker does alter himself or herself. Because thinking is inescapably an activity of a person, and because activity shapes one's identity, the speculative philosopher ceases to be an "existing" person in the eminent sense of one who relates thought to being. Transforming all reality into imagined possibility, one attempts to become what one thinks, but what one becomes is "fantastic."

The self-deception, however, lies in the futility of remaining abstractly in the imagination, for the thinker cannot alter the fact that he or she exists:

> If it is possible for a human being to become anything of the sort [i.e., abstract], and it is merely something of which at most he becomes aware through the imagination [Phantasie], he becomes the pure abstract conscious participation in and knowledge of this pure relationship between thought and

being, this pure identity; aye, this tautology, because this
being which is ascribed to the thinker does not signify that he
is, but only that he is engaged in thinking.[46]

The thinker becomes "fantastic" in forgetting that thinking is an activity, a

movement by an existing person. Instead, one identifies oneself with the

process and object of thinking. But this identification so distorts the activity of

thinking that the very activity is the source of the self-deception. Thus one only

"imagines" that one becomes this relation between thought and being.

The Idealist's attempt to identify the self with abstract thought is,

therefore, self-defeating, and for the same reason that the Romantic's escape into

imagination is self-defeating: the infinite and the finite are not brought into a

fruitful relation. The finitude of the "immediate" and the infinitude of the

"abstract" remain in an unresolved tension that takes its revenge on the Idealist

thinker, just as on the Romantic. In a journal entry from 1846, Kierkegaard

writes:

> By means of abstract imaginative thinking [en abstrakt
> Taenkning] a person wishes to transform himself (although if
> this self-creation were to succeed, it would simply mean his
> annihilation); yet at the same time he does continue to exist
> [existere], to be present [at vaere til], and therefore it can
> never succeed. Even the most persistent abstractedness in a
> human being still cannot wholly renounce immediacy; on the
> contrary, he becomes continually more conscious of it in
> trying to escape it, if for no other reason. The immediate is
> his foothold, and no matter how he may soar, no matter how
> extravagant he becomes in imagination [hvor phantastisk
> udsvaevende], he can nevertheless never completely abandon
> his foothold.[47]

Ironically the abstract thinker who believes in the identity of thought and being

actually lives a dual existence. Half of one's life is spent in abstract, imaginative

thought; the other half in immediacy. The final irony is that despite this imaginative expansiveness, the suppressed immediacy dominates existence. In another journal entry from 1846, Kierkegaard writes:

> The reason so-called immanental thinking has become so fashionable, practically among bartenders, too, is that it so splendidly encourages thoughtlessness in existence [Existents] and yet flatters it so profusely. Once in a while one thinks something in imaginative distance [i phantastisk Fjernhed], a compound of abstraction sub specie aeterni, which wipes out all distinctions--and for daily use exists [existerer] in animal categories (vegetates comfortably, discreetly chats a little with neighbors and the fellow next door, etc.). How infinitely remote most men's so-called thinking usually is from their existence; how rarely does even one single person get any reflective transparency with regard to his thought-existence [Tanke-Existents]; how rare is even the one who is simply aware of this.[48]

Just as Schlegel's imaginativeness leads finally to a "vegetative" existence, so does the Idealist's fantastic thought lead to a vegetative existence in finite categories.

In summary, Kierkegaard's adoption of the Hegelian critique of the Romantics in The Concept of Irony is, in the Climacean writings, turned against Idealism itself. Just as the Romantics flee from reality into the imagination, so too the Idealists, despite their stress on the "concrete" and the "objective," also flee reality by logically and metaphysically confusing possibility for the real. Thus, whereas at first sight the Romantics appear to be the champions of the imagination and the Idealists appear to restrict the claims of the imagination in the interests of the actual, a deeper analysis of Idealist philosophy in this "second level" shows that they too are guilty of an escape into the imagination.

There is yet a third level of analysis, dialectically more developed in incorporating the first two levels, preparatory to Kierkegaard's own account of a proper functioning of the imagination in existence. His response to the fantastic expansion of the imagination of the Romantic and Idealist is not to restrain the excesses of both by dealing the troublesome imagination a final, fatal blow. On the contrary, Kierkegaard argues that their fantastic expansion actually results from a severely truncated notion of the imagination, one that ignores the full scope of the imagination in human life. While agreeing with the speculative philosopher that the imagination cannot grasp the infinite by aesthetic intuition (as the Romantics claim), Kierkegaard denies that the solution is to comprehend the imagination within a broader movement to reason. Rather, the imagination possesses an entire realm of activity of which both Romantics and Idealists are unaware. In the language of the first level of analysis, Kierkegaard argues that a proper understanding of the imagination can lead one to the middle distance between a Romantic expansion of the imagination on the one hand and a speculative denigration of the imagination on the other. In the language of the second level of analysis, Kierkegaard argues that the imagination need not be only fantastic. It is these positive and necessary functions of the imagination that we must examine in the next section.

The imagination in the "simultaneity of factors" in the subjective thinker

In the Postscript's third level of analysis, Kierkegaard depicts the positive functions of the imagination primarily in the section on the "simultaneity of factors" in the existing thinker, a section that expands his reflections in Johannes Climacus on the relation of imagination and dialectic.[49] Kierkegaard begins his constructive account with an attack on the Idealist denigration of the imagination, using their dismissal of the imagination (the first level of analysis) as the foundation for his own positive account (the third level). In language reminiscent of his reflections on myth in The Concept of Irony, Kierkegaard grants that it may be possible, "from a scientific point of view," to make thought the highest stage, and to speak of a world-historical development from poetry to thought.[50] But this is as much as he willing to concede to the Idealists, since their mistake lies in attempting to transfer this world-historical development to individual existence, with ludicrous results:

> It is professed that thought is higher than feeling and imagination [Phantasie], and this is professed by a thinker who lacks pathos and passion. Thought is higher than irony and humor--this is professed by a thinker who is wholly lacking in a sense for the comical. How comical![51]

It is just this ignoring of the proper functions of feeling and imagination that is fantastic (in terms of the second level of the analysis). Kierkegaard continues:

> Just as the whole enterprise of abstract thought in dealing with Christianity and with existential problems is an essay in the comical, so the so-called pure thought is in general a psychological curiosity, a remarkable species of combining and constructing in a fantastic medium, the medium of pure being [i et phantastisk Medium: den rene Vaeren].[52]

Kierkegaard's remedy for this absent-mindedness on the part of speculative philosophy is not simply to supply a modification of the System, for he realizes that any simple modification will itself be accommodated to the System. Rather, he supplies a complete alternative to speculative thought, one that from its foundation prohibits the temptation to dissolve oneself into abstract thinking. The remedy is to reestablish imagination and feeling, along with will, on the same level as thought. Kierkegaard uses this as a decisive argument against speculative thought's obsession with the objective:

> If the understanding [Forstanden], feeling, and will are essential qualifications in a man, belong essentially to human nature, then all this chaff that the world-development now occupies a higher level vanishes into thin air. . . . The great

individual is great simply because he has everything at once.[53]

The starting-point, then, is the fact that the imagination and feeling also have claims on the person. In the language of Either/Or, the aesthetic is not eliminated, but incorporated into the ethical stage. As the motto from Edward Young placed before the first volume of Either/Or says, "Are passions, then, the pagans of the soul? Reason alone baptized?"[54] The passions can indeed be pagans, but they are not for that reason beyond the pale, for there is a logic to feeling and imagination as well as to thought. The problem with speculative thought is that it attempts to subsume the moments of subjectivity within a reflective knowledge of them and so abstract them from existence: "In existence, however, such a principle does not hold. If thought speaks deprecatingly of the imagination [Phantasien], imagination in its turn speaks deprecatingly of thought, and likewise with feeling."[55]

For example, Kierkegaard notes, when speculative thought and logic treat the question of immortality and eternal happiness, these disciplines quite correctly maintain that an eternal happiness (immortality) cannot be delivered by thought. This follows from the distinction between thought and actuality; thought deals with immortality as a concept but cannot prove its actuality. The question of eternal happiness, however, cannot simply be dropped as if it were of no further concern, for the question addresses itself just as much to the affective capacities of the person as to the intellectual. "Having a concern" is not simply an intellectual endeavor; feeling and imagination may continue to be concerned with the question of an eternal happiness even if the results of abstract thought are inconclusive. Like Socrates, whose agnosticism about an afterlife did not weaken his passion concerning it, so too the subjective thinker's imagination and feeling will not allow the question of an eternal happiness to die.[56] Indeed, it is fantastic to be unconcerned with happiness or to "entertain" the possibility of happiness in abstraction instead of as a matter of deep personal concern. Rather, when thought speaks deprecatingly of the imagination and feeling, the latter can urge their own "reasons," that is, their concerned desire for happiness. The person who thinks as an existing human being will have to attend to the "logic" of the imagination and feeling as well as of thought.

As in Johannes Climacus, Kierkegaard's ideal is not anti-rationalism, but a fusion of imagination and dialectic in the subjective thinker, now described as the simultaneity of the factors of thought, imagination and feeling, and will:

> In existence thought is by no means higher than imagination and feeling, but coordinate. . . . The task is not to exalt the one at the expense of the other, but to give them an equal status, to unify them in existence [det Medium, hvori de enes, er i at existere].[57]

This ideal of simultaneity and balance is at the heart of the entire enterprise of the Postscript, as indicated by its subtitle, "A Mimetic-Pathetic-Dialectic Composition, An Existential Contribution." The simultaneity of factors is, of course, hardly an original notion; Kresten Nordentoft calls it "almost a cliché in Danish and German, Goethe-inspired, post-romantic intellectual life," adding, however, that it is "all too easily overlooked when he [Kierkegaard] is labelled 'the father of modern existentialism.'"[58] There is certainly a "classicism" about this ideal, one that warns against construing Kierkegaard as an irrationalist or worshipper of sheer will, and in this sense the Postscript is a "mimic" composition, Kierkegaard's own Phenomenology of Spirit, describing too an itinerarium mentis ad Deum.[59] But, at the same time, Nordentoft fails to do justice to the anti-Idealist force of the simultaneity of factors, the inherent dynamism of the balance, evidenced by Kierkegaard's placing the discussion of "the simultaneity of factors" in a section critical of Idealism.

In using the image of a simultaneity of factors, Kierkegaard appears to have as his target Hegel's The Philosophy of Fine Art, with its subordination of imagination to reason. In a journal entry from 1841 or 1842 Kierkegaard notes that there is a

> passage where Hegel himself seems to suggest the imperfection of thought alone, that not even philosophy alone is the satisfactory expression of human life, or that thus personal life does not fulfill itself in thought alone, but in a totality of kinds of existence [Existents-Arter] and modes of expression. Cf. Aesthetik III, III, p. 440, bottom of page.[60]

In the passage to which Kierkegaard refers, Hegel discusses the superiority of philosophical thought over imagination, but admits that:

> On the other hand, however, this form [of philosophy] is linked with abstraction, . . . so that the concrete man can . . . express the content . . . of his philosophical consciousness in concrete fashion, as permeated with soul and perception, imagination and feeling [Phantasie und Empfindung].[61]

The irony of Kierkegaard's simultaneity of factors, then, is that he argues for a dynamic, indeed, artistic, balance against a philosophy that prides itself on its own balance. In the name of balance, Kierkegaard calls for a restitution of the very faculties the Idealists so often see as disruptive: imagination and feeling. Kierkegaard, in short, argues that speculative philosophy, like Romanticism, fails in its cherished goal of restoring human wholeness. In the simultaneity of factors, he introduces his own understanding of the requirements of that wholeness. In this way Kierkegaard reworks the classical and Hegelian ideal, adapting it to a philosophical outlook that emphasizes becoming rather than being, individual dynamism rather than (despite Hegel's incorporation of movement into thought) an abstract, intellectual stasis.

Kierkegaard stresses imagination and feeling because the wholeness he envisions requires passion. Passion, in Kierkegaard's concept, is a particular form of directed interest that can integrate thought, imagination, and feeling into their proper functions. The Idealists recognize the connection between passion and imagination, but relegate them both to a past stage in the development of spirit. Kierkegaard argues on the contrary that the Romantics are right at least in seeing the importance of imagination and feeling, and once passion is recognized as a prime requisite of the subjective thinker, then it is possible to evaluate the place of the imagination and feeling properly:

> but since we have in our time forgotten what it means to exist sensu eminenti, and since pathos is usually referred to the sphere of imagination [Phantasie] and feeling, the dialectical being permitted to abrogate and supplant it, instead of seeking the union of both in the simultaneity of existence, it has come about in our philosophical nineteenth century that pathos has been discredited, and that dialectics has lost its passion.62

The challenge to Kierkegaard is, then, to redefine the imagination as more than either Idealism's "surpassed medium" or the Romantics' aestheticism. The imagination must also be seen as a passion and an activity characterizing a "higher enthusiasm"--the enthusiasm of the "subjective thinker." This aim is clear in the very terminology Kierkegaard uses to describe the relation between imagination and passion, for he at once opposes passion to mere imagination and yet, in describing the subjective thinker, links passion and imagination intimately.

First, Kierkegaard distinguishes aesthetic passion and existential passion sharply, in terms consistent with his opposition between Phantasie-Anskuelse and Livsanskuelse in his early writings.63 For the Postscript, too, the imagination is predominant in sheer aestheticism. At times Kierkegaard uses the expression "Phantasie-Lidenskab" (imaginative-passion) of the Romantic ironic poet and his passion: "The poet is known by his power to wrestle pathetically with the imaginative passion [Phantasie-Lidenskab] of the infinite in happiness and despair, and comically and wantonly to take the whole Philistine world by the nose."64 And Kierkegaard can speak of the poet's passion as simply "Phantasie":

> The pathos of the poet is therefore essentially imaginative pathos [Phantasie]. An attempt ethically to establish a poetic relationship to reality is therefore a misunderstanding, a backward step. Here as everywhere the different spheres must be kept distinct.65

Thus, Kierkegaard makes a clear distinction between the poet's imagination and existential passion.

Second, Kierkegaard can nonetheless use the same expressions, Phantasie and Phantasie-Lidenskab, for the subjective thinker's passion. Although passion is not identical with imagination, the passion of the subjective thinker includes imagination:

> There is an old say that oratio, tentatio, meditatio faciunt theologum. Similarly there is required for a subjective thinker imagination [Phantasie] and feeling, dialectics in existential inwardness, together with passion. But passion first and last; for it is impossible to think about existence without passion.66

Kierkegaard can suggest an even closer relationship between imagination and passion. Speaking of those who lose poetic enthusiasm and degenerate into philistinism, Kierkegaard says bluntly that "every individual who does not live either poetically or religiously is stupid":67

> And in what does their stupidity consist? . . . In that after having lost the poetic illusion, they have been wanting in the imagination and passion [Phantasie og Phantasie-Lidenskab] to pierce the illusions of probability and penetrate the

apparent reliability of a finite teleology, all of which breaks down as soon as the infinite in a man begins to move.[68]

Here what Swenson and Lowrie have translated as "imagination and passion" is more accurately translated as "imagination and imaginative-passion," intimately linking the two concepts.[69] Kierkegaard, of course, is not confusing the spheres he insists must be kept distinct; the different senses of the expression Phantasie-Lidenskab are not self-contradictory. He is simply making the point that "imagination" and "imaginative-passion" function differently according to the governing interest. Imagination and passion in the aesthetic stage are dialectically lower than the passion of the subjective thinker. When he speaks of it in this way, he is thinking in terms of the second level of his analysis of the Romantics and Idealists in which both become fantastic and are inferior to the existing thinker. But in arguing against the Idealists Kierkegaard employs his first level of analysis, in which the Romantics, despite their faults, are seen as having a firm grasp of the necessity of the imagination that comes back at this dialectically higher level of the subjective thinker. In short, Kierkegaard argues for a third position that secures the imagination a realm of activity and interest directed to existence.

But what allows the imaginative-passion of the aesthetic to become transformed into the concrete imaginative-passion of the subjective thinker? What finally saves the imagination? The answer is the category of "inwardness" (Inderlighed), for inwardness directs passion and imagination to an infinite within the self, rather than (in the words of The Concept of Irony) to an external infinite:

> Art and poetry have been called anticipations of the eternal. If one desires to speak in this fashion, one must nevertheless note that art and poetry are not essentially related to an existing individual; for their contemplative enjoyment, the joy over what is beautiful is disinterested, and the spectator

of the work of art is contemplatively outside himself qua existing individual.70

By contrast, inwardness provides the interest that harnesses the factors of personality, including imagination, in the task of existing. In the Postscript's discussion of Either/Or, Kierkegaard contrasts imaginative and ethical inwardness. The aesthete lives in "imaginative inwardness" [Phantasie-Inderlighed], also described as an "imagination-existence" [Phantasie-Existents].71 But with Judge William

> instead of a world of possibilities, glowing with imagination [Phantasie] and dialectically organized, we have an individual--and only the truth which edifies is truth for you; that is, the truth is inwardness, but please to note, existential inwardness, here qualified as ethical.72

The distinction Kierkegaard employs is between "the medium of imagination" (Phantasie-Mediet or Phantasie-Medium) and "the medium of existence" [Existents]. The poet and speculative philosopher work in the medium of the imagination; the subjective thinker utilizes the imagination in the medium of existence, governed by inwardness: "In passion the existing subject is rendered infinite in the eternity of the imaginative representation [i Phantasiens Evighed] and yet he is at the same time most definitely himself."73 By means of the inwardness of the medium of existence, passion and imagination are transformed and yet maintained. Inwardness directs the imagination to reflect passionately on the conditions of one's own life, creating thereby an image of a task and a desire that leads to ethico-religious striving. In this process, a controlled inner infinite develops that is passionately grounded in the finite conditions of one's existence. The "medium of existence," although in opposition to the "medium of imagination," therefore incorporates the imagination into itself. In short, the distinction between the two media specifies the different uses of the imagination in the different spheres.

In fact, the very model Kierkegaard employs for the subjective thinker's striving in the medium of existence is that of the artist. Referring to the Postscript, Niels Thulstrup writes:

> The subjective thinker's task is to understand himself in his existence . . . and in order to fulfill this task he must use imagination as well as feeling and thinking, that is, he does not accomplish the task "scientifically" (speculatively) but as the title of the work also says, unscientifically, as an artist.[74]

The subjective thinker is an artist aware of the distinction between thought and being, possessing the necessary passion, keeping firmly in view the fact that it is out of the material of life that he or she must forge an existence transparent to the idea. The imagination presents the subjective thinker with possibilities that, raised to ideals in passion and inwardness, are ethically transformed into action. Artistry is at work here, coordinating his or her faculties. Kierkegaard is very direct on this point: "Existing is an art. The subjective thinker is aesthetic enough to give his life aesthetic content, ethical enough to regulate it, and dialectical enough to interpenetrate it with thought."[75] As an art, existence is complex and rich. In describing this richness of subjective thinking, Kierkegaard draws from both Romantic and Idealist conceptions of art and the artist.

First, as the Romantics saw, art holds opposites together, not in a higher synthesis, but in fruitful tension. So too for Kierkegaard, the subjective thinker holds together the opposites of the comic and the tragic. One may "at one and the same time . . . be crushed in spirit and yet free from care," "have one mood rich and full, and also . . . have the opposite mood." The thinker's form will be "as manifold as the opposites he holds in combination." But how close this ideal is to the Romantics' "mixed emotions" Kierkegaard attacked in The Concept of Irony.[76] Kierkegaard can take even the faults of the Romantic artist transpose them into the virtues of the subjective thinker. Once the artist's infinitude is seen to be internal rather than external, and once the simultaneity of factors as a complex, dynamic harmony becomes the ideal, Kierkegaard can incorporate the Romantic insights about human complexity into his picture of the subjective thinker. The subjective thinker "will find an inexhaustible subject for thought in his faith, when he seeks to follow its declension in all the manifold casibus of life."[77]

Second, Kierkegaard employs the Idealist concept of the concreteness of the art object against both Romantics and Idealists. The richness of the subjective thinker's artistry is due to his or her holding the abstract Idea in a proper relation to the concrete, thus achieving the wholeness that both Romantic and Idealist earnestly desire, but cannot attain. Kierkegaard thus gives his argument a final, ironic twist; having thoroughly castigated the Romantics and Hegelians for losing concretion in the abstraction of their imaginations, he demonstrates how the very "elements of concretion" of their own aesthetics can secure the concreteness of the subjective thinker's artistry.

With regard to the Romantics, Kierkegaard in the Postscript redeems the imagination by seeing how it gives one concreteness the Romantics lack--just as in his dissertation Kierkegaard redeems irony in the same way. Of course, the subjective thinker still possesses the abstracting movement of irony and imagination. Like the Romantic ironist, one "takes the whole Philistine world by the nose." But unlike the Romantic, one is master of irony. Wit turns upon irony itself, and is able "jestingly to look in upon the [aesthetic] imaginative passion [Phantasie-Lidenskab] of the infinite."[78] This artist is of a peculiar sort, then, dialectically advanced beyond the Romantic artist, for one will not be as imaginatively expansive; "in comparison with a poet, his form will be abbreviated":

The subjective thinker does not have the poetic leisure to create in the medium of the imagination [Phantasiens Medium], nor does he have the time for aesthetically disinterested elaboration. He is essentially an existing individual in the existential medium [en Existerende i Existentsen] and does not have at his disposal the imaginative medium [Phantasie-Mediet] which would permit him to create the illusion characteristic of all aesthetic production.[79]

This "higher irony" does not dissipate itself into sheer dreaminess; on the contrary, in aesthetic passion the imagination orients itself not only to the ideal, but to the individual and the concrete: "The subjective thinker adds to his equipment aesthetic and ethical passion, which gives him the necessary concreteness."[80] The term "aesthetic passion" here signifies concretion, the incorporation of the unresolved concrete pole that the Romantic poet sometimes imaginatively fled and that sometimes took its revenge when the Romantic lapsed into sheer dreaminess. In the medium of existence aesthetic passion secures the concreteness of the subjective thinker, producing an artistry that avoids the Hegelian charges of the vacuity of the "beautiful soul."

Kierkegaard ironically employs against the Hegelians too their own description of aesthetic concreteness, the concreteness that they believe to be at once art's glory and its limitation. For Kierkegaard, these "limitations" are precisely the virtues of the subjective thinker, for they are higher than rationalism's abstractedness. The subjective thinker exemplifies two Idealist concepts: that in art the imagination is the organ for the concrete, and that the art object is a sensuous medium transparent to the idea. The difference, however, is that in the subjective thinker the imagination is directed to a concrete life, not a concrete work of art; it is existence, not the sensuous medium, that is transparent to the idea, and the idea is made manifest in a concrete individual, not as objective Spirit in the concrete universal.[81] Kierkegaard uses the Hegelian aesthetic of the imagination as the organ for the concrete to his own ends. He redeems the imagination from the ambivalence of Hegelian aesthetics in order to secure the concrete as one pole of the healthy relation of the abstract and the concrete in the individual. The imagination takes its place not as a surpassed moment in the history of spirit, but as a continuing element in the dynamism of the person. The subjective thinker is, then, an artist, one who, in contrast to the pale and etherealized Idealist depicted in the Postscript, can hold the opposites together, maintaining the concretion and definiteness that the rationalist dismisses.

It is from his high estimation of the functions of the imagination in the subjective thinker as artist that Kierkegaard is able to complete his argument against both the Romantic and Hegelian misconstruals of the imagination, which we may summarize briefly. His attack on the Idealists, like that on the Romantics, is ironic. While Kierkegaard appears in The Concept of Irony to reduplicate the Idealist attack on the Romantics, in the Postscript he extends the argument against the Idealists themselves. Kierkegaard's opposition of the two media, imagination and existence, is at once a reduplication and an ironic parody of the Hegelian opposition of the media of poetry and thought. It is a reduplication of the Hegelian opposition, for Kierkegaard affirms that one, indeed, cannot remain in the medium of poetry and imagination; in this the Idealists are right. Kierkegaard agrees with Hegel that art as a "sensuous medium" and the imagination as a "medium" are transformed by spirit and thought. So too, Kierkegaard's new understanding of the imagination in the subjective thinker is a "synthesis" that seeks to unite Romantic and Idealist strengths.

More important, however, is that Kierkegaard's reduplication at the same time parodies Idealism. The parody is that the opposition of the media of imagination and thought leads not away from existence, to a higher conceptual synthesis, but into existence; it leads not away from the imagination, but into a greater imagination. The imagination is not surpassed by thought, for in the "simultaneity of factors" the imagination, like irony, is "mastered," transcending its own medium to enter into the highest levels of subjective existence. Again like irony, the imagination becomes the instrument of the concrete. In contrast, then, to the opposition of imagistic and conceptual thought in The Concept of Irony, which Malantschuk thinks significant, the Postscript so reworks the problem that the imagination is no longer identified, as in Hegel, only with its medium, or with a form of representative or pictorial consciousness, but achieves new functions and extent in subjectivity.

At the same time, in so elevating the imagination Kierkegaard does not abate at all his anti-Romantic polemic. He is at pains to show that although the subjective thinker is an artist, this artistry is unique, in marked opposition to the poetic imagination. This is important to recall because Emanuel Hirsch, among others, has written that Kierkegaard's Romantic side shows pre-eminently in his understanding of the person, in which he transfers Romantic inwardness to Christianity.[82] Wilhelm Anz agrees with Hirsch that Kierkegaard is closer to the Romantics than to Hegel, because they had a sense of the infinite inwardness and irreplaceability of individuality. But Anz rightly corrects Hirsch for thinking that Kierkegaard finds in the poetic the source of his understanding of the person.[83] It is clear from our study that Hirsch's conclusion is too simple. Kierkegaard is certainly interested in forging a concept of the imagination beyond the Idealists, but at the same time he is still just as interested in showing the Romantic imagination to be impossibly shallow. For this reason it is only one-half of the story to say that Kierkegaard is, in Jean Wahl's phrase, the "revenge of Romanticism on the system."[84] Torsten Bohlin is nearer to the truth when he argues that in The Concept of Irony Kierkegaard uses Romanticism polemically against Hegel and Hegel polemically against the Romantics.[85] We would add that the technique of setting opponents over against each other, exhibited obscurely in The Concept of Irony, is clearly evident in the Postscript; the book is a superb example of Kierkegaard's technique of putting dialectic to non-Hegelian, non-synthetic purposes. Our argument, then, is that Kierkegaard's double-edged dialectic allows him to chart a new and distinctive course in forming a concept of the imagination over against those of his contemporaries, Romantic and Hegelian alike.

In summary, for Kierkegaard, both Romantics and Idealists fail to achieve their stated goals of integration and wholeness, either in poetic imagination or in a rationalism that dismisses the imagination. Both are fantastic, primarily because they attempt to solve the problems of wholeness in an aesthetic, disinterested way. The Romantics do this by fixing on imagination as in itself providing the way to wholeness, but in their fixation rob life of its complexity by obscuring the demands of aesthetic integrity and personal self-integration. The Idealists are, if anything, in a worse situation, for in fearful reaction to Romantic excesses, they subsume the imagination within a larger conceptual, objective synthesis, a rational and contemplative wholeness that defeats itself by obscuring imagination and feeling as factors of the self.

For Kierkegaard, however, the problems of wholeness and integration are problems of existence; they are not solved either by escaping existence in aestheticism or by presuming that the "problem of imagination" can be solved in objective reflection. Problems of existence are solved only in the concrete struggles of individual life. For this reason, too, the imagination can only be rightly seen in the context of individual existence. Therefore, in the Postscript, in contrast to The Concept of Irony, Kierkegaard outlines the higher ethical and religious dimensions of the imagination in subjective thinking as an aspect of that true quest for wholeness. His work is an attempt--an imaginative attempt--to map out beyond the worlds of Romanticism and Idealism a realm for the positive functions of the imagination.

We have completed our analysis of the immediate polemical context against which Kierkegaard formulates his understanding of the imagination's roles. But we still have only touched the surface of Kierkegaard's thought on the imagination, for his reflections go beyond the particular, culturally-prominent forms of "diseased imagination," Romanticism and Idealism. Kierkegaard goes on to analyze the imagination as a central aspect of human life. Furthermore, the uses of the imagination in ethical and religious existence are also complex, and, Kierkegaard uncovers a wealth of further dialectical and passional steps for the imagination in the medium of existence. To appreciate the full range and subtlety of Kierkegaard's reflections on the imagination's functions, negative and positive, we must stand back from the polemical context and examine in the next three chapters Kierkegaard's vision of the manifold roles of the imagination in the stages of life. The clue to our study will be Kierkegaard's assertion in The Sickness Unto Death that the imagination is "the capacity instar omnium."

[1] G. W. F. Hegel, Hegels Theologische Jugendschriften, ed. Herman Nohl (Tübingen: Mohr, 1907) 20; the English translation is in H. S. Harris, Hegel's Development Toward the Sunlight, 1770-1801 (Oxford: Clarendon, 1972) 499; see also Charles Taylor 55; Taylor discusses at length this theme of "wholeness" in Hegel.

[2] Hegel, Jugendschriften 16; translated and cited by Stephen Crites, In the Twilight of Christendom: Hegel vs. Kierkegaard on Faith and History, American Acad. of Religion Studies in Religion 2, ed. Willard G. Oxtoby (Chambersburg, PA: American Acad. of Religion, 1972) 29; Harris, ch. IV, uses "Phantasie und Herz" in the chapter title, to describe Hegel's "Frankfurt period" of 1797-1800.

[3] G. W. F. Hegel, Phenomenology of Spirit, trans. A. V. Miller, analysis of the text and fwd. J. N. Findlay (Oxford: Clarendon, 1977) 400.

[4] This is the first section of the third part of the Encyclopädie der philosophischen Wissenschaften im Grundrisse (1817, later editions in 1827 and 1830); Thulstrup, Kierkegaard's Relation to Hegel 380, notes that Kierkegaard read in the Encylopädie, just as he read in much of Hegel: "Only the section on the philosophy of nature in the Encyclopedia seems to have left no mark on Kierkegaard."

[5] G. W. F. Hegel, Hegel's Philosophie des Subjektiven Geistes, with English trans., trans. and ed. M. J. Petry, 3 vols. (Dordrecht: Reidel, 1978), vol. 2, Anthropology 95-97; the standard English translation is by William Wallace, Hegel's Philosophy of Mind (Oxford: Clarendon, 1894), see 17.

[6] Hegel, Subjektiven Geistes 97; Kierkegaard too speaks often of the primacy of the imagination in youth, saying, for example, in Training in Christianity that, insofar as it is a natural capacity, "The imagination is strongest

in youth and decreases with years." Walter Lowrie omits this sentence from his translation; see Søren Kierkegaard, Training in Christianity and The Edifying Discourse which 'Accompanied' It, trans. with introd. and notes Walter Lowrie (Princeton: Princeton UP, 1941) 185 (hereafter, TC); for the Danish, see Søren Kierkegaard, Søren Kierkegaards Samlede Vaerker, ed. A. B. Drachmann, P. A. Heiberg, and H. O. Lange, 2nd ed., 15 vols. (Copenhagen: Gyldendal, 1920-36) 12: 209: "Indbildningskraften er staerkest i Ynglingsalderen, og tager saa af med Aarene."

7 Hegel, Philosophy of Mind 70; Hegel speaks here of non-religious Vorstellung, which engenders a finite Bild, in contrast to a religious Vorstellung and its reference to the Infinite; see Emil L. Fackenheim, The Religious Dimension of Hegel's Thought (Boston: Beacon, 1976) 154-55.

8 Hegel, Philosophy of Mind 75-76.

9 Hegel, Philosophy of Mind 76; Hegel's disciple and biographer, Karl Rosenkranz, gives a fuller treatment than Hegel of the place of the imagination in subjective spirit in Psychology, or the Science of Subjective Spirit (Psychologie, oder die Wissenschaft vom subjectiven Geist), 2nd ed. (Königsberg: Bornträger, 1843) 275-317. Rosenkranz discusses the imagination in the usual Idealist terms, under the headings of the reproductive imagination (die reproductive Einbildungskraft), productive fantasy (die productive Phantasie), and semiotic fantasy (die semiotische Phantasie). Kierkegaard owned the first edition of the book, but nowhere refers to the book's discussion of the imagination. Vigilius Haufniensis gives the book mixed praise in Søren Kierkegaard, The Concept of Anxiety, ed. and trans. with introd. and notes Reidar Thomte, with Albert B. Anderson, Kierkegaard's Writings 8 (Princeton: Princeton UP, 1980) 147-48. Vigilius notes appreciatively Rosenkranz's definition of disposition (Gemyt) as the unity of feeling and self-consciousness; but ambivalence emerges in Vigilius'

footnotes where he says of Rosenkranz's book, "I urge [the reader] to familiarize himself with it, for it is actually a competent book, and if the author, who otherwise distinguishes himself by his common sense and his humane interest in human life, had been able to renounce his fanatical superstitious belief in an empty schema, he could have avoided being ridiculous at times," 147-48n. Kresten Nordentoft says rightly that "psychology, the doctrine of the 'subjective spirit,' is a part of the weakest sections of Hegel's system," and he adds, referring to Rosenkranz and F. C. Sibbern, that "Kierkegaard . . . was unable to learn anything of essential importance from these academic psychologists, who smartly and elegantly enumerated the individual emotional states." He adds that Kierkegaard learned more from the Romantics than from the Idealists on the psychological aspects of the imagination. Kierkegaard's Psychology, trans. Bruce H. Kirmmse, Duquesne Studies: Psychological Series 7 (Pittsburgh: Duquesne UP; Atlantic Highlands, NJ: distr. Humanities, 1978) 389n9.

10 Hegel, Fine Art 1: 56, 381. Kierkegaard was very familiar with this work; see Thulstrup, Kierkegaard's Relation to Hegel 276.

11 Hegel, Fine Art 1: 6.

12 Hegel, Fine Art 1: 9.

13 Hegel, Fine Art 1: 9.

14 Hegel, Fine Art 1: 15.

15 Hegel, Fine Art 1: 381-82.

16 Hegel, Fine Art 1: 54, 383.

17 Hegel, Fine Art 1: 54.

18 From Hegel, Die Idee und das Ideal, cited in Charles Taylor 478.

19 Hegel, Fine Art 1: 120.

20 Hegel, Fine Art 1: 120.

[21] We will return to the relation of <u>Vorstellung</u> and <u>Begriff</u> in Chapter VI, in dealing with the role of imaginative, representational thought in Hegel's and Kierkegaard's understanding of religion.

[22] Hegel, <u>Fine Art</u> 1: 13.

[23] Wellek 333.

[24] It is clear that in <u>Johannes Climacus</u> Kierkegaard is making autobiographical references in identifying dialectic and imagination as the central prerequisites for philosophy. "My imagination [<u>Phantasie</u>] and my dialectic constantly had material enough to operate with, and time enough, free from all bustle, to be idle. For long periods I have been employed with nothing else but the performance of dialectical exercises with an adjunct of imagination, trying out my mind as one tunes an instrument--but I was not really living." Kierkegaard, <u>PV</u> 80. On childhood, storytelling, and imagination, see Kierkegaard, <u>JP</u> 1: 265 (II A 12), n.d. 1837; cf. also Kierkegaard, <u>LD</u> 211 (Letter 149): "Father was always almost impressed with me, for I could depict an idea with lively imagination and pursue it with daring consistency."

[25] Søren Kierkegaard, <u>Johannes Climacus, or De Omnibus Dubitandum Est: A Narrative</u> (hereafter, <u>JC</u>), in <u>Philosophical Fragments</u> and <u>Johannes Climacus</u>, ed. and trans. with introd. and notes, Howard V. Hong and Edna H. Hong, Kierkegaard's Writings 7 (Princeton: Princeton UP, 1985) 120. Cf. Kierkegaard, <u>LD</u> 211 (Letter 149): "A curious thing about Father was that what he had most of, what one least expected, was imagination, albeit melancholy imagination."

[26] Kierkegaard, <u>JC</u> 120.

[27] Kierkegaard, <u>JC</u> 121.

[28] Kierkegaard, <u>JC</u> 237; Kierkegaard later used a similar example in <u>Stages on Life's Way</u>, trans. Walter Lowrie, introd. Paul Sponheim (New York:

Schocken, 1967) 333 (hereafter, <u>SLW</u>), where Quidam records in his diary, "When I was a child a little peat fosse was my all in all. The dark tree-roots which protruded here and there in the profound obscurity were vanished kingdoms and lands, where every discovery was as important to me as are antediluvian remains to the scientist."

[29] Kierkegaard, <u>JC</u> 121.

[30] Kierkegaard, <u>JC</u> 122.

[31] Kierkegaard, <u>JC</u> 122-23.

[32] Hegel, <u>Phenomenology of Spirit</u> 400.

[33] Kierkegaard, <u>CUP</u> 307.

[34] We will examine the imagination's role in the "fantastic" more carefully when we turn in Chapter IV to Søren Kierkegaard, <u>The Sickness Unto Death</u>, trans. and ed. Howard V. Hong and Edna H. Hong, Kierkegaard's Writings 19 (Princeton: Princeton UP, 1980). The term also proves useful to Kierkegaard in his theological polemics, as we will see in Chapter VI.

[35] Cf. McCarthy 3.

[36] Horn 113-15, 150-58; in chs. 5-7 Horn analyzes the mutual influence of Heiberg and Martensen in the 1830's, in which Heiberg shifts closer to a theological understanding of speculation while Martensen is drawn back to Hegelianism.

[37] Nonetheless, Kierkegaard focusses his attack beyond Danish Hegelianism. He denies that Danish Hegelianism as represented by Martensen is his only target. In a draft of an article written in response to Magnus Eiriksson, Kierkegaard says that in the <u>Postscript</u> "the scene is deliberately sustained in such a way that rather than being in Denmark it is in Germany, where, after all, the speculation that 'goes beyond' originates," <u>JP</u> 6: 6596 (X[6] B 128), n.d., 1849-50. See E. Skjoldager, "An Unwanted Ally: Magnus Eiriksson," <u>Kierkegaard as</u>

a Person, vol. 12 of Bibliotheca Kierkegaardiana, ed. Niels Thulstrup and Maria Mikulová Thulstrup (Copenhagen: Reitzel, 1983). 102-08, esp. 106-07.

38 Kierkegaard, CUP 282.

39 Kierkegaard, CUP 284.

40 Kierkegaard, CUP 282.

41 Kierkegaard, CUP 350.

42 Anz 13.

43 Anz 13; see also Søren Kierkegaard, Either/Or, vol. 2, trans. Walter Lowrie, rev. and fwd. Howard A. Johnson (Princeton: Princeton UP, 1959) 175 (hereafter, EO2).

44 Kierkegaard, CUP 288; see also 295.

45 Kierkegaard, CUP 271.

46 Kierkegaard, CUP 112.

47 Kierkegaard, JP 2: 1348 (VII[1] A 143), n.d., 1846.

48 Kierkegaard, JP 1: 1043 (VII[1] A 140), n.d., 1846.

49 Kierkegaard, CUP 307ff.

50 Kierkegaard, CUP 308.

51 Kierkegaard, CUP 269; cf. Kierkegaard, JP 1: 47 (V A 20), n.d., 1844.

52 Kierkegaard, CUP 269.

53 Kierkegaard, JP 3: 3657 (IV C 78), n.d., 1842-43.

54 Kierkegaard, EO1 1.

55 Kierkegaard, CUP 311.

56 Kierkegaard, CUP 310; cf. Ralph Henry Johnson, The Concept of Existence in the Concluding Unscientific Postscript (Nijhoff, 1972) 80ff; C. Stephen Evans, Kierkegaard's "Fragments" and "Postscript": The Religious

Philosophy of Johannes Climacus (Atlantic Highlands, NJ: Humanities, 1983) 68-72, helpfully links passion and valuing.

[57] Kierkegaard, CUP 310-11.

[58] Nordentoft 93-94; balance was of course Heiberg's ideal as well, see Horn 121.

[59] Richard Kroner applies the phrase to the Phenomenology of Spirit in his introduction to G. W. F. Hegel, Early Theological Writings, trans. T. M. Knox, introd. and Fragments trans. Richard Kroner (Chicago: U of Chicago P, 1948) 44; see also Mark C. Taylor, Journeys to Selfhood, for an extended use of this image with regard to Hegel and Kierkegaard.

[60] Kierkegaard, JP 2: 1593 (III C 33), n.d., 1841-42.

[61] Hegel, Fine Art 4: 212; I follow the English translation of this passage found, with the previous quotation from Kierkegaard, in Thulstrup, Kierkegaard's Relation to Hegel 276-77. The German passage is in G. W. F. Hegel, Sämtliche Werke 14: 440.

[62] Kierkegaard, CUP 345.

[63] Kierkegaard, CUP 347.

[64] Kierkegaard, CUP 394.

[65] Kierkegaard, CUP 347; note that Swenson and Lowrie here translate "Phantasie" as "imaginative pathos."

[66] Kierkegaard, CUP 312-13.

[67] Kierkegaard, CUP 408-09.

[68] Kierkegaard, CUP 409.

[69] In the forthcoming translation of the Postscript by Howard V. Hong and Edna H. Hong the provisional reading of this phrase is "imagination and imagination-passion." I am indebted to the Hong Kierkegaard Library, St. Olaf College, for this information.

[70] Kierkegaard, <u>CUP</u> 277n3; in the Swenson and Lowrie translation "eternal" in the first sentence is erroneously given as "external."

[71] Kierkegaard, <u>CUP</u> 226-27.

[72] Kierkegaard, <u>CUP</u> 227.

[73] Kierkegaard, <u>CUP</u> 176.

[74] Thulstrup, <u>Kierkegaard's Relation to Hegel</u> 377.

[75] Kierkegaard, <u>CUP</u> 314.

[76] Kierkegaard, <u>CUP</u> 317, 319; cf. Kierkegaard, <u>CI</u> 301. F. C. Sibbern, the Danish philosopher and novelist, frequently used the expression "mixed emotions"; see Robert J. Widenmann, "Sibbern," <u>Kierkegaard's Teachers,</u> vol. 10 of <u>Bibliotheca Kierkegaardiana</u>, ed. Niels Thulstrup and Marie Mikulová Thulstrup (Copenhagen: Reitzel, 1982) 87. As Widenmann notes, however, for Kierkegaard the dynamism and tensions of mixed emotions preclude the perfect harmony Sibbern envisioned.

[77] Kierkegaard, <u>CUP</u> 314.

[78] Kierkegaard, <u>CUP</u> 394.

[79] Kierkegaard, <u>CUP</u> 319.

[80] Kierkegaard, <u>CUP</u> 313.

[81] We will examine Kierkegaard's concept of concrete personal transparency further in Chapter V on the ethical imagination. For now, the important contrast to keep in mind is that stated by Judge William: "The ethical individual is transparent to himself and does not live <u>ins Blaue hinein</u> as does the aesthetic individual," <u>EO2</u> 262. In <u>Postscript</u> Kierkegaard says, "Abstract thought turns from concrete man to consider man in general; the subjective thinker seeks to understand the abstract determination of being human in terms of this particular existing human being," <u>CUP</u> 315; cf. Kierkegaard, <u>JP</u> 3: 3224 (XI^2 A 107), n.d., 1854: "Personality could be called transparency."

82 Hirsch, serial pagination, 649; cited also in Jean Wahl, Etudes Kierkegaardiennes (Paris: Librairie Philosophique J. Vrin, 1959) 86.

83 Anz 33.

84 Wahl 135.

85 Cited by Capel in Kierkegaard, CI 352.

PART TWO: THE DIALECTIC OF IMAGINATION IN EXISTENCE

CHAPTER FOUR

The Capacity Instar Omnium:

The Imagination in the Intellectual

and Aesthetic Spheres

> The aesthetic and intellectual principle is that no reality is thought or understood until its esse has been resolved in its posse.
>
> --Kierkegaard, Postscript

> I am bound in a chain formed of dark imaginings, of unquiet dreams, of restless thoughts, of dread presentiments, of inexplicable anxieties.
>
> --Kierkegaard, Either/Or I

The Postscript depicts the imagination as a coordinate factor with feeling, will, thought, and passion in an individual life. The Sickness Unto Death continues and deepens this image of a simultaneity of factors by defining the imagination more closely, giving it an even more fundamental role in the picture of the self: as "the medium for the process of infinitizing," the imagination is "the capacity instar omnium [for all capacities]."[1] Examining the meaning of this term will allow us in this and the next two chapters to step back from the immediate polemical context and to see how Kierkegaard broadens his reflections on the entire scope of the imagination in the aesthetic, ethical, and religious stages. So too, the various roles of the imagination will become evident: medium, state, activity, capacity, disposition, and passion.

By identifying the imagination as "the capacity instar omnium," Kierkegaard discerns a wide range of both positive and negative functions for the imagination:

a) The imagination is central to logic, abstract thought, and objective knowledge, which for Kierkegaard is subject to a "quantitative dialectic,"[2] the type of reflection appropriate to objective knowledge of the finite. Here the essential movement is one of abstraction from reality to thought.

b) In the "aesthetic" stage of existence, as we have seen, a similar abstraction occurs, with equal ambiguity, including corruptions of the positive functions of thought in the quantitative dialectic. Kierkegaard unites the intellectual and aesthetic movements as abstracting activities: "The aesthetic and intellectual principle is that no reality is thought or understood until its esse has been resolved in its posse."[3] Turning especially to The Sickness Unto Death and Either/Or, Volume I, we will examine more closely in this chapter the positive and negative functions of the imagination in thinking and in the aesthetic sphere of existence.

c) In Chapters V and VI on the ethico-religious uses of the imagination, we will enter into the imagination's roles in the "qualitative dialectic," which, Kierkegaard says, "belongs to existence [Tilvaerelsen]"[4] and in which the subjective "how" of appropriation is decisive. In particular, Kierkegaard's treatment of aesthetic existence goes beyond his critique of Romanticism and Idealism, placing them within a much broader philosophical and psychological analysis of the aesthetic stages as a universal--and not simply cultured-- disposition of human beings. The aesthetic stage in its turbulence will be revealed as an often dramatic but inadequate way of being imaginative in existence. In Chapter V, relying on The Sickness Unto Death and Either/Or, Volume II, we will turn to the ethical sphere and expand on the Postscript's discussion of the imagination's place in the qualitative dialectic, where subjective thinking unites finite and infinite in the concrete individual. As we will see, the imagination operates here too in a most dialectical fashion, one that in some ways trims back the imaginative profuseness of the aesthetic sphere, yet combines the abstract functions of the imagination present in the aesthetic stage with the movement to the concrete: in contrast to the aesthetic and intellectual principle, "the ethical principle is that no possibility is understood until each posse has really become an esse."[5] Finally in Chapter VI, the role of the imagination in the qualitative dialectic of the religious and Christian spheres will prove to be even more complex.

A visual model would be helpful here, as long as it is not interpreted in too architectonic a fashion. It is as if Kierkegaard sees the capacities of the person organized into an arch, in which the ascending arc represents a) the abstracting capacities and dialectic of the thinker, especially the movement of thought from the actual to the possible, and b) the dynamic, restless movement characteristic of the aesthetic stage as a whole. The descending arc of the model shows the existential side of thought and dialectic, in which one can move from the realm of the possible back to the concrete and actual, in the ethico-religious realm. The model emphasizes, first, that reflection and the aesthetic sphere have much in common, and, second, that the descending arc of the ethical and religious spheres at once moves away from contemplation to action and yet retains reflection and the aesthetic in a dialectically more advanced process. To alter the image, the arch becomes a circle; the imagination abstracts ideals from the given world, then infuses itself in existence, which in turn gives material for future imaginative abstraction. Because of this, neither the ascending nor descending arc is of greater value than the other. In order to make the descending movement of the ethical, one must reach the apex of the possible, of abstraction, and of imagination. But so too, in order to be a self, one must make the descending movement as well.

The locus classicus for Kierkegaard's understanding of the imagination is The Sickness Unto Death. Although Anti-Climacus begins by analyzing a negative use of the imagination, that of the fantastical (Det Phantastiske) in despair, his remarks have a wider applicability, for he gives the imagination a central place in both the quantitative and qualitative dialectics of the self:

> As a rule, imagination [Phantasien] is the medium for the process of infinitizing [det Uendeliggjørendes Medium]; it is not a capacity, as are the others--if one wishes to speak in those terms, it is the capacity instar omnium [for all capacities]. When all is said and done, whatever of feeling, knowing, and willing a person has depends upon what imagination he has, upon how that person reflects himself-- that is, upon imagination. Imagination is infinitizing reflection [den uendeliggjørende Reflexion], and therefore the elder Fichte quite correctly assumed that even in relation to knowledge the categories derive from the imagination. The self is reflection, and the imagination is reflection, is the rendition of the self as the self's possibility. The imagination is the possibility of any and all reflection, and the intensity of this medium is the possibility of the intensity of the self.[6]

Two points in this paragraph deserve special attention. First, the passage indicates a role for the imagination in thought and knowledge. The imagination is "the possibility of any and all reflection"; "even in relation to knowledge . . . the categories derive from the imagination." Second, the passage illuminates aesthetic existence; because the imagination is "the medium for the process of infinitizing," it describes not only thought but the aesthetic sphere of existence. In the remainder of this chapter we must examine how the imagination as the capacity instar omnium functions in both thought and aesthetic existence.

Imagination and thinking

As for Kant and the Idealists, so too for Kierkegaard, the imagination is basic to thinking. Yet while he inherits the vocabulary of idealism, Kierkegaard nonetheless formulates a strongly anti-speculative concept of thought. Thinking for Kierkegaard is an activity of the individual, in which the imagination plays a central role. In this respect he is closer to Kant than to either British empiricism or Hegelian speculation.

As we have seen in discussing the simultaneity of factors in the Postscript, Kierkegaard isolates the essential problem of Hegelian philosophy as a "living in possibility" in which the thinker becomes fantastic. Behind this lies not only Kierkegaard's ethical concern, but his consistent and prolonged reflection on logical categories and epistemology. Kierkegaard's primary interest is not, of course, as logician or epistemologist, but these disciplines concern him greatly, since he believes clarity in logic and thought can guard against the confusion of thinking with existing. When the functions of abstract thought are distorted, as he believes speculation distorts them, they become fantastic, but abstract thought is certainly legitimate. Kierkegaard, therefore, is hardly an irrationalist; rather, he clarifies concepts concerning different kinds of thinking, their powers and limits. The Hegelian error is finally, for Kierkegaard, so subtle and insidious because in the guise of epistemology it distorts the true functions of knowledge and thought.

To illumine this point, Kierkegaard distinguishes within the quantitative dialectic between "abstract thought" and "pure thought," abstract thought being legitimate, and pure thought "fantastic."[7] The imagination as the movement from actuality to possibility, from esse to posse, is basic to both abstract thought and pure thought. In a journal entry from 1842 or 1843, Kierkegaard reflects on the imagination's role in abstract thought: "to what extent does the imagination

[Phantasien] play a role in logical thought, to what extent the will, to what extent is the conclusion a resolution."[8] The answer is that, in logical thought, the imagination abstracts from existence to possibility; further, such imaginative abstraction, the creation of possibilities, is endless unless halted by the will.[9] In the important section in the Postscript on the possibility of a logical system, Kierkegaard comments further on the imagination's role in logic:

> in order to throw some light on the nature of logic, it might be desirable to orient oneself psychologically in the state of mind of anyone who thinks the logical--so as to determine what kind of dying away from the self is involved, and how far the imagination [Phantasie] plays a role in this connection.[10]

This "dying away from the self" is not meant pejoratively. It is akin, rather, to the same process that Kierkegaard mentions in Philosophical Fragments when he says that "I never reason in conclusion to existence, but I reason in conclusion from existence."[11] To think logically requires a dying away from the self as an existent being, a suspension, or brief "forgetting," in which the thinker abstracts general concepts from the particulars of temporality. In 1848 Kierkegaard notes in his journal:

> The abstract can produce a prodigious effect. If I say in a talk: there where the road turns, there by the gate where the hired man stands--pure abstractions. . . .
> The gate can be a hundred thousand gates; the hired man can be millions.
> This is the eternal one of the imagination [Dette er Phantasiens evig Eet]. Just like the eternal "once upon a time" of the imagination: then man goes out into the morning of life.[12]

Kierkegaard holds that if one merely keeps the essence-being distinction in mind, and remembers that one not only thinks but exists, one will suffer no harm. But the danger is that this distinction will be obscured because of the imagination's powers of abstraction leading to "pure thought." Enchanted by the powers of abstraction, Hegelian logic falls into the error of "pure thought" by systematically obscuring the distinction between logical essences and being. It posits a fantastic identity between thought and being, subject and object, the inner and the outer, especially in claiming movement in logic.[13] But Kierkegaard, relying on Aristotle and Trendelenburg, believes that "the concept of movement is itself a transcendence that has no part in logic."[14] The thinker's imagination generates abstract concepts that are purely hypothetical possibilities, neither "existing" nor "moving."[15]

Despite the fantastic misuse of imagination in the "pure thought" of Hegelian logic, imagination nonetheless is for Kierkegaard the necessary condition for abstract thought and the science of abstraction, logic. In abstraction one rightly takes the givens of the world and distills the posse from the esse: in this the mind exercises its proper sovereignty in ranging widely and freely over the things of the world. The mind is not tied, for example, to this hired man, but is able to consider the "hired man" as a concept, a general term applicable to many instances. This imaginative generalization establishes a range of uses for an expression, necessary for thought and communication.

Kierkegaard describes this abstraction in Johannes Climacus, where he opposes, somewhat cryptically, immediacy and reality on the one hand, and mediacy and ideality on the other:

> What, then, is immediacy? It is reality itself [Realitet]. What is mediacy? It is the word. How does the one cancel the other? By giving expression to it. . . .
> Immediacy is reality; language is ideality; consciousness is contradiction [Modsigelse]. The moment I make a statement about reality, contradiction [between my statement and the reality or actuality I speak about] is present, for what I say is ideality.[16]

With language comes a split between reality and ideality. Ideality, in the humble sense of the general or the abstract, first emerges in the exercise of the imagination in language. Indeed, ideality, as abstract thought and its structural forms and rules (logic), is possible only because of the operation of the imagination.

It is interesting that Kierkegaard speaks of the imagination in connection with the state of immediacy prior to the split between reality and ideality. This immediate state Kierkegaard calls "soulishness" or the "psychical" as opposed to the "physical." "Soul," as John Elrod notes, "refers essentially to the imagination."[17] The power of the soul is "the origin of those imaginative thought productions in which the self may lose itself when it fails to act."[18] The imagination plays, then, a double role, first, as the immediate state of dreaming soulishness prior to the split of immediacy into reality and ideality, and second, as the activity of abstracting into which this state develops.

This process of abstraction from immediacy, and the related reality and ideality split, Kierkegaard denotes by the important term "reflection."[19] In The Sickness Unto Death the imagination is called "the possibility of any and all reflection" and "the medium for the process of infinitizing." These phrases, we must repeat, have primarily an existential force, but they also apply to logical and cognitive matters as well. As soulish immediacy, the imagination is basic to "the possibility of any and all reflection," and as "the medium for the process of infinitizing" the imagination is reflection. Because of these multiple senses of "imagination," as soulishness and as reflection, Kierkegaard can, first, see the imagination as a state, either the dreaminess of immediacy or the self-forgetfulness of the reflective fantastic. But, second, he can see the imagination as a capacity rightfully exercised in an activity, that of infinitizing.[20]

For Kierkegaard it is crucial to be clear that thinking begins with one's given state of immediacy and is an activity of an individual thinker. The Hegelians are "fantastic" partly because they neglect these facts; this neglect leads them to suppose that one can start without presuppositions in philosophy. For the Hegelians, Kierkegaard charges, the starting point of logic and philosophy is the "immediate," defined, however, "as the most abstract content remaining after an exhaustive reflection."[21] But for Kierkegaard the starting point is "immediacy," not as the abstract result of an immanent movement of thought, but as a) the given, and b) the individual will to begin: "Whenever a beginning is made, on the other hand . . . such a beginning is not the consequence of an immanent movement of thought, but is effected through a resolution of the will, essentially in the strength of faith."[22] Again, because thinking is primarily a human activity for Kierkegaard, rather than the movement of thought itself, the first stage of the philosophical task--indeed the human task--is to start with the given and from that to will abstract generalization. Denying movement to logic means that thought is a human activity. Kierkegaard's picture is of the particular individual who is in a certain environment, learning, along with speech, the world of the ideal. The imagination of the individual then is an element, along with will, in Kierkegaard's substitute for the self-moving Hegelian concept. By contrast, Kierkegaard makes the imagination logically and cognitively significant by using it in his psychological account of how an individual comes to think, an account that displaces the Hegelian movement of thought itself. By naming this capacity "imagination," Kierkegaard grounds this movement in the capacity of the person, thus securing the significance of the individual in cognition.

To complete this picture of imagination's place in thinking, we must now turn to the particular roles of the imagination in a) the origin of categories, b) theoretical consciousness, and c) objective knowledge. Throughout we will see Kierkegaard's orientation to thought as an individual activity and endeavor.

a) The origin of categories

That Kierkegaard sees thought as an activity is the key to understanding his assertion in The Sickness Unto Death that the imagination is the "origin of the categories," a notion Kierkegaard cites from "the elder Fichte."[23] Now we have already seen that Kierkegaard is unfailingly critical of Fichte's absolute ego, which he calls "fantastic," inasmuch as it attempts to find an immanent union of subject and object in knowledge. Kierkegaard argues for their separation, and the approximate character of knowledge. In the Postscript, Kierkegaard notes that knowledge, if empirically considered, is always an approximation; and if idealistically considered, it is something objective, in which case "thought must be pointed away from the subject."[24]

Without falling into the Fichtean errors of identifying subject and object, or of holding the imagination to have a transcendental creative function, Kierkegaard nevertheless agrees with Fichte that the imagination operates in the origin of the categories, including the a priori categories. Unlike Fichte, however, Kierkegaard accounts for the origin of the categories without positing an "absolute ego" as the whole source of the objective world. Kierkegaard would never say, with Fichte, that "all things exist only in and through yourself."[25] As will be recalled from Chapter I, Fichte's point, in the passage to which Kierkegaard alludes, is that Kant showed the regulative character of the categories. Yet, Fichte argued, Kant could not decisively defeat scepticism, since Kant did not show that objects are posited in the same "moment" in which the categories arise. That is, scepticism can be overcome only by showing that the objects of knowledge are given in and with the categories.[26]

Kierkegaard's approving nod to Fichte does not mean that he adopts Fichte's metaphysics; Kierkegaard at most adopts something of the Fichtean analysis of consciousness for his own purposes. Despite the fact that in epistemological questions Kierkegaard is essentially on the side of the sceptics rather than the idealists, he accepts a restrained notion of the a priori.[27] In reflection, the ideal and real are posited over against one another, and the imagination helps generate the synthetic a priori categories applicable to contingent knowledge, plus the necessary logical laws of thought. The a priori is both a gift and a task; it is an activity, and yet something not simply generated by the self. In an early journal entry, Kierkegaard reflects on logic as being something like prayer:

> The development of a priori basic concepts is like a prayer in the Christian sphere, for one would think that here a person is related to God in the freest, most subjective way, and yet we are told that it is the Holy Spirit that effects prayer, so that the only prayer remaining would be to be able to pray, although upon closer inspection even this has been effected in us--so also there is no deductive development of concepts or what one could call that which has some constitutive power--man can only concentrate upon it, and to will this, if this will is not an empty, unproductive gift, corresponds to this single prayer and like this is effected, so to speak.[28]

The passage is interesting, for on the one hand Kierkegaard links the "origin of categories" to human activity "in the freest, most subjective way," and yet on the other hand, in the midst of this activity, something emerges without our will, i.e., "the development of a priori basic concepts." It is only by concentrating upon concepts that concepts emerge, it is only by categorizing that categories emerge, and therefore thought is primarily an activity of the individual. But on the other hand, logic and thought are not simply, in modern parlance, conventional, a matter of conscious agreement on the laws of thought or the a priori; they are given.

The activity of the imagination, then, not only posits the ideal realm as opposed to the real in the beginning of language, but, as part of that activity, gives rise to the categories "receptively." Kierkegaard's agreement with Fichte, therefore, seems to center in the notion that the categories arise "with" the objects. Prior to this, the objects are the undifferentiated given, and hence are not objects. In this sense, Kierkegaard can agree with Fichte that the categories arise with the objects of knowledge.[29] But true to his basic orientation to a "critical empiricism," Kierkegaard is not prepared to go any further than this. Kierkegaard's interest is not primarily epistemological, but when, in The Sickness Unto Death, he writes "even in relation to knowledge, the categories derive from the imagination," such a remark is not evidence of an idealism at odds with the general tenor of his thought. It shows, rather, even more strongly the essential feature of Kierkegaard's understanding of knowledge in an age dominated by Idealism: knowledge is the result of human activity, the imagination is part of that activity, and in the operations of the imagination in positing the ideal and the real, certain a priori concepts are given.

b) Theoretical consciousness

When we turn to the place of the imagination in knowledge proper, we must deal first with Kierkegaard's description of imagination in The Sickness Unto Death as "the possibility of any and all reflection." Kierkegaard applies the term "infinite reflection" to thought and existence, but, as we have seen, when applied to thought (the quantitative dialectic), it signifies the abstractive and polarizing activities of mind necessary to logical thought and knowledge. But there is another stage beyond reflection that is necessary for knowledge, "theoretical consciousness."[30] In Johannes Climacus, the claim is made that theoretical consciousness brings reality into relation with ideality in objective knowledge.[31] In reflection the terms are two, for example, ideality and reality; in consciousness, the terms are three:

> For when I say, I am conscious of this sensory impression, I am expressing a triad. Consciousness is mind, and it is remarkable that when one is divided in the world of mind, there are three, never two. Consciousness, therefore, presupposes reflection.[32]

If theoretical consciousness is somehow beyond reflection in self-consciousness, what is the imagination's role in this? In reflection one is absorbed in ideality as such; in theoretical consciousness the thinker is aware of the self setting up the dualities between ideality and reality, bringing the world of the ideal and real together.[33] The imagination is implicitly active in this, providing abstractions from the pole of ideality in reflection.

c) Objective knowledge

The imagination plays a part also in objective empirical knowledge itself, for theoretical consciousness deals with objective knowledge, and not just the conditions of that knowledge in the thinker. As we have seen, theoretical consciousness has disinterested knowledge as its aim but this can be of two kinds, either empirical or idealistically-conceived knowledge.[34] In the latter case we deal with a conformity of thought and being, e.g., in logical matters, in which the basic principle is tautology. But in empirical knowledge, there is a disjunction between thought and being; truth becomes an object, that is, something objective, and if thinking is an activity, as Kierkegaard maintains, the question arises as to how one moves to truth in objective knowledge.

The answer Kierkegaard gives is that all objective knowledge is an approximation, an overcoming of uncertainty, since in the move to objective knowledge one must go from the realm of possibility to reality. We can explain this using Climacus' example in Philosophical Fragments of the transition from asserting "there is" a star to asserting that "the star has come into existence." One first observes the star in immediate cognition. But even though the observer has not perceived the star's coming into existence, he or she goes on to apply "ideality" to this perception, that is, the concept of "having come into existence." One says, "I know the star has come into existence." For Kierkegaard, this knowledge is arrived at not by logical certainty but in an active overcoming of doubt by an exercise of belief (Tro).[35] Kierkegaard's point is that with regard even to objective knowledge, in this case "historical" knowledge of a past event, an element of belief is involved; pace Hegel, even though the star's having come into existence is a past event, neither the event nor our knowledge of it is necessary. If there is belief in objective knowledge, the observer must make a "leap," an attribution of ideality ("having come into existence") to the reality (the star).

Because the ideal is applied to the real, this move to belief in the star's having come into existence is an exercise of imaginative understanding. Hence another feature of the imagination's role emerges, for in objective knowledge the imagination participates in the willed "descent" to actuality, analogous both to the will acquired in logic (in ending reflection) and to the individual's descent to the real in ethico-religious subjectivity. Here too, resolution is important, for in historical knowledge "the conclusion of belief is no conclusion but a resolution."[36] Belief in the star's having come into existence emerges not with the necessity of logic but from applying concepts like "having come into existence" to the givens of experience.

The imagination, in summary, ranges broadly in the quantitative dialectic. As the "medium of the process of infinitizing" it plays an important role in abstract thought and logic, reflection, soulish immediacy, the origin of the categories, theoretical consciousness, and in objective empirical knowledge. As both activity and state, and as both abstracting and concretizing, the imagination is central to thinking. Kierkegaard's epistemological concern with questions of knowledge centers, of course, in his attempt to outline the bounds of subjectivity and objectivity, and it emerges from his conviction that abstract thought is the activity of an individual thinker. Thinking is not simply passively receiving sense-impressions or actively associating sense data as in empiricism, as if the mind were a tabula rasa. Nor is thinking simply tracing the movements of objective spirit, as in idealism. But to say simply that Kierkegaard is generally Kantian in his understanding of thinking misses the flavor of his reflections. Thinking for Kierkegaard is an individual act that requires imagination; it involves projection, sympathy, insight, and suggestion. Precisely because it requires imagination to be a thinker, thinking is for Kierkegaard an eminently human activity.

To be sure, universal as the imagination is, it is in the intellectual and artistic realms also a gift that one can develop. This is seen especially in Kierkegaard's reflection on, and practice of, the dialectician's and the poet's creation of imaginative possibilities of existence. The dialectician creates possibilities of thought "algebraically," sketching the relationship between conceptual possibilities; as a psychologist the dialectician possesses insight and the presentiment (Ahnelse) to predict and map out the results of different situations in human life. The poet deals in possibilities as well, but in particular imagined figures. As Howard V. Hong and Edna H. Hong write: "What distinguishes the poet is a kind of imagination that shapes the possibilities in palpable form, in the form of 'ideal actuality.'"37 When these capacities merge in a "poet-dialectician" who creates a thought-experiment (Tankeexperiment) in a concrete psychological portrait of a fictitious figure, the result for Kierkegaard is what the Hongs translate as "imaginary construction" (Experiment), or "experimenting a character" (experimentere en Figur).38 In the exercise of this imaginative sketching of existential possibilities Kierkegaard turns to his primary concerns, not with the quantitative dialectic of thought, but with the qualitative dialectic of the stages of existence. It is to Kierkegaard's imaginative analysis and depiction of the roles of the imagination in those stages that we must turn in the remainder of this and the next two chapters.

Imagination and the aesthetic sphere of existence

In turning now to the aesthetic forms of existence, Kierkegaard's central philosophical interest emerges, the anatomy of the categories of subjectivity. So too, his greater interest in the imagination emerges, not in epistemological questions, but in the service of a philosophy dedicated to plumbing the depths of the human heart. Possibility gains an added significance, for no longer is possibility concerned only with the realm of ideality, with the possible in general, but with possibility for the person. And imagination gains an added significance, for no longer is it employed simply as the instrument that posits the ideal, but it is engaged in the processes attending a person's subjectivity.

In analyzing the imagination in the aesthetic sphere, some preliminary remarks will orient us to Kierkegaard's vocabulary. Again we turn to the passage from The Sickness Unto Death in which the imagination is called "the medium of the process of infinitizing," the "capacity instar omnium":

> Imagination is the medium for the process of infinitizing; it is
> not a capacity, as are the others--if one wishes to speak in

those terms, it is the capacity _instar omnium_ [for all capacities]. Imagination is infinitizing reflection, and the imagination is reflection, is the rendition of the self as the self's possibility. The imagination is the possibility of any and all reflection, and the intensity of this medium is the possibility of the intensity of the self.[39]

Kierkegaard gives a series of equivalences: the self is reflection, and imagination is reflection; imagination is "the rendition of the self as the self's possibility"; imagination is also the possibility of reflection, and as such is the possibility of the intensity of the self.

As we have seen, Kierkegaard closely links the imagination with reflection, but reflection refers to existence as well as to the abstract, quantitative dialectic.[40] Positing ideals, the imagination extends one's horizon beyond the immediately given, and in this sense is the "possibility of all reflection." Imagination is then called the medium for the process of infinitizing, the reflection of the process, and the possibility of all reflection. The complexities of this may be simplified by using the image of the mirror, for just as a mirror reflects an image, so too the imagination is a mirror on which the process of infinitizing shines the realm of possibility, giving back a picture of a possible self. But to alter the image, the imagination as the medium of that process becomes in effect identical with the process: the imagination is the activity, the process of infinitizing itself.

This passage speaks too of imaginative reflection as either "finite," tied to the immediate, or expansively "infinite." If infinite, reflection becomes endless, both in the sense of being unceasing and also unlimited in its scope. "Infinite reflection" can be either a positive or negative term in Kierkegaard's vocabulary, since it can refer a) positively, to abstract thought, b) negatively, to advanced forms of the aesthetic life, including the fantastic, or c) positively, to ethical and religious concern. Our interest in this section is how aesthetic existence involves either finite or infinite imaginative reflection in the sense of b). In the next chapter we will turn to c) infinite reflection in the ethico-religious stages.

We have seen that for Kierkegaard the imagination is a medium, an activity, and a state. Just as important is his remark that it is "not a capacity, as are the others," but is the capacity instar omnium: "When all is said and done, whatever of feeling, knowing, and willing a person has depends upon what imagination he has, upon how that person reflects himself, that is, upon imagination."[41] Kierkegaard here alters the analysis of the imagination somewhat from that of the Postscript's simultaneity of factors. Whereas in the Postscript Kierkegaard uses "imagination" almost synonymously with "feeling," here he distinguishes them. One can have a feeling in a "fantastic" way (or more positively, in an "imaginative" way). But feelings can also be "sluggish," "heavy," "constricted," or "narrow." To say that the imagination is "not a capacity, as are the others" indicates that this imaginative expansiveness can be predicated of other activities, whether of knowing, feeling, or willing. When one has an imaginative feeling, one is experiencing not two feelings, but one; to be "imaginative" can describe not only a discrete activity ("imagining"), but "how" a person does other things. Furthermore, to say a person is imaginative can point not only to individual episodes of imagining, but to the quality of the person's entire life, in Kierkegaard's words, "how that person reflects himself." For example, whereas one can say that "Constantin Constantius imagined his future trip to Berlin for half an hour," one can also say that "Constantin is an imaginative person to have planned such a trip." In the first instance an activity is denoted, in the second a disposition of a person.[42]

Here emerges a new aspect of the imagination, far beyond the epistemological functions. The stirrings of the imagination lead not only to a grasp of the world in a cognitive way, but also in an affective way and, moreover, an affective way that may be long-term. First, the imagination as the capacity instar omnium underlies the emotional life as the expansive and driving force behind the great array of moods and emotions in human life--compare the association of imagination with feeling in the Postscript's simultaneity of factors.[43] Yet, second, the affections are not irrational; the imagination as the capacity instar omnium links the affections with the intellect; the capacity to imagine is fundamental to both. The link is this: just as the imagination is a condition for cognition, taking one beyond the limited horizon of the given, so too the imagination is a condition for feeling, in that a person entertains possibilities and idealities affectively. Or to put it conversely, to have a mood or emotion is to respond to a particular image of a possibility. To be melancholy, for example, entails believing the world justifies melancholy. For this reason, the cognitive and the affective are closely related; diseases of the intellect--such as the intellectual-fantastic--affect one's emotional life.[44]

Because of this fundamental connection of thinking and feeling, Kierkegaard discerns a logic to moods and emotions. Indeed, his writings, including the journals and The Concept of Irony as well as the formal authorship, provide an extended attempt to analyze the logic of moods and emotions, using both "algebraic," terse philosophical treatises (such as The Concept of Anxiety and The Sickness Unto Death), and "lyrical" literary presentations.

For Kierkegaard the imagination is central to understanding emotions, and the role of the imagination in moods and emotions is complex. In general, the imagination is the power behind the turbulence of moods, for the imagination presents possibilities to a person that evoke a mood. Thus, there is in one sense an ascending level of the moods according to their relative "imaginativeness" and dynamism, from the first stirrings of emerging spirit in the immediate aesthetic to the highest flights of the fantastic and of self-conscious, infinite aesthetic reflection. In numerous portraits and sketches, both of mythic types like Don Juan and lyric-dramatic figures like Cordelia Wahl and Johannes in the "Diary of a Seducer," Kierkegaard maps the terrain of the emotional life analyzing the progression to the imaginative-fantastic.[45] At every stage, the imagination both presents a possibility to a person and is itself increased as a capacity in the reaction of mood. Yet one can recoil from an imaginative possibility, retreating from the threat of imaginative expansiveness by sinking to a lower level of immediacy in which the imagination continues to function, but less expansively.

In either case, whether the movement is to an expanded or reduced imagination, a person lives out a variation of the unresolved tension between the infinite and the finite that we first identified in the Romantic ironist. In The Sickness Unto Death and elsewhere Kierkegaard presents a broad anatomy of the diversity of the imagination's diseases. Underlying the description of the aesthetic sphere is his understanding that aesthetic existence is a state of despairing imbalance--a lack of simultaneity--between, on the one hand, the infinite and possibility as products of the imagination and, on the other hand, the finite and the necessary elements of existence. As Anti-Climacus says in The Sickness Unto Death: "The forms of despair may be arrived at abstractly by reflecting upon the constituents of which the self as a synthesis is composed."[46] Shortly we will consider these forms of despair analyzed in The Sickness Unto Death and their dread-filled confrontations with possibility, but we must first see how the imagination operates in the primal stirrings of spirit that give rise to this dialectic of the infinite (and possibility) and the finite (and necessity).

Kierkegaard's concept of the "soulish" is, again, the starting point for the emergence of the imagination. As we have seen, a person is a duality. The self, even though unreflected and slumbering, is already a synthesis of finitude and infinitude, but as a merely negative unity: "A human being is a synthesis of the infinite and the finite, of the temporal and the eternal, of freedom and necessity, in short a synthesis. A synthesis is a relation between two. Considered in this way, a human being is still not a self."[47] By means of mythic or literary figures Kierkegaard describes the original positing of this duality; as we have seen, in Johannes Climacus Kierkegaard writes of language as the originating point of the duality of ideality over against reality. Related to this is another "origin" myth, that of the human being as a synthesis of the bodily and soulish.[48] The original state of the human being, prior to the separation of the bodily and soulish, is the dreaming state, which Kierkegaard in The Concept of Anxiety identifies with innocence and ignorance: "Innocence is ignorance. In innocence, man is not qualified as spirit but is psychically qualified in immediate unity with his natural condition. The spirit in man is dreaming."[49]

But this dreaming state is already a restless state, for in dreaming "the spirit projects its own actuality, but this actuality is nothing, and innocence always sees this nothing outside itself."[50] The imagination, by implication, operates in this "primal anxiety," in which even in the state of dreaming, the spirit, not yet awake, begins to project possibilities, hardly in a conscious manner, but, ironically, as "nothing." Kierkegaard finds examples of this stage of dreaming in the Page in Mozart's "The Marriage of Figaro," and, historically, in a paganism that preserves the childlike.[51] The Page, in the first step of the immediate stages of the erotic, is troubled by his emerging sense of separation.[52] In him the sensuous awakens to a deep but sweet melancholy. An amorphous desire is aroused for an object, but there is yet no separate object: "Desire and its object are joined." The desire is for a non-differentiated object: "The object of desire is dawning, and is so near that it is within the desire."[53] In this stage primal anxiety just begins to be aware of freedom and possibility.[54] And because the desired object is, in a sense, not possessed, there is melancholy here too: "The sensuous awakens, not yet to movement, but to a hushed tranquillity; not to joy and gladness, but to deep melancholy."[55] Thus even in the primal anxiety typified by the Page and evident in the child's "seeking for the adventurous, the monstrous, and the enigmatic," the imagination is at work.[56] The spirit, although dreaming, is restless, relating itself to itself as anxiety.[57]

In the development of the individual, however, the imagination comes to have a more discrete role in childhood and youth. In Christian Discourses (1848) Kierkegaard contrasts the dreaminess of childhood with that of youth. The child is active and turned outward in dreaminess, not yet separating the self from its surroundings, but "its senses are open to every impression, the child being sheer life and movement, alert attention all the day long."[58] The dreaminess means that the child does not differentiate itself sufficiently even from sense-impressions. There is not yet a discrete world apart from self-perception. On the other hand, the youth is awake too in passion, but the spirit, Kierkegaard makes clear, is still asleep at this stage; the youth "is more turned inward, but in imagination [Indbildningen]; he dreams, or it is as though everything about him were dreaming."[59] Here too, the youth makes little discrimination between the self and the world, but in place of the child's confusion of itself with the external world, the youth's dreamy imagination absorbs the external world into the content of the dream.[60] In the words of Kresten Nordentoft, it is this youthful imaginativeness "which forms the transition to the crisis of identity which is discussed in The Concept of Anxiety as the fall into sin."[61] The imagination tenses, reaching a point where dreaminess sets one over against immediacy. Possibility looms in reflection, and from this dream state one emerges to find oneself in sin by a qualitative leap.

In The Sickness Unto Death Kierkegaard treats the result of this development from soulishness to the state of sin in his analysis of sin as despair.

Despair arises from an imbalance between possibility and necessity--in other words, an imbalance in which the imagination is central.[62] Important to note immediately--and a point we will return to later--is that these opposite kinds of despair exist on the unconscious as well as conscious levels; one need not be aware of despair in order to be in despair. Kierkegaard's dispositional account of the imagination, describing not only "what" a person does, but "how" he or she does it, here serves to support his claim that despair is unconscious. Because the imagination is the capacity instar omnium, it need not denote "imaging" as a conscious activity. Kierkegaard believes that despair may be unconscious, that it is possible to classify people according to whether they continue in a despairing imaginativeness, or whether--and this is much more common--they fall into a despair that stifles youthful enthusiasm. But a perceptive observer can detect the avoidance involved in all forms of despair, even unconscious despair.

Of the four major forms of despair Anti-Climacus sketches in The Sickness Unto Death, the first two, the despair of infinitude and of possibility, exhibit the imagination's expansiveness, while the second two forms, the despair of finitude and necessity, show the frustrated, self-destructive, and narrow imagination that recoils from possibilities, yet ironically still is restlessly present in the human being.

1) When the imagination generates only dreams, one can fall into the despair of infinitude. The proper dialectic of infinitude and finitude is the concrete, in which the imagination prepares one for concrete action.[63] But in this form of despair, the ascending movement of infinitizing is the sole movement. The individual never becomes concrete, because the movement is halted at the point of infinitizing: the self becomes fantastic. In this section of The Sickness Unto Death Kierkegaard summarizes his polemic against the

Romantics and Idealists as living self-contradictions. At the same time, by identifying their despair as only one form among others, Kierkegaard locates the Romantics and Idealists as merely unusually sophisticated representatives of a universal human illness.

The three forms of the fantastic are those of feeling, knowing, and willing.[64] In all of these forms, the "fantastic" undercuts the feeling, knowing, and willing of the person, by self-deceptively presenting a picture of the self that is never realized in action.

In fantastic feeling, a person becomes abstract in his or her emotions, concerned, for example, about the fate of an abstraction like "humankind as a whole" while having no regard for particular persons or for loving action. The effects of entertaining fantastic feelings are cumulative, Kierkegaard argues, and eventually the person becomes abstractly sentimental. As we saw in the analysis of the Romantics, such feeling is finally self-contradictory and undermines itself, for in sentimentality, generous feelings become divorced from any appropriate object; feeling drifts and becomes moodiness, unattached to an object.

One can also be "fantastic" in knowing. Knowledge can become fantastic when it is unrelated to self-knowledge--as in the speculative philosophers. Knowledge expands, but is unrelated to the conditions of the knower. According to Kierkegaard's rule for knowledge--that increase in knowledge be edifying--such knowledge is fantastic. It reveals, ironically, a desire to avoid self-knowledge by turning all knowledge away from the self and to external concerns.

Fantastic willing occurs when a person makes grandiose plans, but cannot attend to the small part of the task at hand. The very notion of "planning," that a plan entails a purpose effected in action, is undercut, since the person's will never executes the imagined plan. Fantastic planning is finally no planning at all.

These forms of the fantastic indicate once more the dispositional aspect of the capacity instar omnium. The fantastic finally describes the person in general and not only particular acts: "when feeling or knowing or willing has become fantastic, the entire self can eventually become that."65

2) The despair of possibility is a variation on the despair of infinitude, but more advanced dialectically:

> Inasmuch as the self as a synthesis of finitude and infinitude is established, is kata dynamin [potential], in order to become itself it reflects itself in the medium of imagination [Phantasiens Medium], and thereby the infinite possibility becomes manifest.66

The dialectic of possibility and necessity is the basis of freedom, and so is a more advanced state than the synthesis of infinite and finite. Now a person recognizes the importance of the concrete (as the synthesis of the infinite and the finite), but he or she must now take a step to freedom.67 One is able to imagine a possible concrete self or selves, but the question is, "Which self should I become?" In the despair of possibility one fails to attend to necessity, the givens of life, and entertains one possibility after another, or a possibility entirely unrelated to the conditions of life. Kierkegaard says that the "mirror of possibility"

> is no ordinary mirror: it must be used with extreme caution, for, in the highest sense, this mirror does not tell the truth. That a self appears to be such and such in the possibility of itself is only a half-truth, for in the possibility of itself the self is still far from, or is only half of itself.68

To summarize, in the despair of infinitude and of possibility the imagination plays a new part. It first delivers possibility, but, second, it then responds to possibility in these particular expansive varieties of despair. We see a dual function for the imagination, for not only does it give rise to possibility, eliciting dreaminess and anxiety, but now, as accentuated, it becomes a particular form of an expansive imbalance in the human synthesis.

At the dialectically opposite pole from the expansive imaginative forms of despair stand those forms that, while suppressing imagination, cannot extinguish the imagination entirely.

3) The despair of finitude is due to a lack of infinitude; a person loses all venturesomeness and becomes entirely determined by finite, temporal interests. Anti-Climacus is quick to point out that this despair is not limited to the mediocre or to philistines, for it can also be found in persons of talent and intelligence. Rather, the despair of finitude occurs when the crowd, "the others," form one's identity, and instead of developing one's own "angularity" and uniqueness, one finds it "far easier and safer to be like the others, to become a copy, a number, a mass man."[69] Such a despair, so common in the modern world, is seldom noticed; it is the despair of the person who by a series of tiny adjustments to his or her surroundings becomes accepted, comfortable, risking nothing, thereby suppressing the spontaneity of primitive imaginativeness.[70]

4) This spiritlessness appears also in the despair of necessity, in which a person, consciously or not, faces the loss of possibility. Possibility is like the air we breathe, for possibility means that there is space for one's further development, but necessity is suffocating.[71] In the advanced form of this despair, a person confronts, ironically, a dreadful possibility that threatens possibility: "Picture a man who with all the shuddering revolt of a terrified imagination [Indbildningskraft] has represented to himself some horror as a thing absolutely not to be endured."[72] Should this horror come to pass, the person will be in despair; life will become narrow, and "humanly speaking his destruction is the most certain of all things--and the despair in his soul fights desperately to get leave to despair." Kierkegaard goes on to relate this despair to

the need for God, because "for God all things are possible," and faith is the fight for possibility.[73] Apart from God, however, this despair of necessity continues to fester either quietly in the form of triviality or more self-consciously as fatalism. The lowest form, triviality, appears in philistinism, a complete suppression of the stirrings of the spirit:

> Bereft of imagination [Phantasi], as the philistine-bourgeois always is, whether alehouse keeper or prime minister, he lives within a certain trivial compendium of experiences as to how things go, what is possible, what usually happens. In this way, the philistine-bourgeois has lost his self and God. In order for a person to become aware of his self and of God, imagination must raise him higher than the miasma of probability, it must tear him out of this and teach him to hope and to fear. . . . But the philistine-bourgeois mentality does not have imagination, does not want to have it, abhors it.[74]

The extent of this spiritual degradation becomes apparent when Kierkegaard compares the philistine-bourgeois unfavorably to the fatalists or determinists, for at least the latter "have sufficient imagination to despair of possibility, sufficient possibility to discover impossibility."[75] The fatalist has a sense of possibility, but also of its loss, or non-existence, whereas the philistine thinks that he or she has control of the world, "leads possibility around imprisoned in the cage of probability, exhibits it, imagines itself to be the master."[76]

The frightfulness of the despair of finitude and of necessity is that they so often involve a suppression of the imagination, an abdication of one's birthright to imagine. Despair thus is a symptom not only of youthful expansiveness, but of maturity. Indeed, when a person has become most adjusted to the world, one may then be most in despair, partly from having sacrificed that original restlessness of the imagination: "Over the years, an individual may abandon the little bit of passion, feeling, imagination, the little bit of inwardness he had and embrace as a matter of course an understanding of life in terms of trivialities."[77]

But unimaginative as these forms of despair are they cannot quench the restive imagination entirely. The suppressed imagination will inevitably take its revenge. Even in the unconscious despair of finitude and necessity, in which it appears defunct, the imagination actually continues to move restlessly.[78] In his analysis of unconscious despair in The Sickness Unto Death, Kierkegaard indulges in a play on words that relates the imagination to the willful ignorance and self-deception of unconscious despair. The unconscious despairer "imagines [indbilder] himself to be happy, although considered in the light of truth he is unhappy, he is usually far from wanting to be wrenched out of his error [Vildfarelse]."[79] At this level the imagination provides one with a delusion; in one sense, the imagination ironically allows a successful suppression of the threatening possibilities that the imagination itself presents. But in another sense this delusion, though successful, is never secure, since it is continually on the defensive and can be easily upset. Despair (Fortvivelse) is perplexity (Forvildelse), and ignorance of despair simply adds error (Vildfarelse).[80] The security of delusion is a reactive use of the imagination, covering a simultaneous restlessness of the suppressed spirit that can break out once the security is disturbed:

> The relation between ignorance and despair is similar to that between ignorance and anxiety (see The Concept of Anxiety by Vigilius Haufniensis); the anxiety that characterizes spiritlessness is recognized precisely by its spiritless sense of security. Nevertheless, anxiety lies underneath; likewise, despair also lies underneath, and when the enchantment of illusion is over, when existence begins to totter, then despair, too, immediately appears as that which lay underneath.[81]

Aesthetic existence, then, covers many forms of imaginative life. The imagination is present in the initial stirrings of primal anxiety, in the expansiveness of youth, and in the despair of the infinite and of possibility. Though suppressed, it is present even in spiritless philistines sunk in the despair of finitude and of necessity, where self-deception is a cocoon the imagination spins to protect one from disturbing yet beckoning thoughts of possibility.

So far in Anti-Climacus' analysis, "despair" is a diagnostic concept applicable to all persons whether conscious of their despair or not, and in which the imagination may function in various ways. But in The Sickness Unto Death and elsewhere in the literature, Kierkegaard also analyzes, as Vincent McCarthy argues, how one in the aesthetic sphere may be disturbed by progressively more serious crises of mood, from irony through anxiety and melancholy to conscious despair.[82] In general, the moods represent progressive increases in consciousness, opening up new horizons, giving a person greater scope for the operation of the imagination. Yet there is nothing necessary about this hierarchy of moods; one does not naturally develop from one mood to the next. Whatever level of consciousness achieved, one may remain at that level, advance to the consciousness of the next level, or even regress to a more restrictive despair of finitude or necessity, one that is, nonetheless, more self-aware than the earlier state of mere spiritlessness. In these crises the imagination is a logical and genetic condition for all the moods, since the moods are reactions to the possibilities the imagination opens up to an individual.[83]

The role of the imagination in this dialectical movement through the moods to progressively greater levels of consciousness can be summarized briefly. In irony, examined at length in Chapter II, the drive of the individual is toward the infinite and away from the finite. One unsuccessfully attempts to escape the finite in an effort to transcend the philistine-bourgeois world. The imagination of the despair of infinitude and the despair of possibility is at the heart of irony, but as we saw in Kierkegaard's criticism of the Romantics, the heights of irony never escape the finite.

The levels of anxiety, beyond that of primal anxiety, also signal the attempt to acknowledge the demands of imagined possibilities. Unlike irony, anxiety confronts the person not only with the promise of possibility, but with the fear of possibility as well. Anxiety is "a sympathetic antipathy and an antipathetic sympathy."[84] At its more advanced levels, the anxious person begins to be aware of the eternal, but still only externally, in the form of poetry and art, which finally are, says the pseudonym Vigilius Haufniensis, "no more than the atonement which imagination [Phantasien] offers.... Eternity is gilded with the tinsel of imagination, and one longs for it."[85]

Kierkegaard closely associates this advanced anxiety with the greater degree of inwardness found in the dialectically more advanced mood of melancholy, which is "an overbalance of imagination." The longing for the eternal so prominent in poetry and art becomes a sad awareness that one lacks the eternal. Kierkegaard self-consciously associates melancholy with the imagination, as is clear from an annotation in his personal copy of Either/Or:

> The first part [of Either/Or] contains melancholy (egotistic-sympathetic) and despair (in reason and passion). The second part therefore teaches despair and choosing oneself. Even the essay on Don Juan has melancholy, an enthusiasm which robs him of understanding, a dreaming, almost deranged reveling in fantasy [Phantasie]....
> Fantasy like this always creates melancholy; therefore the first part is melancholy.[86]

The remedy for this and all moods is a progression to a state of conscious despair, in which one acknowledges that a fundamental unconscious despair has been at the bottom of all the moods, whether expansive or restrictive. Despair becomes conscious when one develops a concern for the eternal and recognizes one's spiritual failure to relate the temporal and the eternal. In conscious despair one sees the inadequacy of the aesthetic stage, moves to the boundary between the aesthetic and the ethico-religious spheres, and thus is in a position possibly to make the leap to the latter.[87]

In The Sickness Unto Death, Anti-Climacus dwells in detail on two roles the imagination plays in the crisis of conscious despair. First, conscious despair arises when one imaginatively focusses not on an object over which one despairs, but on oneself. For example, in the conscious despair of weakness (willing not to be oneself), a person sees that despair over a lost love is actually a total despair over oneself; in weakness the person wishes not to be oneself. Ironically, while in unconscious despair the imagination erected an obscuring shield of security, now the imagination, as the infinitizing capacity, takes one to self-conscious clarity of total despair. Second, having become conscious of despair, one can choose to remain in despair, either in the despair of weakness (willing not to be oneself) or of defiance (willing to be oneself apart from God). In either case, consciousness is raised to an extremely high level and the imagination of delusion falls away. Yet the imagination can now become the final refuge of a conscious, continuing despair. Let us examine these two roles of the imagination in despair more closely.

First, the imagination is a key element in a person's becoming conscious of despair. In analyzing the despair of weakness (not willing to be oneself), Kierkegaard recapitulates the range of despair from the unconscious despair of pure immediacy to the consciousness of the despair of weakness. In pure immediacy an external event may awaken one's dormant despair: "Whenever some event or the expectation of it wrenches him out of his brute-transformation, dread which dwells deeply within him awakens and casts him into despair, in which he essentially was."[88] Yet the despair can be of a very low form, a mere comic wish to be another person: "When immediacy despairs, it does not even have enough self to wish or dream that it had become that which it has not become."[89] At a higher level a self-reflective despair develops in which the "imagination [Phantasi] discovers a possibility that, if it eventuated, would thus become the break with immediacy";[90] the advance here, of course, is that one can foresee the possibility rather than merely experiencing it if and when it occurs. This despair is the most common, and Kierkegaard calls it despair over the earthly or over something earthly.[91]

Now one can move from this spot either back into immediacy or else forwards. The backward movement consists in stifling the feared event that would cast one into conscious despair.[92] The forward movement is to recognize the extent of one's vulnerability, that there could be an occurrence or an element in one's character that would cast one into despair. Such a person begins to be aware of the eternal within, since "reflection helps him to understand that there is much he can lose without losing the self."[93] But now the imagination can move; the despairer sees that suffering over something earthly (the particular) is a despair over the earthly in toto. The imagination increases despair, pushing one into a deeper crisis calling for resolution:

> When the self in imagination [Phantasi] despairs with infinite passion over something of this world, its infinite passion changes this particular thing, this something, into the world in toto; that is, the category of totality inheres in and belongs to the despairing person.[94]

This, Kierkegaard adds, is "a genuine advance in consciousness of the self," since it is an initial expression for the full despair of weakness, that of "despair over oneself" and "of the eternal."[95] Despair focusses on its true source, the weakness within the self that avoids the eternal: "The person in despair himself understands that it is weakness to make the earthly so important, that it is weakness to despair."[96]

This brings us to the second major role the imagination plays in conscious despair. One now stands poised at the brink of an even more fearful despair, the conscious choice to remain in that state. Kierkegaard argues that the choice to remain consciously in despair takes two forms, the despair of weakness (willing not to be oneself) and the despair of defiance (willing to be oneself apart from God). The imagination operates differently in each. In the despair of weakness, the self stands at a crossroads; one can turn to faith and seek help, or continue in an "inclosing reserve" [Indesluttethed].[97] If one spurns faith and chooses this reserve, one hates the weakness, aristocratically isolates oneself, brooding over the relation to the eternal, yet deceiving oneself that this weakness does not have an element of pride and defiance in it. The imagination in one way ceases, for the possibility of escaping weakness is closed, yet the imagination continues in a fixated form, in which one pores over the self-image of weakness, loving one's refined solitude.

The despair of defiance continues the despair of weakness, for in defiance the "inclosed" despairer becomes conscious of why he or she does not want to be a concrete self.[98] It is also the most dialectically advanced form of conscious despair, for now the imagination is potentiated to the highest degree, fully conscious of the most abstract possibility of the self; it is the despair of possibility taken to a higher level. Yet, unlike the despair of infinitude and of possibility, the imagination here does not simply entertain possibilities, but with cool control chooses one image of the self regardless of the actual self, defying both the gift and task of actuality:[99]

> With the help of this infinite form, the self in despair wants
> to be master of itself or to create itself, to make his self into

the self he wants to be. . . . He does not want to put on his
own self, does not want to see his given self as his task--he
himself wants to compose his self by means of being the
infinite form.[100]

The despair of defiance can be active or passive. In the active variety "the

self is its own master, a king without a country," "always building only castles

in the air."[101] The self dwells on his or her existence with infinite interest, but

builds nothing solid and can arbitrarily create the self over again. Kierkegaard's

prototype for this active form of despair is Johannes the Seducer who, as we will

shortly see, is more complex than the phrase "active defiant despair" would lead

one to believe.

In the passive variety the defiant one's despair is "to be unwilling to hope

in the possibility that an earthly need, a temporal cross, can come to an end."[102]

Some obstacle or defeat prevents one from being the self one wishes to be. And

so one defiantly and with self-pity fixates on the hurt, nurturing in seclusion an

"inwardness with a jammed lock," and stays awake with "demonic cleverness"

to keep "despair closed up in inclosing reserve."[103] Limiting as this passive

variety of defiant despair is, the despairing person still has imagination enough to

see at once the self one is called to be, the self one wills to be, and the concrete

element that stands in the way, "some difficulty or other . . . the Christian

would call a cross, a basic defect."[104] The despairing person would escape this

if possible, but, being less adept at "imaginative constructing" than the active

defiant one, is unsuccessful; "in a Promethean way, the infinite, negative self

feels itself nailed to this servitude."[105] Nevertheless, the person still refuses

help, is defiant, and imaginatively active, dramatizing the self as a tragic figure,

convinced that "this thorn in the flesh gnaws so deeply that he cannot abstract

himself from it."[106] Thus, although less imaginative than the active defiant one

at constructing an alternative self, the passive one recruits imagination in an attempt to celebrate the self as a suffering tragic hero. The attempt becomes, however, nothing but a self-contradictory fixation on that thorn in the flesh.

In The Concept of Irony Kierkegaard argued that Romantic irony results in a reductio ad absurdum in its self-contradiction. Kierkegaard's analysis of the moods, especially that of despair in The Sickness Unto Death, extends that method to all the moods. In anxiety, melancholy, and despair, as much as in irony, the actual and the ideal, necessity and possibility, passivity and activity, are in a restless relation. Even at its highest levels, the despair of defiance undermines its own imagination. Despair by definition cuts off possibility, and even in its most imaginative forms, despair spells the end of possibility. Instead of being open to a future of further development, despair restricts the imagination to substanceless dreams in an endless, fruitless, and at last self-destructive manner.

The way in which even the active variety of defiant imaginative despair undermines its own imaginativeness and possibility is best seen by contrasting the two imaginative eroticists, Johannes in "The Diary of the Seducer," in Either/Or Volume I, and Julius in Schlegel's Lucinde. For Kierkegaard, Johannes is, as many critics have noted, a dialectic advance on Julius.[107] In one sense Johannes' imagination attains the victory over the actual world that Lucinde's Julius sought unsuccessfully. Julius is only at a lower level of self-consciousness, an ironist especially subject to the revenge of the actual in his "vegetative" ideal of life. But whereas Julius is passive and langorous, satirizing Prometheus' aspirations, Johannes is wildly active. Whereas in Lucinde the sexes mingle in a primal unity that suppresses consciousness and individual identity, in "The Diary of the Seducer" the eroticist heightens the split between the "masculine" (as spirit or idea) and the "feminine" (as nature, the concrete, or "material") to a demonic degree.

Johannes strives for a complete triumph of the imagination over the actual. He not only creates himself in his imagination, he also seeks to create Cordelia after his image.[108] Subtly he brings her to the stage of reflection he occupies: "Light have I made her, light as a thought."[109] Apprehending Cordelia as an ideal, he sees her as living "in a world of fantasy [i Phantasiens Verden]."[110] He desires sexual union with Cordelia, but his seduction is primarily of spirit rather than flesh. Identifying himself with the mythic, Johannes plays Amor to Cordelia's Psyche, and exclaims on the eve of the seduction, "Everything is symbol; I myself am a myth about myself, for is it not as myth that I hasten to this meeting?"[111] Ronald Grimsley writes:

> As he [Johannes] gazes steadfastly at the image mirrored in his own consciousness, . . . the dividing line between reality and imagination becomes blurred. Detaching himself more and more from outward things in order to contemplate the imaginative possibilities of his own inner being, he moves uncertainly between the two 'worlds' of fact and phantasy.[112]

Johannes' imagination becomes completely enclosed within itself, actively defiant in self-assertion, subjecting all other persons to the demands of his infinite self-creativity, thinking only of his next experiment in imagination. The seduction complete and Cordelia abandoned, Johannes immediately turns his attention to the next variation on the theme of seduction. The diary ends with Johannes planning that experiment: "It would . . . really be worth while to know whether or not one might be able to poetize himself out of a girl, so that one could make her so proud that she would imagine that it was she who tired of the relationship."[113] In a complex hierarchy of imaginative irony, Johannes hovers completely above not only his own but also his victim's emotions in a complicated dance of deception.

Yet Johannes' final deception is a self-deception. Although the embodiment of active, defiant possibility and hardly a "vegetative soul" like Julius, in the end Johannes' possibilities and prospects are few, except to develop the taste for ever more highly refined intellectual pleasures. "Possibility" in the aesthetic sense is all he has, for possibility is his escape from the despairing recognition that he is without hope. For all his triumph of imaginative creativity, even Johannes the Seducer, the most ethereal and imaginatively adept of Kierkegaard's characters, ends in the self-contradiction that the active pursuit of endless possibility leads finally to no possibility in the true sense. The imagination can conquer, but at the expense of the true possibility the imagination holds out. The editor of Either/Or, Victor Eremita, suggests that Johannes is a production of the restless mind of "A." If so, "A's" own musings in the Diapsalmata are appropriate to sum up the bondage that the aesthetic imagination even in its highest flights can create for itself:

> What is the power that binds me? How was the chain made with which the Fenris wolf was bound? It was wrought from the sound of a cat's paws walking over the ground, from women's beards, from the roots of rocks, from the nerves of bears, from the breath of fishes, and the spittle of birds. And thus I, too, am bound in a chain formed of dark imaginings [Indbildninger], of unquiet dreams, of restless thoughts, of dread presentiments, of inexplicable anxieties. This chain is "very supple, soft as silk, elastic under the highest tension, and cannot be broken."[114]

* * *

As medium, state, activity, capacity, disposition, and passion, the imagination is a protean power in the intellectual and aesthetic realms. It lies at the heart of logic, cognition, and the emotional life, from the first stirrings of anxiety to the most highly developed aesthetic reflectiveness. The imagination as the capacity _instar omnium_ is a restless factor in a person's life, ceaselessly active. In the aesthetic life, the imagination beckons and opens possibilities for the self to which the aesthetic stage in all its varieties is a response. But all the forms of the aesthetic--ironic or philistine, demonic or spiritless, whether accentuating or suppressing the imagination--cannot resolve the dialectic of the infinite and the finite. For all its powers, the imagination cannot give wholeness.

Yet, as we saw in Chapter III on the simultaneity of factors, the extent of the imagination's powers is not exhausted in the aesthetic sphere. Harnessed in the ethical sphere, the imagination becomes even more dialectical. It is to these manifold functions of the imagination in the ethical sphere that we must now direct our attention.

[1] Kierkegaard, <u>SUD</u> 31; the Danish is "Evnen <u>instar omnium</u>." <u>Sickness</u> was written in 1848 and published on July 31, 1849, under the Christian pseudonym Anti-Climacus. Kierkegaard for a time considered publishing it under his own name, <u>JP</u> 6: 6517 (X^2 A 147); see also the Hongs' "Historical Introduction," <u>SUD</u> xv-xvi.

[2] "All logic is quantitative dialectic or modal dialectic, for everything is and the whole is one and the same," Kierkegaard, <u>JP</u> 1: 759 (VII^1 A 84), n.d., 1846. That the quantitative dialectic deals with finitude should not obscure that it includes "infinite" functions; see Malantschuk 305-06, and Diem 34; as Johannes Climacus says, thought as an activity can go on endlessly: "Reflection has the remarkable property of being infinite," Kierkegaard, <u>CUP</u> 102.

[3] Kierkegaard, <u>CUP</u> 288.

[4] Kierkegaard, <u>JP</u> 1: 759 (VII^1 A 84), n.d., 1846.

[5] Kierkegaard, <u>CUP</u> 288.

[6] Kierkegaard, <u>SUD</u> 30-31.

[7] Kierkegaard, <u>CUP</u> 278-79.

[8] Kierkegaard, <u>JP</u> 3: 3658 (IV C 89), n.d., 1842-43.

[9] Cf. Kierkegaard, <u>CUP</u> 103: "Only when reflection comes to a halt can a beginning be made, and reflection can be halted only by something else, and this something else is something quite different from the logical, being a resolution of will."

[10] Kierkegaard, <u>CUP</u> 106.

[11] Søren Kierkegaard, <u>Philosophical Fragments</u> (hereafter, <u>PF</u>) in <u>Philosophical Fragments</u> and <u>Johannes Climacus</u>, ed. and trans. with introd. and

notes Howard V. Hong and Edna H. Hong, Kierkegaard's Writings 7 (Princeton: Princeton UP, 1985) 40.

[12] Kierkegaard, JP 1: 4 (VIII[1] A 622), n.d., 1848; cf. JP 2: 2166 (X[3] A 275), n.d., 1850, where Kierkegaard remarks, in a very different context, that of his reflections on the evils of the press in his day, "Ultimately an abstraction is related to man's fantasy [det Phantastiske], and fantasy is an enormous power"; cf. also JP 1: p. 759, cited above, where Kierkegaard describes the quantitative dialectic, based on the principle of identity, as that in which "everything is and the whole is one and the same."

[13] Kierkegaard, CUP 112. Niels Thulstrup, Commentary on Kierkegaard's Concluding Unscientific Postscript with a New Introduction, trans. Robert J. Widenmann (Princeton: Princeton UP, 1984) 9lff.

[14] Kierkegaard, CA 13. For a brief account of Kierkegaard's studies in logic, see Diem 15-20; we will examine the place of movement, kinesis, in the next chapter when we discuss the ethical stage of existence.

[15] See Paul L. Holmer, "Kierkegaard and Logic," Kierkegaardiana 2 (1957): 25-42.

[16] Kierkegaard, JC 167-68.

[17] John W. Elrod, Being and Existence in Kierkegaard's Pseudonymous Works (Princeton: Princeton UP, 1975) 38-39; Elrod's study has informed my own remarks, although I depart from him at several points.

[18] Elrod 38; Elrod's emphasis.

[19] On the Hegelian background of "reflection," see G. W. F. Hegel, Hegel's Logic, trans. William Wallace, fwd. J. N. Findlay, 3rd ed. (Oxford: Clarendon, 1975); Mark C. Taylor, in his comparative study of Hegel and Kierkegaard, Journeys to Selfhood 173 and 237, stresses the distinction between these two related forms of abstraction, as "reflexion" and "reflection." Whereas

the first, reflexion, refers to the activity of setting out the poles of, for example, ideality and reality, the second, reflection, refers to the abstracting power of the mind. They are, however, closely related for Kierkegaard, since "reflexion," as the activity of setting up these poles, and reflection, as the abstracting power, are continuous activities. Elrod notes this connection between the two aspects of abstraction, and the relation of the imagination to both, when he writes of "reflection" that "it cannot stop itself when it reaches the point of its most abstract determination. Reflection is halted only by individual resolve, and it assumes its proper task when it is brought into a functional coherence with imagination. The function of imagination representation is crucial to the establishment of the two poles of the self's being which are necessarily prerequisite for the emergence of consciousness" (47).

[20] We will further analyze soulishness and reflection in the next section on the aesthetic sphere. Elrod puts too fine a point upon the distinction between imagination and reflection when he says, "reflection establishes reality and ideality, in contrast to the imagination, which explores all possibilities in the limitless realm of infinity" (48). The relation between imagination and reflection is closer than his, as indicated by Anti-Climacus when he says in SUD that "imagination is reflection, is the rendition of the self's possibility," and "the imagination is the possibility of any and all reflection" (31)

[21] Kierkegaard, CUP 103.

[22] Kierkegaard, CUP 169.

[23] Fichte, Grundriss des Eigenthümlichen der Wissenschaftslehre (3, VII) in Fichte.

[24] Kierkegaard, CUP 171.

[25] Fichte, The Vocation of Man, cited in Hart 359.

26 For a brief account of Fichte on this point, see Hart 358; a phenomenological study of Fichte's concept of the imagination questions the usual identification of his philosophy as "an absolute idealism which fell short of its mark" on the way to Hegel, and sees Fichte's interest to be precisely in finitude rather than the infinite or absolute; see T. P. Hohler, Imagination and Reflection: Intersubjectivity: Fichte's Grundlage of 1794. Martinus Nijhoff Philosophy Library 8 (The Hague: Nijhoff, 1982).

27 Robert Perkins, quoted in Crites, Twilight 22n1, misses this in his otherwise accurate summary of Kierkegaard's epistemology: "All objective knowledge for Kierkegaard is empirical, and is in every sense an approximation. Tautologies may indeed be necessary, but the empirical facts of the world are not necessary, and the knowledge of them is not necessary. Thus there is a distinction between the Kantian phenomena and the Kierkegaardian approximation. For Kierkegaard . . . there is no element of the a priori. Objective knowledge is an approximation, but more like Hume's scepticism than Kant's synthetic a priori." Kierkegaard is indeed convinced that objective knowledge is an approximation. And the empirical facts of this world and our knowledge of them are not necessary. But it is overstating the case to say that "for Kierkegaard . . . there is no element of the a priori." Kierkegaard's criticism of the a priori is directed against the Hegelian stress on necessity, and not against the Kantian notion of the imagination's playing an a priori role in knowledge of the contingencies of the empirical world.

28 Kierkegaard, JP 2: 2257 (II A 301), December 2, 1838.

29 Thus Kierkegaard speaks of the categories as deriving not from thought, but from being, e.g., JP 1: 240 (IV C 91), n.d., 1842-43; cf. JP 1: p. 507: "Categories are abbreviations of existence" (VII[1] A 249). Malantschuk glosses this as "thought abbreviates (foreshortens) and conflates the

circumstances of existence in certain major concepts (categories)," JP 1: p. 507. Malantschuk implies that "category" for Kierkegaard refers primarily not to a priori categories, but to the philosopher's development of concepts in the activity of reflecting on existence. Kierkegaard's "categories," he says, "are first and foremost existential concepts," JP 1: p. 507. This is true, but, as we have seen, Kierkegaard's interest in logical matters extends beyond "existential concepts" alone.

30 Elrod 47.

31 In contrast to theoretical consciousness, practical consciousness in the existential dialectic brings ideality into relation with reality.

32 Kierkegaard, JC 169, Kierkegaard's emphasis.

33 Elrod 49-51.

34 Kierkegaard, CUP 169ff.

35 In the Postscript the claims of scepticism are more strongly stated. While Kierkegaard can say in the Fragments that immediate sensation and immediate cognition cannot deceive (PF 81), in the Postscript "The apparent trustworthiness of sense is an illusion" (CUP 280). In the Fragments the star's existence is immediate; in the Postscript even that is called into question. Thus, in the latter book, even in the case of asserting either immediate sensation, or the existence of objects, an element of belief is entailed, a leap is made, and one applies possibility and ideality to the actual (in this case, the actual sense impression). This does not negate Kierkegaard's understanding of the a priori element in objective knowledge, but is precisely an application of the a priori.

36 Kierkegaard, PF 84; Kierkegaard denies in the Fragments that historical belief is knowledge, but this is not to deny that the theoretical consciousness (and therefore the imagination) is at work, or to deny that the historical involves knowledge. The point, rather, is that in historical knowledge,

as in all forms of objective knowledge, including logic, the conclusion is not simply the conclusion of an argument, but a resolution. In addition to knowledge, will is operative and the result is "belief."

[37] Howard V. Hong and Edna H. Hong, "Historical Introduction," Fear and Trembling and Repetition, by Søren Kierkegaard, ed. and trans. Howard V. Hong and Edna H. Hong with introd. and notes, Kierkegaard's Writings 6 (Princeton: Princeton UP, 1983) xxiv.

[38] Hong and Hong, "Historical Introduction," Fear and Trembling and Repetition xx-xxi. See also Howard V. Hong, "Tanke-Experiment in Kierkegaard," Kierkegaard: Resources and Results, ed. Alastair McKinnon (Waterloo, Ontario: Wilfrid Laurier UP, 1982) 39-51 and Robert L. Perkins' response, "Comment on Hong" 52-55.

[39] Kierkegaard, SUD 30-31.

[40] Helmut Fahrenbach, Kierkegaards existenzdialektische Ethik (Frankfurt am Main: Klostermann, 1968) 16ff; Elrod 43-53.

[41] Kierkegaard, SUD 31.

[42] We will return to this topic in discussing the dispositional aspects of the imagination in the ethical sphere of existence. The literature on "dispositions," "occurrences," and "events" in contemporary philosophical psychology is, of course, immense. The starting-point is still, however, Gilbert Ryle, The Concept of Mind; see especially ch. 2 on the "knowing-how" and "knowing-that" distinction, ch. 5 on dispositions and occurrences, and ch. 8 on the imagination and "picturing in the mind." The "knowing how-knowing that" distinction as it applies to Kierkegaard's concept of faith and to contemporary language philosophy is perceptively analyzed by Andrew J. Burgess, Passion, "Knowing How," and Understanding: An Essay on the Concept of Faith, American Acad. of Religion Diss. Series 9, ed. H. Ganse Little, Jr. (Missoula,

MT: Scholars, 1975). Kierkegaard's dispositional account of the imagination does not entail his abandoning or even criticizing the "event" or "activity" account; he combines them. Neither does Kierkegaard in his dispositional account of the imagination criticize the supposed "internal" quality of the imagination. Yet, as we will argue in Chapters V and VI, Kierkegaard's emphasis on the ethico-religious uses of the imagination stresses the need for embodying any "imagined self" in "external" action.

[43] On the distinction between moods and emotions, see Robert Roberts, "Kierkegaard on Becoming an 'Individual,'" Scottish Journal of Theology, 31 (1978): 133n2; the most thorough study of moods in the aesthetic sphere is Vincent A. McCarthy, The Phenomenology of Moods in Kierkegaard.

[44] This is not to say, however, that a person is necessarily self-conscious in relating moods to beliefs; as we will shortly see, one can be victim of a vague despair without linking it with one's beliefs, or even being aware of it. Nonetheless, a diagnostic observer can locate the root of despair in the person's beliefs.

[45] Elrod 15-16.

[46] Kierkegaard, SUD 29.

[47] Kierkegaard, SUD 13.

[48] Kierkegaard, SUD 43.

[49] Kierkegaard, CA 41; Kierkegaard here relies on Rosenkranz's Psychologie, see Nordentoft 21.

[50] Kierkegaard, CA 41.

[51] Kierkegaard, EO1 60ff; Kierkegaard, CA 42, 96ff.

[52] Nordentoft 22.

[53] Kierkegaard, EO1 76, 74.

[54] "Anxiety is freedom's actuality as the possibility of possibility," Kierkegaard, CA 42.

[55] Kierkegaard, EO1 74.

[56] Kierkegaard, CA 42.

[57] Kierkegaard, CA 44.

[58] Søren Kierkegaard, Christian Discourses and The Lilies of the Field and the Birds of the Air and Three Discourses at the Communion on Fridays, trans., introd., and notes Walter Lowrie (Princeton: Princeton UP, 1940) 113 (hereafter, CD).

[59] Kierkegaard, CD 113.

[60] Nordentoft 33-34, links this passage to the second and third stages of the immediate erotic, the child correlating to Papageno, and the youth to Don Juan.

[61] Nordentoft 34.

[62] Kierkegaard, SUD 13.

[63] Kierkegaard, SUD 29-30.

[64] Kierkegaard, SUD 31ff.

[65] Kierkegaard, SUD 32.

[66] Kierkegaard, SUD 35.

[67] Kierkegaard, SUD 30.

[68] Kierkegaard, SUD 37.

[69] Kierkegaard, SUD 34.

[70] Kierkegaard, SUD 33.

[71] Kierkegaard, SUD 40.

[72] Lowrie's translation here better conveys the sense; Søren Kierkegaard, Fear and Trembling and The Sickness Unto Death, trans., introd., and notes Walter Lowrie (Princeton: Princeton UP, 1954) 171.

[73] Kierkegaard, SUD (Lowrie's trans.) 171.

[74] Kierkegaard, SUD 41, in the Hongs' translation.

[75] Kierkegaard, SUD 41.

[76] Kierkegaard, SUD 42.

[77] Kierkegaard, SUD 59.

[78] This is because spiritlessness is not simply an absence of spirit, but a suppression of spirit; see Kierkegaard, CA 44 and 95, and SUD 46-47. In the development of the history of spirit, the age of innocence is over, and spiritlessness since the advent of Socrates and, at a higher level, Christianity, is in a defensive posture over against spirit. See, for example, Kierkegaard, EO1 59ff.

[79] Kierkegaard, SUD 43.

[80] Kierkegaard, SUD 44.

[81] Kierkegaard, SUD 44; cf. Kierkegaard, CA 96: "Viewed from the standpoint of spirit, anxiety is also present in spiritlessness, but it is hidden and disguised."

[82] McCarthy, esp. 127ff.

[83] John Elrod is right to say that "The first volume of Either/Or is a representation of the complex hierarchy of aesthetic existence possibilities which range from complete immersion in facticity-finitude-(Don Juan) to its dialectical opposite, total immersion in imagination-infinitude-(Johannes the Seducer)," Elrod 37n26. Yet this should not obscure the presence of the imagination at the primitive stages of the aesthetic sphere, including the dreaming of the immediate sensuous, or the suppressed restlessness of the imagination in the less expansive moods. Neither should one ignore the dialectical increase of finitude and necessity at the higher levels of despair--the despair of necessity, e.g., can be at

a higher level of the "hierarchy" than sheer spiritlessness. In other words, the imagination plays various roles in the dialectic of moods.

[84] Kierkegaard, CA 42.

[85] Søren Kierkegaard, The Concept of Dread, trans., introd., and notes Walter Lowrie, 2nd ed. (Princeton: Princeton UP, 1957) 135-36.

[86] Kierkegaard, JP 1: 907 (IV A 213), n.d., 1843. See also Ronald Grimsley, "Kierkegaard and the Don Juan Legend," Søren Kierkegaard and French Literature: Eight Comparative Studies (Cardiff: U of Wales P, 1966); Louis Mackey, Kierkegaard: A Kind of Poet (Philadelphia: U of Pennsylvania P, 1971) 15. Cf. Kierkegaard, EO2 24, for Judge William's analysis of melancholy; also, CA 43n, for Vigilius Haufniensis' analysis.

[87] McCarthy 96.

[88] Kierkegaard, CD 69.

[89] Kierkegaard, SUD 53.

[90] Kierkegaard, SUD 54.

[91] Kierkegaard, SUD 56-57.

[92] Kierkegaard, SUD 58.

[93] Kierkegaard, SUD 54-55.

[94] Kierkegaard, SUD 60.

[95] Kierkegaard, SUD 60.

[96] Kierkegaard, SUD 61.

[97] Kierkegaard, SUD 63.

[98] Kierkegaard, SUD 67.

[99] Kierkegaard, SUD 67; cf. McCarthy 99.

[100] Kierkegaard, SUD 68.

[101] Kierkegaard, SUD 69.

[102] Kierkegaard, SUD 70.

[103] Kierkegaard, SUD 72-73.

[104] Kierkegaard, SUD 70.

[105] Kierkegaard, SUD 70.

[106] Kierkegaard, SUD 70.

[107] As early as 1877, Georg Brandes notes the relation between Julius and Johannes, see Malantschuk 218n96; Mullen 658. Paulsen (74) argues against drawing too close a connection between Julius and Johannes.

[108] Kierkegaard, EO1 439; Hirsch 154.

[109] Kierkegaard, EO1 433.

[110] Kierkegaard, EO1 331, 336.

[111] Kierkegaard, EO1 439; see also Arild Christensen, "Zwei Kierkegaardstudien," Orbis Litterarum 10 (1955): 47-48.

[112] Ronald Grimsley, "Kierkegaard and the Don Juan Legend: (2) Kierkegaard and Laclos," Grimsley 36.

[113] Kierkegaard, EO1 440.

[114] Kierkegaard, EO1 33. On Johannes as a production of "A's" mind, see EO1 9; cf. McCarthy 107n1.

CHAPTER FIVE

The Capacity Instar Omnium:

The Imagination of Repetition

in the Ethical Sphere

Every man possesses in a greater or lesser degree a talent which is called imagination, the power which is the first condition determining what a man will turn out to be; for the second condition is the will, which in the final resort is decisive.

--Kierkegaard, Training in Christianity

To recall the arch model we used, it is only when a person's reflection descends from the world of possibility and ideality back to the concrete reality of ethical action that one enters the realm of true self-concern. In the language of Johannes Climacus, one moves from theoretical consciousness to practical consciousness, from concern with objective thinking to concern with subjective thinking, from the disinterest that marks the aesthetic sphere to interestedness. As we will see, "reality" gains an added significance not simply as the given or the actual, but as the task of the ethical person, concretely realized in time, for "the ethical reality of the individual is the only reality."[1]

But just as the imagination takes on many dialectical forms in the intellectual and aesthetic realm of possibility, so too the imagination becomes dialectical in the ethical stage and, even more so, in the religious stages of existence. We have already seen how Kierkegaard rehabilitates the artistic in the simultaneity of factors, identifying a subjective artistry that makes life transparent to the idea. We will now investigate this in more detail by examining, first, in this chapter, Judge William's understanding (in Either/Or, II, and Stages on

Life's Way) of the functions of the imagination in the ethical sphere of existence, and then, in Chapter VI, the more complex dialectic of the religious spheres, illustrated in particular by three figures from the Kierkegaardian literature, the young man of Repetition, Quidam in Stages on Life's Way, and another unnamed young man in Training in Christianity. Here too the imagination as medium, activity, passion, capacity, and disposition are prominent.

When Judge William, in his correspondence to "A," analyzes his young friend's lack of equilibrium, he singles out the imaginative despair into which the aesthete has fallen, a despair composed of irony and dreaminess, mental virtuosity and self-evasion:

> You are constantly hovering above yourself, but the ether, the fine sublimate into which you are volatilized, is the nullity of despair. . . . You have got the notion that "life is a fairy tale." You are capable of spending a whole month reading nothing but fairy tales, you make a profound study of them, you compare and analyze, and your study is not barren of result--but what do you use it for? To divert your mind; you let the whole thing go off in a brilliant display of fireworks. You are hovering above yourself, and what you behold beneath you is a multiplicity of moods and situations which you employ to find interesting contacts with life.[2]

Despite the fact that despair is the source of the aesthete's disordered existence, the Judge's remedy is to recommend that the aesthete accentuate his despair to the utmost: "So, then, despair with all your soul and with all your mind."[3] From the despairing uses of imagination at the brink of the ethical, Judge William beckons the aesthete to pass through that despair with all of his passion and leap to a new form of existence. From the height of the ascending arc of the abstracting and aesthetic functions of the imagination, the ethical sphere holds out the promise of a returning movement, a second arc, back to the concrete from which the imagination originates. The ethical, of course, has already come under our inspection. We have seen the importance of actuality as gift and as task in The Concept of Irony. So too, we have seen some of the ethical functions of the imagination in the artistic, passionate inwardness of the subjective thinker in the Postscript. But it is in Either/Or, II, that Kierkegaard elaborates his reflections on actuality and on the artistry of ethical thinking and existence.

At first glance, Kierkegaard's analysis of the ethical stage in Either/Or (and Stages) says little on the imagination. The target is aestheticism, especially Romantic aestheticism, rather than the anti-imaginative aestheticism of speculative philosophy. As we saw in Chapter III, Johannes Climacus in "A Glance at a Contemporary Effort in Danish Literature" observes that the first part of Either/Or "is an imagination-existence [Phantasie-Existents] in aesthetic passion"; in the second part, "instead of a world of possibilities, glowing with imagination [Phantasie] and dialectically organized, we have an individual."[4] In an important sense the Judge has left behind the fevers of the imagination for the sake of becoming an individual.

Yet, prosaic as he may be, the Judge maintains like Johannes Climacus that the aesthetic is not lost in the ethical, but rather that there is an equilibrium of the aesthetic and the ethical in the composition of personality. The Judge even admits an ironic admiration for Schlegel's Julius, of whom he can say:

> In one of the tales of the Romantic School which evinces the greatest genius, there is one character who has no desire to write poetry like the others among whom he lives, because it is a waste of time and deprives him of the true enjoyment--he prefers to live. Now if he had the right conception of what it is to live, he would have been the man for me.[5]

The Judge can even speak, like Johannes Climacus, of the ethical person as an artist.[6] In his own way, stressing certainly the balance and harmony of the ethical, Judge William does have a version of the simultaneity of factors. Like

Johannes Climacus, he sees the imagination flourishing in realms beyond the aesthetic sphere of existence.

The heart of Judge William's reflections on the imagination's movements in the ethical sphere occurs in his discussion of the relation between the "actual self" and the "ideal self." Analyzing this discussion will allow us to consider the imagination's role in constituting an ethical personality. We will examine how in the ethical sphere of existence the imagination relates to a variety of factors: the significance of choice, the role of kinesis as a transition as well as a separation between possibility and actuality, the manner in which the ethical utilizes the imagination's powers as the organ of the concrete, and how the imagination is ingredient in the "inner infinity" of the ethical. We will then be able to see how truly non-Hegelian Kierkegaard's picture of the self is, despite his use of Hegelian terms. This will show, too, the imaginative elements in the movement of "repetition," especially as they throw light on Kierkegaard's understanding of ethical disposition, "truth," and "reality." The imagination will emerge, then as a remarkably supple ethical category, indispensable to an understanding of Kierkegaard's reflection on the moral life.

Let us begin with the relation of the "actual self" and the "ideal self" in ethical action, a relation that corresponds to the movements of abstraction and of concretion in the existential dialectic. The movement of the ethical is twofold, beginning with the concrete, the given actuality, abstracting from this to possibility; in this way the ethical movement duplicates the aesthetic, and it provides the aesthetic element in the ethical. But beyond the aesthetic movement, the ethical takes the picture of the possible self that the imagination has presented, and makes it a goal of action. In the depiction of the self in The Sickness Unto Death, Kierkegaard describes this in a manner completely congruent with Judge William's understanding:

> Inasmuch as the self as a synthesis of finitude and infinitude is established, is kata dynamin [potential], in order to become itself it reflects itself in the medium of imagination [Phantasiens Medium], and thereby the infinite possibility becomes manifest. The self is kata dynamin [potentially] just as possible as it is necessary, for it is indeed itself, but it has the task of becoming itself. Insofar as it is itself, it is the necessary, and insofar as it has the task of becoming itself, it is a possibility.[7]

This is, in effect, a concise summary of Judge William's more detailed discussion of the relation of the actual self and the ideal self in Either/Or; it is this detail that we must now examine.

There are two stages in the movement of the ethical person between the actual and ideal self. The first stage of movement is that beginning with the actual self, the "necessary" element of the given characteristics of the person; the second stage is the actualizing of the ideal self. Turning to the first movement, it is important to note the differences between the aesthetic movement to possibility and the ethical movement to the ideal. While both the aesthete and the ethical individual begin with the actual self, the aesthetic person does not accept the actuality of his or her existence as a gift, a given, but "views himself in his concretion and then distinguishes inter et inter. He regards some things as belonging to him accidentally, other things as belonging to him essentially."[8] That is to say, the aesthete examines the given capacities and talents and chooses those which he or she will make the center of existence. But this is not true choice, since it is an attempt to exercise complete lordship over one's life. Instead of accepting the givens of existence, the aesthete, in despair of possibility, stands back from the concrete self and sovereignly decides which elements shall and shall not be part of personality. Yet, Judge William charges, the aesthete in reflexive irony never regards even the essential elements as truly essential, but flits from one "essential" possibility to another, "for so long as a man lives merely aesthetically one thing belongs to him as accidentally as another, and it is merely for lack of energy an aesthetic individual maintains this distinction [between essential and accidental elements]."[9] Thus, the aesthete is in despair, regarding even the "essential" elements of personality as adventitiously given and hence "external" to the self.

The ethical person also begins with the actual self, and also makes the same distinction between accidental and essential elements, but to much different ends:

> He who lives ethically abolishes to a certain degree the distinction between the accidental and the essential, for he accepts himself, every inch of him, as equally essential. But the distinction returns, for when he has done this he distinguishes again, yet in such a way that for the accidental which he excludes he accepts an essential responsibility for excluding it.[10]

The ethical person does not claim total sovereignty over his existence. One may, indeed will, choose to develop certain capacities and leave others, but the ethical person does so with a sense of the gift-quality of the neglected talent as well. Furthermore, the ethical person does not flee into possibility in a sheer negation of the finite. Rather, one takes the given element and "infinitizes" it in imagination. In The Sickness Unto Death, Anti-Climacus describes this as "an infinite moving away from [oneself] in the infinitizing of the self."[11]

The danger at this point of infinitizing is great, of course, for in this infinitizing one can easily shirk the responsibility of moving on to action. Anti-Climacus uses the mirror metaphor to describe how one begins with the actual self, and also this danger at the point of possibility:

> Even in seeing oneself in a mirror it is necessary to recognize oneself, for if one does not, one does not see oneself but only a human being. The mirror of possibility is no ordinary mirror; it must be used with extreme caution, for in the

highest sense, this mirror does not tell the truth. That a self appears to be such and such in the possibility of itself is only a half-truth, for in the possibility of itself the self is still far from or is only half of itself. Therefore, the question is how the necessity of this particular self defines it more specifically.[12]

Judge William answers this last question by arguing that "necessity" is where a person can acquire "information" about one's actual self.

Ethical infinitizing, then, is to be distinguished from aesthetic infinitizing in several ways. First, the motive is not sheer dreaminess or escape, a flitting from one possibility to another; it is directed to the end of concrete action. Second, the imaginative movement begins with a concentrated investigation or inventory of the actual self, distinguishing the essential and then moving to idealize it imaginatively: "Ethically, the ideality is the real within the individual himself."[13] Reflection on the actual self is an anchor for the infinitizing movement of the imagination. In this way the "ideal self" that is infinitized in imagination is, if rightly used, not a false image, but rather a projection based on the actual self, a "half-truth." Third, the imagination in one sense is limited. The ethical person, instead of suffering from the melancholic's "overbalance of imagination," restricts the breadth of imagination and concentrates on a particular possibility. Yet, fourth, in the concentrated moment of ideality the primary function of the imagination in the ethical sphere is to engender pathos and resolution. Johannes Climacus writes of this juncture between imaginative representation and striving in remarkable terms:

> It is only momentarily that the particular individual is able to realize existentially a unity of the infinite and the finite which transcends existence. . . . In passion the existing individual is rendered infinite in the eternity of the imaginative representation, and yet he is at the same time most definitely himself.[14]

But the Judge too can speak of pathos: "It is not so much a question of choosing the right as of the energy, the earnestness, the pathos with which one chooses."[15] The pathos of choosing one's imaginative ideal does not produce will, but the ideal inspires resolution rather than melancholic, yearning lassitude; resolution "is the ideality brought about by a purely ideal reflection, it is the earned capital required for action."[16] For this reason Judge William says that a chosen ideal is a person's "possibility (or to avoid an expression so aesthetical) that it is his task."[17] Seeing one's possibility as task, a person unites wishing with willing; a possibility that is freely chosen becomes "related to the self as a morally binding authority."[18]

At this point the ethical person begins to enter the second movement, that of the transition between the imagined ideal self and the actual self. The central distinguishing feature of this transition is choice. But what is choice? Judge William argues that one makes a formal choice, first of all, to become a self rather than any particular self:

> But what is it I choose? Is it this thing or that? No, for I choose absolutely, and the absoluteness of my choice is expressed precisely by the fact that I have not chosen to choose this or that. I choose the absolute. And what is the absolute? It is I myself in my eternal validity.[19]

What makes a choice "absolute" or ethical, rather than simply a decision to limit one's possibilities, is that the ethical choice includes a formal decision to see one's particular choice, whatever it is, under the eternal obligation of the ethical. In choosing to be a married man, Judge William chooses not simply a particular state of social life; he also chooses to see that decision as an infinitely binding choice, lasting a lifetime, recruiting new commitment daily. Ethical choice gives vigor to the imagination by opening up the prospect of a continuing love for his wife that defeats the erosion time brings; he achieves an inner infinity grounded in the sense that "I ought" and "I can." The imaginative possibility, now a task, shows him the "eternal." A new sense of the eternal emerges, for now, in Gregor Malantschuk's words, "the eternal in man comes to the fore and as such must be interpreted as the ethical in the proper sense, which from its side poses a task for man."[20] The "eternal" is central to any chosen ethical task; it is universally applicable to all the choices different people make and to the different choices that any one person may make in his or her lifetime. In all this, the "eternal" opens up the future to a person. In short, for Kierkegaard, to be a self is to exercise the ability to choose freely the self one is to be; in choice a person gains sovereignty over the self, but Judge William notes in an image that hearkens back to the aesthete's defiance, ethical sovereignty is unlike "the very embarrassing sovereignty which characterizes a king without a country."[21] In ethical choice one rules over the territory of the self, one's dreams, and imaginings becoming transformed into a concretely constituted actual self.

We are now at the pinnacle of a proper abstraction in the ethical life, in which the eternal is shown in its fullness. But to have a possibility as a task of constituting a concrete self, one must make the second movement of the self in which imaginative passion culminates in a descent back to finitude. In Anti-Climacus' phrase, the self engages in "an infinite coming back to itself in the finitizing process."[22] Judge William says, "the individual chooses himself as a concretion determined in manifold ways."[23] Having stressed the powers of infinitude and abstraction, Kierkegaard is not about to slip back into what he considers the Hegelian absorption of finitude into the infinite.[24] The self is now posited as individual spirit's active synthesizing of possibility and necessity in which freedom takes one beyond abstract possibility to the concrete: "But what, then, is this self of mine? If I were required to define this, my first answer would be: It is the most abstract of all things, and yet at the same time it is the most concrete--it is freedom."[25]

The movement from sheer abstract freedom to freedom's concrete actualization is kinesis ("movement" or "becoming"). Kinesis is one of the most crucial categories in Kierkegaard's thought, for by means of it he performs the subtle dialectical task of separating the spheres of possibility and actuality, thought and existence, and yet relating them in a dynamic way. Kinesis separates, on the one hand, the realm of the abstract and contemplative and, on the other hand, the realm of action, preventing a speculative confusion between them. Yet kinesis is also a term of transition between possibility and actuality: "kinesis is difficult to define, because it belongs neither to possibility nor to actuality, is more than possibility and less than actuality."[26] Since kinesis "mediates" between possibility and actuality, between the quantitative and qualitative, there is not a sheer contrast between them. For all Kierkegaard's interest in ruling out an Hegelian mediation by dialectically separating the two realms, he does not divorce them; such an undialectical divorce would in effect condemn actuality and action to the realm of the unintelligible, which is never Kierkegaard's intention. In kinesis, freedom as movement, one relates ideality and possibility to actuality so that possibility "informs" or "infuses" actuality. As Johannes Climacus says in the Postscript, movement is "the inexplicable presupposition and common factor of thinking and being, and . . . their continued reciprocity."[27] Indeed, kinesis is related to passion, in that passion's imaginative enthusiasm in striving provides the resolution needed for ethical action.

Because kinesis dialectically both separates and relates the possible and the actual, it is the key to understanding how the imagination becomes incorporated in ethical passion, how Johannes Climacus' simultaneity of factors in the subjective thinker operates. Becoming a concrete, finite individual in ethical striving does not exclude, but dialectically incorporates, the ascending movement of imagination. This means that both strands of Kierkegaard's polemic, against the Romantics and Idealists, are summed up in his emphasis on the moment of kinesis. Against aestheticism, the ethical person knows that the ideal self is only a "half-truth"; the very point of ethical striving is that one is not yet the ideal. So too, Kierkegaard can speak of the ethical need "to minimize the medium of imagination and to will to have only the medium of existence."[28]

But on the other hand, against Idealist rationalism, in the ethical kinesis from possibility to actuality, the imagined ideal that is anchored in the actual, held before one's concentration, and translated into actuality, becomes ingredient in the self beyond "the medium of imagination." Because kinesis is the transition between the realm of possibility and actuality, existence is infused with imagination. In ethical action leading to the concrete, one never simply flees from imaginative possibility into necessity, for in that case the ethical ideal would be lost and the ethical would be indistinguishable from "necessity's despair due to lack of possibility." Quite the contrary, the choice of a particular concrete self (which includes necessity) is always mediated through the imagination.[29] Conversely, the person's possible self always becomes concrete; otherwise one would lapse into "possibility's despair due to lack of necessity." The ethical not only raises the actual to the ideal, but finds the ideal's fulfillment in a definite, concrete life shaped by the ideal.

Judge William discusses this entire movement, leading to the concrete, in his reflections on the ideal self and the actual self. In an important albeit ponderous and lawyerly passage, Judge William speaks of the ethical person's self-knowledge:

If I desired to be clever I might say at this point that the
individual knew himself in such a way as Adam "knew" Eve
in the Old Testament sense of the word. By the individual's
intercourse with himself he impregnates himself and brings
himself to birth. This self which the individual knows is at
once the actual self and the ideal self which the individual has
outside himself as the picture in likeness to which he has to
form himself and which, on the other hand, he nevertheless
has in him since it is the self.

The Judge explains this cryptic remark:

Only within him has the individual the goal after which he
has to strive, and yet he has this goal outside him, inasmuch
as he strives after it. For if the individual believes that the
universal man is situated outside him, that from without it
will come to him, then he is disoriented, then he has an
abstract conception and his method is always an abstract
annihilation of the original self. Only within him can the
individual acquire information about himself. Hence, the
ethical life has this duplex character, that the individual has
his self outside himself and in himself.

The Judge then analyzes the use the ethical person makes of this ideal self once it
is discovered:

When the individual knows himself and has chosen himself
he is about to realize himself, but as he has to realize himself
freely he must know what it is he would realize. What he
would realize is in fact himself, but it is his ideal self which
he acquires nowhere but in himself. If one does not hold fast
to the fact that the individual has the ideal self in himself, his
Dichten und Trachten [thought, aspirations, endeavors,
studies] remain abstract.[30]

Here we see how the imagination functions fully in the ethical, for the

ideal self, anchored to the actual and directed to the concrete, is also, because of

that anchoring, the ideal "other." Three aspects of this deserve comment. First,

as we have seen, imaginative reflection on the actual self engenders the ideal self

of possibility and so gives an "inward infinity": "only within himself can the

individual acquire information about himself."[31] "The individual has the ideal in himself"[32] because the past, given self is the basis of the idealized self's goal. In contrast to the aesthete who finds only an external infinity, the actual self gives to the ethical person, in the shape of the ideal self, an internal infinity of possibilities. Yet, second, the ideal self, grounded in the actual, is "external" too, as an ideal task pointing one to the future. In this sense the ethical person chooses a self "absolutely distinct from his former self, for he has chosen it absolutely";[33] the individual has this ideal self "outside himself as the picture in likeness to which he has to form himself."[34] It is the universal ideal. Third, the ideal self as "another" points beyond an abstract self to a concrete self:

> But although he himself is his aim, this aim is nevertheless another, for the self which is the aim is not an abstract self which fits everywhere and hence nowhere, but a concrete self which stands in reciprocal relations with these surroundings, these conditions of life, this natural order.[35]

This passage is of great importance, for Kierkegaard here unites two senses of the imagination, as the organ of possibility and the organ for the concrete. The advance of the ethical imagination over the aesthetic imagination is that, in terms reminiscent of the simultaneity of factors, the imagination is the source not only of possibility, but of "aesthetic concreteness" aimed now at ethical concretion. The ideal of the union of the finite and infinite in the concrete which we examined in the Postscript's simultaneity of factors is here clarified in terms of the artistry of the ethical person. Judge William describes a dynamic harmony of possibility and necessity, and the restlessness of the imagination in the aesthetic sphere now finds its rightful place in the simultaneity of factors.

Furthermore, not only is the imagination now the servant of the concrete as well as of the possible, but the imagination, which usually distances and so yields only an "external infinity," now ironically opens up the realm of the "inner infinite" Kierkegaard first defined in The Concept of Irony. The imagination provides the abstraction from the given, and so "internally" generates an "external" ethical ideal that, as a goal that is acted upon, becomes truly "internal." The ideal is my ideal, and yet it stands apart from me as my goal; it is an external goal, and yet it points to the concrete self I strive to become.

In this combination of the ideal as "internally" generated and yet "external" as the universal ideal pointing to the concrete "other," Kierkegaard dialectically unites two different notions of what it is to be an individual, in a manner confirming our earlier argument that Kierkegaard goes beyond both Romanticism and Idealism on the imagination. One notion of the individual is the Romantic idea of self-development as a cultivation of uniqueness: a person must nurture his or her own unduplicable gifts. The other, Idealist notion of individuality stresses not the uniqueness but the singleness of the ethical individual as formed by a universally binding obligation. In willing the universal, a person becomes individuated by the commitment to that universal. Kierkegaard combines these two notions, deliberately tempering the Romantic stress on uniqueness with the universal demand of the ethical, and yet seeing in the universal ethical demand the fulfillment of the Romantic desire for

> When the ethical individual has completed his task, has fought the good fight, he has then reached the point where he has become the one man, that is to say, that there is no other man altogether like him; and at the same time he has become the universal man.[36]

In the ethical, one must repent oneself out of the individualistic Romantic desire for uniqueness by repenting oneself into the public world of universally-binding ethical action; but the result of this repentance into the ethical world is that the quest for uniqueness is fulfilled.[37] Ironically, the Romantic goal of an inner infinity by way of the imagination is rewarded, but only through seeking a goal that is held "outside" one as the ideal.

Thus, strangely enough, this ideal "external" self, this imagined "other" as the goal of striving, allows one to attain both "concreteness" and an "inner infinity." This complex picture of the self--actual, ideal, and concrete; infinite and finite; possible and actual--reveals how for Kierkegaard the self is not a substance but a dynamic, ordered relation of factors. For Kierkegaard, the self is best understood, as Herbert Fingarette puts it, by "the metaphor of . . . a community rather than a collection."[38] Moreover, to be truly a self, in the ethical sense, means that one's identity cannot be described apart from that ideal imagined self. As Judge William says, for the ethical person, "the picture in likeness to which he has to form himself" is one part of his "duplex character."[39]

The imagination then is not the self, but to be a self one must be imaginative. Again, in Anti-Climacus' words,

> Every man possesses in a greater or less degree a talent which is called imagination [Indbildningskraften], the power of which is the first condition determining what a man will turn out to be; for the second condition is the will, which in the final resort is decisive.[40]

The imagination is the first necessary condition for becoming a self, since in the imagination one first forms a notion of what it is to be a self, which then becomes part of one's self-identity; a self emerges who unites finitude and infinitude, necessity and possibility, reality and ideality in a concrete way exhibiting freedom.

In many respects, as scholars have noted, Kierkegaard echoes Hegel in this picture of the self as composed of dynamic factors, including an external ideal that is internalized in a process governed by spirit.[41] But one difference between Hegel and Kierkegaard is on the place of the imagination in this picture. As will be recalled from the discussion of the simultaneity of factors in Chapter III, Kierkegaard, unlike Hegel, is explicit about the imagination's part in this.

Kierkegaard accentuates thereby the self's freedom, passion, and spontaneity and also the sense of the concrete that the individual spirit, wielding the imagination, alone can give. Hegel, by contrast, is concerned with this process as it leads rationally to objective spirit.[42] For Kierkegaard, the development is to subjectivity; for Hegel the development of the self is a development to objectivity. Most evidently in The Sickness Unto Death the analysis of the dynamic self quite seriously uses Hegel's form of the self as dynamic, but with a content, in particular the dynamism and concreteness of the imagination, that undermines the thrust toward objectivity in Hegel's analysis of the self. Hence, Kierkegaard's critique of Hegel is not a critique of the Hegelian picture of the self; the definition of the self at the beginning of the first part of The Sickness Unto Death is not a parody of Hegel. But to say only this ignores the fact that the content that Kierkegaard gives to the picture of the dynamics of the self, with its stress on the imagination's role in existence, is a condemnation of Hegel.[43]

The anti-Idealism of these dynamics is most clearly seen when the "arch" leading up to possibility and then down to actuality becomes a "circle." This two-fold continuous process, this movement along the circle, this recovery of the disturbed balance in existence, is Kierkegaard's crucial category of "repetition" (Gjentagelsen). In repetition a person raises reality to ideality, and then repeats that possibility in actuality.[44] Repetition is imaginative because it requires diagnostic perception and originality to sift out the confusions and imbalance one finds in oneself.[45] The imagination in repetition becomes an instrument for achieving subjective transparency (Gjennemsigtighed), which we have already seen is the "artistic" element of the ethicist.

In ethical repetition's transparency, one's past, present, and future are linked together in continuity. Aesthetic existence is fragmented; the ironist, for example, lives in a state in which "the most contrary feelings are allowed to displace each other"; the ironist is "now . . . a god, now a grain of sand."[46] But the healthy operation of the imagination is quite different; the imagination gives continuity to a person's life and links one day to another by grasping the past and the future. The past is made into a present ideal, and this ideal is focussed again in the move to concrete realization in the present and future. This is why Kierkegaard associates the imagination so often with memory.[47] Memory allows a person to see the past as one's own past, and to connect that past self with the present self and the future self in a creative way.

Yet in repetition the imagination is oriented also to the future, grasping the future as possibility; the "eternal" in ethical striving is for Kierkegaard, in one sense of the word, simply the "future" in the possibilities it opens to the individual.[48] Directed to the future, the imagination is at the heart of expectation as well as memory:

> Expectation and the future are inseparable thoughts. He who expects something is preoccupied with the future. . . . It is precisely man's greatness, the proof of his divine heritage, that he can occupy himself with the future; for if there were no future, neither would there have been a past, and if there were neither past nor future, then would man be enslaved like the beasts, his head bent toward the earth, his soul ensnared in the service of the moment.[49]

The past and future, memory and expectation, are fruitfully rather than fantastically related, however, only by living in the present. The dilemma of the "unhappiest man" in Either/Or, I, shows how frightening is an existence in imagination that fails to relate the past and the future,

> for the future he has already anticipated in thought, in thought already experienced it, and this experience he now remembers, instead of hoping for it. Consequently, what he hopes for lies behind him, what he remembers lies before him.[50]

It requires imagination to bring the past before one in memory; it requires imagination to be related to the future. Yet the task is to imagine both past and future without dissolving oneself in the medium of imagination.

In ethical existence, by contrast, the imagination helps to constitute a real self and so becomes an element in the continuity of the self from the past to the present and future. To put it another way, the imagination can become part of the ethical person's disposition. As we have seen, the imagination can be dispositional in the aesthetic sphere in a fantastic way. But in the ethical sphere the imagination as a disposition comes into its own. Contrary to popular portrayals of Kierkegaard's thought, to be ethical is not only "making choices" as if--to use Iris Murdoch's phrase--the self were merely an "agent, thin as a needle," who "appears in the quick flash of the choosing will."[51] Kierkegaard's picture of the ethical self is much richer, concerned with the ethical person's continuity through time in developing long-term dispositions. In the ethical sphere, not only the will but the imagination is raised to a constant factor in one's life. The ethical person not only does ethical deeds, but with originality envisions a way of life and acts upon it responsibly. The ethical person does not simply "image" at particular times, but is dispositionally imaginative. The imaginativeness of the ethical life, therefore, fulfills the aim of possessing a simultaneity of factors.

The ethical person's dispositional continuity as a self gives continuity to the emotional life as well. The moods of the aesthetic stage, episodic and arbitrary, give way to long-term emotions; being tied to commitments and beliefs, they can support an individual over a lifetime. As the Judge indicates, his love for his wife is a continuing, sustaining emotion that checks moods.[52]

Furthermore, this passional and dispositional infiltration of the imagination into the full extent of one's life gives content also to Kierkegaard's concept that "truth is subjectivity." In the imaginative passion and originality with which the ethical person adheres to and wills the ideal, he or she "apprehends the truth": "When the question of truth is raised subjectively, reflection is directed subjectively to the nature of the individual's relationship."[53] In case the truth is objectively uncertain,

> the subject merely has, objectively, the uncertainty; but it is this which precisely increases the tension of that infinite passion which constitutes his inwardness. The truth is precisely the venture which chooses an objective uncertainty with the passion of the infinite.[54]

The imagination looks to the idea, and sees both the beauty of it (the aesthetic element) and the task it entails. As it becomes realized, the individual is formed to that image. In short, one becomes what one imagines, and so becomes oneself. In Diem's words, "truth is subjectivity" means that "every aspect of the ego participates equally in this being in the truth."[55]

Not only is the imagination integral to "truth," it is also integral to Kierkegaard's understanding of the concept "reality." In a solitary sentence shortly before the section on the simultaneity of factors in the Postscript, Kierkegaard writes, "Subjectivity is truth, subjectivity is reality."[56] The importance of this cannot be underestimated, for although Kierkegaard does not believe that the imagination creates reality, neither does the imagination produce "unreal" dreams in opposition to rational "reality." As we saw in the last chapter on the role of the imagination in knowledge, the picture that emerges is more complex than either Romantic or Idealist concepts of truth and reality. The imagination does not in itself deliver "reality," as the Romantics thought. On the other hand, the imagination does not deal with "unreality" either, as the Hegelian rationalists tended to think; Kierkegaard does not adopt the standard rationalist picture of "reason" correlating with "reality" or "truth," and "imagination" correlating with "unreality." For Kierkegaard there is, quite simply, no such thing as a single relation of imagination and reality. The imagination does not have a set cognitive or metaphysical significance in and of itself, but only as deployed in different activities and interests. The imagination is ingredient in knowing truth and reality, but the relation between the imagination and reality differs according to the stage in which one stands. In the intellectual and aesthetic spheres, the imagination construes "reality" as possibility and relates to it objectively. But for the subjective thinker, in concrete reflection on ethical and religious interests motivated by passion, the imagination is a condition for knowing truth and reality in subjectivity. The imagination equips people to apprehend their world in particular ways, aesthetically, ethically, and even religiously. The imagination and reality do have a relation then, but the relation is not univocal, and not determined simply by defining the characteristic of the capacity of the imagination "in itself."

The imagination's role in ethical existence shows again just how dialectical Kierkegaard's understanding of the imagination is, for the "imagination" denotes a medium of possibility, an activity of idealizing, a passion that contributes to resolution, an organ for the concrete, and a capacity or disposition that describes not only what the ethical person does, but how he or she does it.57 When we stand back to survey the scope of Kierkegaard's dialectic of the imagination, it is striking how far Kierkegaard has come from the narrowly architectonic and schoolish understanding of the imagination. In the philosophical tradition the "imagination" is taken in a nominative sense, construed as a single faculty or form of thought believed to have certain abilities as such. By calling it the "capacity instar omnium," indeed, hesitating to call it a capacity at all, Kierkegaard breaks that traditional "nominative" interpretation of the imagination. In describing this wide range of uses Kierkegaard indicates that it is not "the imagination" as a faculty that is <u>instar omnium</u>. Rather, the expression "capacity <u>instar omnium</u>" points to the immense variety of ways of being imaginative that Kierkegaard describes in his literature: the intellectual and the aesthetic, the ethical, and as we will shortly see, the religious.

With regard to ethics, however, the central significance of the imagination is finally that being ethical is a way of being imaginative. This means that the imagination is not a gift alone--certainly not a gift belonging to genius or talent alone--but is part of the ethical task itself. With ethical maturity comes an obligation to refine one's imaginative abilities as well; one can wish and work for a more sensitive ethical imagination, striving for the continuity and harmony that repetition promises.

The harmonious dynamism of ethical repetition is not, however, Kierkegaard's final word on "being imaginative." We must turn now to the religious spheres of existence, for here the manifold uses of the imagination as the "capacity <u>instar omnium</u>" take on an even deeper dialectical complexity.

[1] Kierkegaard, CUP 291.

[2] Kierkegaard, EO2 203.

[3] Kierkegaard, EO2 213.

[4] Kierkegaard, CUP 226 and 227; cf. what the Judge says in SLW 171: "Whatever may be the misfortune with which the melancholy man contends, be it never so concrete, it constantly has for him an admixture of fantasy [Phantasi] and hence of abstraction."

[5] Kierkegaard, EO2 141.

[6] Kierkegaard, EO2 291.

[7] Kierkegaard, SUD 35.

[8] Kierkegaard, EO2 264.

[9] Kierkegaard, EO2 264.

[10] Kierkegaard, EO2 265.

[11] Kierkegaard, SUD 30.

[12] Kierkegaard, SUD 37; the mirror image figures in Purity of Heart (1847), where Kierkegaard discusses the need of having stillness in order to use the mirror and warns of the danger of forgetting that one even has such a mirror in one's "pocket," Søren Kierkegaard, Purity of Heart Is To Will One Thing: Spiritual Preparation for the Office of Confession, trans. and introd. Douglas V. Steere, Cloister Library (New York: Torchbook-Harper, 1948) 61, 108.

[13] Kierkegaard, CUP 289.

[14] Kierkegaard, CUP 176.

[15] Kierkegaard, EO2 171.

[16] Kierkegaard, SLW 158.

[17] Kierkegaard, EO2 256.

[18] Elrod 57.

[19] Kierkegaard, EO2 218.

[20] Malantschuk 344; cf. Ilham Dilman: "'You ought to want to behave better.' In other words, whether [one] cares to behave better or not he cannot escape the judgment that he ought to. That is why Kierkegaard speaks of the vocation with which the better self is identified as 'eternal,'" Ilham Dilman and D. Z. Phillips, Sense and Delusion, Studies in Philosophical Psychology, ed. R. F. Holland (London: Routledge, 1971) 84.

[21] Kierkegaard, EO2 256; cf. Anti-Climacus' reference to the person who despairs defiantly as "a king without a country," SUD 69.

[22] Kierkegaard, SUD 30; Anti-Climacus adds to the phrase cited above, "But if the self does not become itself, it is in despair, whether it knows that or not."

[23] Kierkegaard, EO2 256.

[24] See Hegel, Logic 136ff.

[25] Kierkegaard, EO2 256.

[26] Kierkegaard, JP 1: 258 (IV C 47), n.d., 1842-43.

[27] Kierkegaard, CUP 100.

[28] Kierkegaard, JP 1: 973 (X^1 A 393), n.d., 1849.

[29] Malantschuk 344.

[30] Kierkegaard, EO2 263-64.

[31] Kierkegaard, EO2 263.

[32] Kierkegaard, EO2 264.

[33] Kierkegaard, EO2 219.

[34] Kierkegaard, EO2 263.

[35] Kierkegaard, EO2 267; cf. 219.

[36] Kierkegaard, EO2 261; see also Steven Lukes, Individualism, Key Concepts in the Social Sciences, ed. Philip Rieff and Bryan R. Wilson (Oxford: Blackwell, 1973), ch. 1; Lukes uses Friedrich Schlegel and the Schleiermacher of the Monologen as examples of a Romantic individualism of uniqueness. I am indebted on this point to Professor Gene Outka.

[37] On "repentance," see Kierkegaard, EO2 220.

[38] Herbert Fingarette, Self-Deception, Studies in Philosophical Psychology, ed. R. F. Holland (London: Routledge, 1969) 85. On "substance" in Kierkegaard, see Diem 36; cf. Mark Taylor, Kierkegaard's Pseudonymous Authorship 94ff.

[39] Kierkegaard, EO2 263.

[40] Kierkegaard, TC 185; Kierkegaard's use of Indbildningskraft rather than Phantasi(e) has no philosophical significance for him, in contrast to the Romantic and Idealist distinctions.

[41] See Reidar Thomte, "Historical Introduction," CA xi-xii, for a summary of Crites' and Mark Taylor's position, plus Thulstrup's cautions; Crites, Twilight 70n; Mark Taylor, Kierkegaard's Pseudonymous Authorship 104ff; Thulstrup, Kierkegaard's Relation to Hegel 355 and n31; the relevant Hegel passage is Phenomenology of Spirit, "Preface," esp. sec. 22, p. 12.

[42] Anz 49ff, stresses Kierkegaard's offense at Hegel's trust in objective spirit, seeing this as central to the critique of Hegel; Mark Taylor, Kierkegaard's Pseudonymous Authorship 104n49, admits that Hegel's primary concern in discussing "purposive activity" is with reason.

[43] Mark Taylor, Kierkegaard's Pseudonymous Authorship 104n50, is correct that Kierkegaard's definition of the self is not, strictly, a parody, but Taylor fails to see that Kierkegaard can at once seriously reduplicate and yet parody Hegel's definition of the self.

[44] Elrod 53, 228-29.

[45] "The earnest person is earnest precisely through the originality with which he returns in repetition," Kierkegaard, CA 149.

[46] Kierkegaard, CI 301.

[47] Kierkegaard, TC 185.

[48] Diem 72.

[49] Søren Kierkegaard, "The Expectation of Faith," Edifying Discourses: A Selection, trans. David F. and Lillian Marvin Swenson, ed. with introd. Paul L. Holmer (New York: Torchbook-Harper, 1958) 13. As Stephen Crites has written: "Human becoming is not merely the actualization of inherent potentialities, like the maturation of a tree. As members of a biological species human beings do of course share in that natural process. But concurrent with it is this form of becoming that owes more to the fevers of the imagination than it does to natural growth and decay," Stephen Crites, "Pseudonymous Authorship as Art and as Act," Kierkegaard: A Collection of Critical Essays, ed. Josiah Thompson, Modern Studies in Philosophy, ed. Amelie Oksenberg Rorty (Garden City, NY: Anchor-Doubleday, 1972) 186; cf. Kierkegaard, SUD 58.

[50] Kierkegaard, EO1 223.

[51] Iris Murdoch, The Sovereignty of Good (New York: Schocken, 1970) 53.

[52] For a parable of the contrast between mood and emotion, see Judge William's story of the Dutch orientalist, EO2 313-15. On emotions being conceptually shaped, see Søren Kierkegaard, On Authority and Revelation: The Book on Adler, or a Cycle of Ethico-Religious Essays, trans. and ed. Walter Lowrie, introd. Frederick Sontag, Cloister Library (New York: Torchbook-Harper, 1966) 163.

[53] Kierkegaard, CUP 178.

[54] Kierkegaard, <u>CUP</u> 182.

[55] Diem 38.

[56] Kierkegaard, <u>CUP</u> 306.

[57] Thus, Elrod and Fahrenbach, in an attempt to oversystematize Kierkegaard's reflection on the imagination, take too narrow a view of the scope of the imagination, understanding it primarily in its more technical sense as the infinitizing capacity, without exploring the suggestiveness of calling it "the capacity <u>instar omnium</u>." See Elrod 34; Fahrenbach 16-17.

CHAPTER SIX

The Capacity <u>Instar Omnium</u>:

The Imagination of Repetition and Reversal

in the Religious Spheres

Christianity always puts contradictions together.
--Kierkegaard, <u>Judge for Yourselves!</u>

As important as the imagination is in the ethical stage, it is, in Judge William's presentation to "A," somewhat domesticated. The central image of the ethical life, marriage, lends an aura of comfort and settledness to the Judge's conception of the imagination's functions, especially when contrasted to the maelstrom and midnight cries of the aesthete. Even his ethical religion is ordered and balanced. The Judge is a "subjective thinker," but the simultaneity of factors he achieves, the balance he maintains, is only one way of reaching simultaneity.

At the far side of the ethical life there emerges an imaginative restlessness, a spiritual growth that, still seeking the balance the ethical craves, can break the bonds of ethical harmony. Already in the sermon by his friend the Jutland pastor that Judge William appends to his letters to "A" as an "Ultimatum," there is a hint of coming storms. The pastor ends his sermon with these words, the full import of which is beyond the Judge:

> Do not check your soul's flight, do not grieve the better promptings within you, do not dull your spirit with half wishes and half thoughts. Ask yourself, and continue to ask until you find the answer. For one may have known a thing many times and acknowledged it, one may have willed a thing many times and attempted it; and yet it is only by the deep inward movements, only by the indescribable emotions of the heart, that for the first time you are convinced that

what you have known belongs to you, that no power can take it from you; for only the truth which edifies is truth for you.[1]

Beyond the ethical sphere, Kierkegaard's literature chronicles spirits who heed the pastor and do not check their souls' flights, who continue to ask until they find answers, who attend to the deep inward movements, and the indescribable emotions of the heart. For these figures the call to test themselves in their imaginative infinity, and to make of that infinity a concrete self, takes them beyond the Judge's somewhat prosaic stance, to realms in which the demands of simultaneity are beset by more conflicts and challenges than the Judge can know.

This is not to say that the religious imagination emerges only above the ethical sphere. In 1845 Kierkegaard published under his own name Three Discourses on Imagined Occasions, in which he speaks of the lower levels of the God-relationship. Kierkegaard begins by lyrically describing the worship of the pagan, which Kierkegaard associates with youth. In primitive religion, the awe of the unknown finds expression in nature worship:

> When the forest darkens at the evening hour, when at night the moon loses its way among the trees, when in the forest the wonders of nature lurk for their prey . . . then suddenly the pagan sees a wondrous effect of light which grips him, then he sees the Unknown, and worship is the expression of wonder.[2]

More fully developed, this religion of paganism bears close resemblance to the Romantic sublime--even in the use of sea-images that Kant, for one, employs in the Critique of Judgment. Kierkegaard writes:

> When the sea lies still and inexplicable in its profundity, when wonder gazes dizzily down into it until it is as though the Unknown were rising up, when the waves of the sea roll monotonously towards the shore and overwhelm the soul by the power of uniformity, when the rush whispers before the wind and whispers again and so must desire to confide something to the listener--then he worships.[3]

And when self-reflective, such wonder fixes on a pantheistic God:

> If the wonder defines itself, then its highest expression is that
> God is the inexplicable All of existence, as this is sensed by
> the presentiment of imagination in the least things and in the
> greatest, everywhere.[4]

Lest the reference to the Romantics be missed, Kierkegaard immediately adds:

> What once was the content of paganism is experienced again
> in the repetition of every generation, and only when it has
> been outlived is that which was idolatry reduced to a careless
> existence in the innocence of poetry. For poetry is idolatry
> refined.[5]

For Kierkegaard, such a wonder is not completely negative; he writes at about this same time that "Wonder is the natural point of departure for the fear of God," and he bemoans the common fact "that reflection should eliminate wonder."[6]

But such a religion of wonder and imagination remains a low form of religion. According to Johannes Climacus, it does not even qualify as a God-relationship.[7] Kierkegaard again deliberately places the entire cultural force of Romantic religiosity and sentiment on the lowest rung of spiritual life. Spirit works in contrasts and tensions, and the spiritual life begins not with wonder but only with sin-consciousness and sorrow.[8]

In this religion of awe, one has barely touched the realm of Christian categories. Indeed, before one reaches that level of sin-consciousness, there is a complex progression through higher spheres of conflict. Those levels are represented, first, by ethical religion and, second, by the forms of pre-Christian religiosity leading up to and including "Religion A." We will analyze the progression through these stages, and to the brink of Christianity, by turning our attention to the religious crises of two nameless, imaginative young men Kierkegaard presents in Repetition (1843) and Stages on Life's Way (1845).

The imagination in the ethico-religious spheres prior to Christian faith

The ethical too has its religion, formed by the passionate relation to the ethical ideal. Speaking of a hypothetical ethical man, the Judge speculates on his reflections when, after many years, he realizes that the goals of his youth will be unfulfilled. In this situation the ethical man turns to the One who knows best how to judge ethical passion:

> I demand [an] umpire, a connoisseur, I demand an eye which seeth in secret, which doth not grow weary of seeing. . . . I demand an ear which hears the labor of thought, which divines how my better nature twists itself out of the torture of temptation. To that umpire I will look up, after His applause I will aspire, even though I am not able to deserve it. And when the cup of suffering is held out to me, I will not fix my glance upon the cup but upon Him who holds it, I will not stare at the bottom of the cup if at once I have not drained it, but will fix my gaze immovably upon Him from whom I receive it.[9]

For Judge William, worship and the God-relationship flow naturally from ethical passion.

But the religious sphere of existence begins properly with the inadequacy of the ethical to provide the balance the Judge promises. The reason for this is evident when we recall the full definition of the self Anti-Climacus gives in The Sickness Unto Death, that the self, to escape despair, must be related not only to its own elements, but also to the power that constitutes it.[10] The "overbalance of imagination" that is the mark of melancholy can now reappear, even after the ethical stage. In numerous sketches and literary presentations, Kierkegaard depicts figures who can find no rest in the ethical sphere. They are in Kierkegaard's literature usually young men, marked by intense imagination, bringing to mind Anti-Climacus' comment, "Why I wonder did Socrates love youths--unless it was because he knew men!"[11]

The young man in Repetition (by Constantin Constantius, published in 1843), and Quidam in Stages on Life's Way (edited by Hilarius Bookbinder, 1845), in particular exhibit the tensions of imagination when their attempts to effect repetition are stretched to the breaking-point. The repetition of an ideal is not necessarily a simple matter. Ideals can conflict with one another, the ideal of being a poet with the ideal of being a married person; or the ethical itself can become a temptation.[12] The dislocations of mood can return; anxiety and despair can mount.

Repetition portrays two figures who possess imagination, figures who represent the ironic, detached imagination on the one hand, and the passionate imagination on the other. Constantin Constantius, the first, is a psychologist and ironist; the unnamed young man in the book represents the passionate imagination.[13] Constantin speaks with insight concerning the imagination's powers in possibility. He discourses eloquently on the right use of the theater, which allows one

> to split himself up into every possible variation of himself, and nevertheless in such a way that every variation is still himself. Such a wish, of course, expresses itself only at a very early age. Only the imagination is awakened to his dream about the personality; everything else is still fast asleep. In such a self-vision of the imagination, the individual is not an actual shape but a shadow, or more correctly, the actual shape is invisibly present and therefore is not satisfied to cast one shadow, but the individual has a variety of shadows, all of which resemble him and which momentarily have equal status as being himself. As yet the personality is not discerned, and its energy is betokened only in the passion of possibility.[14]

Eloquent as Constantin is about the imagination's formative influence, his own imagination is on a dialectically lower level than that of the young man. His imagination, like that of "A" in Either/Or, I, easily falls into boredom. His somewhat farcical attempt to capture repetition aesthetically by returning a second time to Berlin results in depression: "My mind was sterile, my troubled imagination constantly conjured up tantalizingly attractive recollections of how the ideas had presented themselves the last time, and the tares of these recollections choked out every thought at birth."[15] Constantin recognizes the young man's powers, that "he had unusual mental powers, particularly imagination [Phantasie]."[16] Constantin sees further that the young man's great imagination contained the seed of his present troubles, because, "as soon as his creativity was awakened, he would have enough for his whole life. . . . Anyone with that nature does not need feminine love."[17]

Ironically, the young man had become caught precisely in that passionate collision brought about by love for a young woman. His love for her awakens in him poetic ideality--but it becomes obvious to him that she is only the occasion for the ideality, and, like Constantin, he falls into the pains of recollection. But the young man, more advanced than Constantin, stands in the ethical sphere and refuses to poeticize himself out of the relationship and into an imaginative ether. Instead he makes the movements of subjectivity, penetrating with imagination and passion the "compounded feelings" of his love experience, that he is "happy, unhappy, comic, tragic."[18]

While Constantin may speak of the importance of the theater as providing models for one's possibility, it is the young man who in passion seeks such a model for his life. Caught in the anguish of his dilemma, he turns not to the theater but to Job, who fights "the disputes at the boundaries of faith."[19] The young man exclaims:

> If I did not have Job! . . . I lay the book, as it were, on my heart and read it with the eyes of the heart, in a <u>clairvoyance</u> interpreting the specific points in the most diverse ways. . . . Every word by him is food and clothing and healing for my wretched soul."[20]

The power of Job's example is that he represents the category of the "ordeal," which, the young man writes to Constantin, "is not aesthetic, ethical, or dogmatic--it is altogether transcendent," in that it "places a person in a purely personal relationship of opposition to God, in a relationship such that he cannot allow himself to be satisfied with any explanation at second hand."[21] This God is not the God of the ethical, for such a God would be divorced from the young man's situation.[22] Beyond the demands of the universal with its ethical repetition, in which one acts with the thought of the eternal, stands a religious striving that takes one into conflicts beyond the ethical. As Constantin says:

> On the one side stands the exception, on the other the universal, and the struggle itself is a strange conflict between the rage and impatience of the universal over the disturbance the exception causes and its infatuated partiality for the exception.[23]

For the imagination this means that in religion a person seeks not the "first immediacy" of the aesthetic, but a second immediacy after loss and suffering. "Repetition," Johannes Climacus tells us,

> is at bottom an expression for immanence, so that persistence in despair gives possession of the self, persistence in doubt, possession of the truth. . . . The young man has the intuition that if repetition is to come into being it must be as a new immediacy, so that the repetition itself is a movement <u>in virtue of the absurd</u>, and the teleological suspension <u>a trial</u>.[24]

Like Job, the young man makes Job's trial his own. Struggling with the paradigm of one who maintained his innocence before God, the young man concludes that Job's repetition consists in the fact that he lost his case before God and so won all in repetition.[25] But unlike Job, the young man finds that repetition is purely inward. He regains his lost immediacy, not by being able to return to the young woman, but by finding that his beloved has married another. Ironic as this is, the young man nonetheless discovers that his inner split has been healed: "I am myself again. This 'self' that someone else would not pick up off the street I have once again. The split that was in my being is healed; I am unified again."[26] He regains too the elasticity of his imagination. Newly self-integrated, possibility opens, and he discovers himself free to be a poet: "It is over, my skiff is afloat. In a minute I shall be there where my soul longs to be, there where ideas spume with elemental fury. . . . I belong to the idea."[27]

The young man in one sense enters the religious sphere of existence, and in another sense does not, and so he provides a good case by which we may both compare and contrast the ethical and religious spheres of the imagination. If we may believe Constantin, the young man makes only a brief foray into the religious sphere, and becomes simply "a religious poet," an exception that only "constitutes the transition to the truly aristocratic exceptions."[28] And he adds that if the young man "had had a deeper religious background, he would not have become a poet."[29] Yet, on the other hand, the young man is on the borderline of the religious.[30] The repetition he achieves is not ethical, but religious. Constantin writes:

> His soul now gains a religious resonance. This is what actually sustains him, although it never attains a breakthrough. His dithyrambic joy in the last letter is an example of this, for beyond a doubt this joy is grounded in a religious mood, which remains something inward, however. He keeps a religious mood as a secret he cannot explain, while at the same time this secret helps him poetically to explain actuality. He explains the universal as repetition, and yet he himself understands repetition in another way, for although actuality becomes the repetition, for him the repetition is the raising of his consciousness to the second power.[31]

The young man's new inwardness is more profound than the ethical can give. The conflict between the ethical universal and his situation creates a need for a reintegration that the universal cannot provide. The public persona of the ethical sphere, exhibiting an external transparency of life, is not adequate to the inner adjustments the young man requires. Although he flees to Sweden to work out his dilemma, the young man, it should be remembered, is outwardly calm; the change is inward. He must come to terms with the ethical conflict in which he finds himself, and the only means of achieving his lost spontaneity is by a change in his self-understanding. Whereas for the ethical person the universal requirement rules, for the religious person there is the need for a "dialectic of inward transformation"--the imagination is turned to a new ideal, that of an eternal happiness in relation to God, and its inward appropriation.[32] As Frater Taciturnus says in Stages on Life's Way:

> This is the difference between the aesthetic and the religious
> ideality. The aesthetic is higher than actuality before
> actuality, that is to say, in illusion; the religious is higher
> than actuality after actuality, that is, by virtue of a God-
> relationship.[33]

But because this new ideality comes after the ethical, the religious paradigm differs from the ethical paradigm. Johannes Climacus says of Job--the young man's model--that he is not possible as an ethical ideal, because "the religious paradigm is an irregularity. From the ethical point of view a trial is unthinkable, since it is precisely by always being valid that the ethical is the universally valid."[34] Job engages the young man's imagination as a paradigm because Job's complaints echo his own sorrows, his own loss of spontaneity, and his own questioning of God. But such a paradigm is highly particularized, addressed to an "individual." Job illustrates in small the painful sense of the loss of possibility (including imagination and spontaneity) and its recovery in the religious sphere. The movement of the young man's imagination, suffering from the loss of possibility, focusses on how to regain that possibility. How can one recover equilibrium and move on to new possibilities for the self? The answers, for Kierkegaard, all touch the religious sphere, and all involve the training of the imagination to strive for a new possibility.[35]

Because the religious sphere is a quest for possibility, the imaginative moods of the aesthetic sphere return to indicate a serious imbalance. Despair in particular returns in these higher spheres of existence beyond the ethical. In The Sickness Unto Death, Anti-Climacus writes that finally the only saving remedy for "necessity's despair due to lack of possibility" is to find refuge in the belief, by virtue of the absurd, that "for God everything is possible."[36] "Imagine," says Anti-Climacus,

> that someone with a capacity to imagine terrifying nightmares has pictured to himself some horror or other that is absolutely unbearable. Then it happens to him, this very horror happens to him. Humanly speaking, his collapse is altogether certain--and in despair his soul's despair fights to be permitted to despair, to attain, if you please, the composure to despair. . . . At this point, then, salvation is, humanly speaking, utterly impossible; but for God everything is possible! That is the battle of faith, battling, madly, if you will, for possibility, because possibility is the only salvation. At times the ingeniousness of the human imagination can extend to the point of creating possibility, but at last--that is, when it depends upon faith--then only this helps: that for God everything is possible.[37]

The need for possibility engenders the God-relationship. But the extent to which the sufferer relies upon one's own resources, including imagination, differs within the religious sphere. The young man of Repetition believes "in virtue of the absurd," and therefore against all possibility, yet in resolution of his dilemma he still assumes that one is capable of the movements of faith.[38] Even though one turns to God when the imagination falters in procuring possibility, the resources for the God-relationship are within. For this reason, although the young man can correctly say that the category of repetition is "entirely transcendent," Johannes Climacus is also correct in saying that "the category of repetition is at bottom an expression for immanence."[39] Repetition is an immanent category; one experiences it as coming "from within," even when, as in the case of the young man, the movement is by virtue of the absurd and in reliance on the God-relationship.

The Postscript identifies the distinction between the religion of immanence and that of transcendence as the difference between Religion A and Religion B (Christianity), and the hinge of the difference is "sin-consciousness." The more Religion A is developed dialectically, the more urgent becomes the question of the religious person's own ability to procure possibility. At the "lower" levels of the religious sphere, sin is not an issue. While Abraham in Fear and Trembling (1843) is a source of wonder, his faith is not miraculous; it is still in the realm of immanence. It is rather when the religious person confronts the question of guilt preventing repetition that the possibility of attaining wholeness is questioned. The imagination is active still throughout Religion A, investigating the subjective thinker's relation to God, but the increasingly disturbing discovery is that the individual does not possess the possibility that is life's breath. In the dialectic of Religion A, described in such detail by Johannes Climacus in the Postscript, the progression moves from an attempt to ground one's existence in the God-relationship, followed by suffering at the discovery of the great gulf between God and the believer, and arriving finally at the guilt that results from this discovery.[40] Throughout these developments one imaginatively holds to the ideal of the God-relationship, in deepening subjectivity, and investigates the "hard spots" that resist one's total reliance upon the absolute.[41] Although the sense of one's need for further reliance upon God grows stronger in Religion A, so too do the doubts about one's ability to accomplish that total reliance.

Because the subjective thinker's capacities are intensified in the religious sphere, his or her imaginative powers increase in the apprehension of guilt as well. In The Concept of Anxiety Vigilius Haufniensis recounts how one is educated by imagination to perceive the extent of one's guilt, that guilt is a qualitative and not a quantitative matter, and therefore that "if a man is guilty, he is infinitely guilty."[42] But as is evident already in Repetition, acknowledging one's infinite guilt is more difficult than Vigilius' succinct statement would lead one to believe.

Kierkegaard returns to this theme of guilt in Stages on Life's Way, where another nameless figure, known only as "Quidam," reveals a story similar to that of the young man in Repetition.[43] But Quidam's concern focusses on the question of whether he is "guilty or not guilty?" Quidam too has great imagination and dialectical skill, but in lengthy and obsessive diary entries he struggles to find the right "imaginative construal" of his situation.[44] More than Repetition's young man, who finds a resolution in the aesthetic-poetic realm on the border of the religious, Quidam is much more inwardly directed, reserved, and taciturn.[45] His imagination concerns itself with the secret sources of the melancholy that prevents marriage: "What is my sickness? Melancholy. Where is the seat of this sickness? In the power of imagination [Indbildningskraften], and possibility is its nutriment."[46]

In morning diary entries that trace the history of his broken engagement, and midnight entries written a year later, Quidam probes his inner life, gathering memory into an investigation of the mystery of his identity, finding the source of his melancholy in the urge to a God-relationship. The religious relationship haunts him and probes him with the question of his guilt. Frater Taciturnus,

Quidam's observer, analyzes the imaginative prerequisites for such a collision.

Quidam, says Frater Taciturnus,

> must be aesthetically developed in imagination [Phantasi] and
> must be able to conceive the ethical with primitive passion in
> order to be properly offended at it, so that the pristine
> possibility in the religious man may break its way out in this
> catastrophe. Therefore melancholy must have accompanied
> him through the previous stages.[47]

The aesthetic and ethical stages together prepare Quidam for the religious struggle, the richness and restlessness of the aesthetic stage joined with the ideality and passion of the ethical stage.

Quidam's imagination brings him, however, to a comic-tragic situation; he idealizes the woman he loves in an effort to probe his own suffering. But, typical of the extreme inwardness of these suffering young men, it is only just when she is about to forget him that his troubled imagination fixes on her, and "in the illumination of his own ideality, she is transformed into a gigantic figure."[48] No longer possessing the imaginative profuseness of his youth, Quidam says that he nevertheless has found in the young woman a focus that intensifies his imagination:

> The period of childhood is now long past, hence on the score
> of imagination [Phantasie] I have less to contribute--so
> greatly am I changed. But the object of my contemplation
> has not become very great in proportion to advancing age.
> There is one person, one only, about whom everything
> turns. Upon that girl I gaze and gaze until I produce out of
> myself what perhaps I should never have managed to see.[49]

Torturing himself with the question of his own culpability, he still

> cannot get to the point of repenting, because it is as though it
> were still undetermined what he is to repent of; and he cannot
> find repose in repentance, because it is as though he ought
> constantly to be doing something, undoing what was done,
> if that were possible.[50]

Quidam's imagination does not extend as far as total guilt; as Frater Taciturnus tells us, Quidam is groping after the notion of sin.[51]

But Quidam's hesitant and obsessive stance on the edge of total guilt and sin-consciousness, as feverishly imaginative as it is, is symptomatic of the dilemma of the imagination in the religious sphere. Quidam at once yearns for new spontaneity, and fears the conclusion to which he is hurtling, that the imagination cannot procure any more possibility by itself (except the possibility of obsessive reserve), and that it is only in repentance, in admitting that before God one is always in the wrong, that one can escape a spiritual dead-end. Just as the understanding pushes to its own downfall in the confrontation with the paradox of its limits in self-understanding, so too the imagination as the faculty of infinitizing pushes the realm of openness and possibility to the point of its own downfall. The next dialectical step is that the guilty one makes the movement Vigilius Haufniensis describes as the infinitizing of guilt; recognizing that one is totally guilty before God, one becomes aware too of how impossible it is to realize the imagined ideal of total reliance upon God. At this point one stands fully in Religion A, comprehending "the contradiction of suffering in self-annihilation, although within immanence."[52]

The limits and necessity of the imagination in Christian faith

As with all Kierkegaard's stages, one can remain in these levels of religion with their unresolved suffering. But in the encounter with Christ, at the brink of "Religion B" or Christianity, new possibilities emerge. One can be offended by the God-incarnate, or one can respond in the passion of faith. If the response is faith rather than offense, the imagination engages in an even more complex dialectic; in one sense the imagination is defeated and yet in another sense the imagination at last finds its highest calling and most healthy spiritual integration. It is this dialectic of the imagination in faith that we must now carefully analyze.

In Section A we will examine Kierkegaard's understanding of the failure of the imagination, despite its passion, to comprehend the God-incarnate. We will then be able to describe Kierkegaard's attack on contemporary theologians, both right-wing and left-wing Hegelians, who gave the imagination a methodological place in the human comprehension of God.

But once Kierkegaard has secured the limits of the imagination, he speaks also of the necessity of the imagination in the Christian sphere in what we can term an imagination of "repetition through reversal." In Section B, therefore, we will outline the necessity of the imagination by examining four elements of this imagination: (1) the imagination of disanalogy as a via negativa in apprehending (not comprehending) Christ; (2) the imagination's role in apprehending Christ as contemporaneous with the believer; (3) the imagination's role in "faith as a happy passion"; and (4) the place of the imagination in the important Kierkegaardian concept of the imitation of Christ (Kristi Efterfølgelse). In considering this fourth area we will conclude by examining the imaginative dialectic in yet another young man, this time presented by the Christian pseudonym Anti-Climacus in Training in Christianity (1850).

A. The limits of the imagination in the Christian sphere

It is in the suffering person's encounter with the paradox of Christ that the imagination encounters reversal and defeat. We can examine this moment of encounter from both the immanent (human) and transcendent (divine) sides. From the immanent side, the imagination, poised between Religion A and Religion B, reaches its highest pitch as a dynamic factor within the person. The imagination's interest in and hope for possibility continue throughout the entire religious stage of existence. And the imagination throughout the religious is still oriented to the ideal as a task.[53] This is no less the case in Religion B, of which Johannes Climacus says in the Postscript that it "is the decisive part only in so far as it is combined with the pathetic to create new pathos."[54]

On the other hand, the person in this position discovers, while still on the side of immanence, that although pathos continues, the capacity of the imagination to deliver possibility falters. The religious person's reliance on God for possibility--a constant theme throughout the religious sphere--now ironically reveals that one can no longer rely on one's own imagination to obtain possibility. As Anti-Climacus says: "At times the ingeniousness of the human imagination can extend to the point of creating possibility, but at last--that is, when it depends upon faith--then only this helps: that for God everything is possible."[55]

Turning to God for possibility is to admit the failure of one's own possibilities and the defeat of the imagination. The imagination of repetition comes to an end at the breach of consciousness in the leap to Christian faith. The optimism of the spheres of immanence, all the way to the point of sin-consciousness, rests on the assumption that repetition is possible, but sin-consciousness means that repetition is not possible. A higher despair appears, an admission that the elements of the personality are not integrated and will not be successfully related to God as "the Constituting Power." Such despair, when recognized, is identical with sin-consciousness. Anti-Climacus sums up the dilemma of the religious person as it culminates in despair and sin:

> The greater the conception of God, the more self there is; the more self, the greater the conception of God. Not until a self as this specific single individual is conscious of existing before God, not until then is it the infinite self, and this self sins before God.[56]

The "infinite self" potentiated by the imagination ends in sin. This sin is defined precisely as the disequilibrium of despair, unresolved finally either by the spheres of the ethical or of immanent religion: "Sin is: before God in despair not to will to be oneself, or before God in despair to will to be oneself."[57] In the quest for the God-relationship, the elements of the self, including the imagination, cannot be reintegrated by the imagination, even with the help of passion. In Religion A such a resolution is still assumed, but in Christianity the believer learns that, in the language of the Fragments, one does not have the truth within, subjectivity is untruth, and one is a sinner in all respects, whether in reason, feeling, will, or imagination. Since despair is unresolved, the imagination is caught in its disequilibrium. It is only by becoming "a person of a different quality or, as we can also call it, a new person" who recognizes both the self's lack of truth and the externality of truth, that possibility can be restored to one.[58]

The dialectical shape of the sinner's despair can be clarified further by seeing it from the transcendent standpoint, that of the sinner's encounter with Christ as the Absolute Paradox. Confronting the God-incarnate brings one beyond guilt to the state of sin-consciousness as a breach in one's self-understanding. The expression for this breach is that of a paradoxical collision of reason and understanding with what it cannot comprehend; the paradox is "the ultimate passion of thought."[59] In other words, the attempt to understand oneself, of which Socrates in the Fragments is the prototype, meets with failure. The human capacities of reason, understanding, and reflection all seek this collision, but thereby effect their own downfall. Because Kierkegaard is concerned to combat the claims of Idealist rationalism, he speaks of "Reason" or "understanding" rather than imagination in this context, but given the close association of the imagination with reflection, it is clear that the imagination is included within this broad concept of "Reason."[60]

In Philosophical Fragments Johannes Climacus proposes for the reader a "thought-project" in which, unlike Socrates, who believed the truth was within the disciple, there is a Teacher who stands against the assumption that one has the truth within oneself. The "paradox" of the relation between this Teacher and disciple is that the kind of passion the disciple needs to understand this Teacher is of a radically different kind from his or her earlier passion.[61] The heart of the paradox is not only that it requires a confession of sinfulness, of the lack of one's possibility, but that the Teacher intensifies the break with one's natural religious self-understanding. The only way to attain a new identity, a new possibility, is to base it, not on one's own powers as in the lower forms of religion, but on the actuality of another person. Christ the Absolute Paradox, the Incarnate suffering God in time, both cancels the possibility of the sinner, and also claims that one's frustrated possibility can only be fulfilled by believing in his actuality.

In Religion B Kierkegaard reverses the entire pattern he has developed in the ethical sphere and in Religion A of how one relates "actuality" and "possibility." In the ethical sphere and in Religion A the imagination raises one's own actuality to possibility as an ideal task; whatever another person does, that is, another person's "actuality," is irrelevant to whether I can or ought to do something. But in the encounter with Christ, actuality is higher than possibility; one can no longer generate a possibility for one's own life, and furthermore, it is only another person's actuality--that of Christ as an historical individual in time-- who can reopen possibility for the disciple. In relying on God for possibility, one relies on the God in time. This historical individual thus becomes of infinite importance to one. Christ and the atonement he offers relieve one of the burden of an independent quest for wholeness by way of the imagination; to appropriate the atonement one needs to accept the forgiveness of the Teacher and reverse one's self-understanding, seeing oneself as a sinner, without possibility, before one can regain possibility.

It is crucial, however, to see this reversal of the imagination primarily as salvation. From the side of immanence the imagination has encountered its own limits. To understand oneself as a sinner in the encounter with the transcendent Christ confirms that failure; but to rely on Christ is to rediscover possibility for the self in complete reliance on God.

Nonetheless, because, as Kierkegaard believed, he lived in an age that transformed the Incarnation from God's salvation of sinners into humanity's apotheosis into divinity, he felt that the Incarnation had first a negative significance as the definitive barrier against all Romantic or Idealist hopes of direct access to the deity. First, the Incarnation frustrates any attempts to grasp the divine by means of feeling, reason, or imagination. Kierkegaard here extends his strictures against the Romantic imagination's grasp of the divine, and applies the same arguments against all forms of imaginative comprehension of the divine, aesthetic, ethical, or theological. Second, the historical aspect of the Incarnation is the key to blocking those attempts, for the Incarnation places the actuality of Christ over against any human possibility, including the imagination.

With these two points in mind, we can now locate Kierkegaard's polemical position against the wide array of those who, despite their great philosophical and theological differences, saw in Christ a direct access to the transcendent. In Kierkegaard's lights, persons as diverse as Bishop Mynster, Schleiermacher, Hegel, Martensen, and D. F. Strauss, in one way or another, held in common a view that Christianity is accessible to persons in aesthetic categories. Kierkegaard sees these figures as spiritually akin, for all of them, in diverse ways, see Christ "fantastically," in the medium of the imagination. As we saw in Chapter III, "the medium of the imagination" served Kierkegaard in linking the Romantics and Idealists; it now serves him theologically, for by it he can locate the common error that binds these thinkers together. That error is to see Christian faith as accessible to anyone in aesthetic immediacy, whether imaginative or reflective.

The broadest and most common form of this is a sentimental religiosity that is a low form of unreflective immediacy. Kierkegaard attacks childish Christianity in the Postscript as one form of the fantastic, in which Christianity is rendered in "the medium of fantasy [Phantasie-Anskuelsens Medium]."[62] Kierkegaard is especially harsh about Bishop Mynster's references to "quiet hours in holy places" where "it is pleasant, even enjoyable, to commune with the highest once a week by way of the imagination."[63]

But Kierkegaard polemicizes also against more reflective theoretical efforts to find a human point of contact with the divine. Whatever their differences, Kierkegaard sees immediacy at the heart of the dogmatics both of the schools of Schleiermacher and of Hegel.

Kierkegaard had great admiration for Schleiermacher. If we can take Vigilius Haufniensis to be speaking for Kierkegaard, Schleiermacher understood the dogmatic task correctly to "begin with the actual in order to raise it up into ideality," which, of course, is a function of the imagination.[64] And his skill in doing this shows Schleiermacher to be, in contrast to Hegel, "a thinker in the beautiful Greek sense, a thinker who spoke only of what he knew."[65] But very early Kierkegaard made up his mind about the inadequacy of Schleiermacher's theology:

> What Schleiermacher calls "religion" and the Hegelian dogmaticians "faith" is, after all, nothing else than the first

immediacy, the prerequisite for everything--the vital fluid--in an emotional-intellectual sense the atmosphere we breathe-- and which therefore cannot properly be characterized by these words [religion and faith].[66]

Against this, Kierkegaard insists that faith is "a second immediacy," and he objects to the reduction of Christian categories to feeling.[67]

The aesthetic sphere includes not only, however, Romantic immediacy, but also, as we saw in Chapter III, the reflected immediacy of Idealism. For Hegel, of course, the imagination plays a great role in religious and Christological issues, for it is by means of the distinction between representation (Vorstellung) and concept (Begriff)--one of the most complex, ambiguous, and historically significant distinctions in the Hegelian philosophy--that Hegel, too, attempts to find a limited but, perhaps, necessary role for the imagination in religious concern. Vorstellung for Hegel refers to the Infinite, whereas non-religious Vorstellung engenders a merely finite Bild.[68] The distinction is clearly stated in the Phenomenology of Spirit, where Hegel says that in revealed religion Vorstellung as a

> form of picture-thinking constitutes the specific mode in which Spirit, in this community, becomes aware of itself. This form is not yet Spirit's self-consciousness that has advanced to its Notion [Begriff] qua Notion: the mediation is still incomplete. This combination of Being and Thought is, therefore, defective in that spiritual Being is still burdened with an unreconciled split into a Here and a Beyond. The content is the true content, but all its moments, when placed in the medium of picture-thinking, have the character of being uncomprehended [in terms of the Notion]. . . . Before the true content can also receive its true form for consciousness, a higher formative development of consciousness is necessary; it must raise its intuition of absolute Substance into the Notion, and equate its consciousness with its self-consciousness for itself.[69]

This state of religious imagery in <u>Vorstellung</u> is, for Hegel, a state of partial immediacy that must be further mediated in philosophical thought. Religious imagery is a form of consciousness that points to the universal truth, but fails to grasp it in its universality as a concept.[70]

Kierkegaard's countermove, however, is to expand the category of "immediacy" to include not only <u>Vorstellung</u> but <u>Begriff</u> as well. Kierkegaard avoids the question of which form of thought or consciousness--<u>Vorstellung</u> or <u>Begriff</u>--gives the desired generality. For Kierkegaard the issue is irrelevant, since any attempt to comprehend the divine, whether by means of religious images or philosophy's pure concepts, is still within the realm of immediacy. Kierkegaard wishes rather to raise the question from that of the level of discourse or form of consciousness to a different level entirely, that of the truth--and untruth--of subjectivity. With the question shifted, the arguments concerning the adequacy of <u>Vorstellung</u> or <u>Begriff</u> as forms of thought are quite beside the point.

Kierkegaard's recasting of the question allows him to criticize equally those who attempt to retain the religious significance of <u>Vorstellung</u> (the right-wing Hegelians) and those who argue that <u>Vorstellung</u> must give way to <u>Begriff</u> (the left-wing Hegelians). For Kierkegaard, this internecine theological warfare is waged between parties who are equally fantastic.

The right-wing Hegelians say that Christianity may indeed be translated into conceptual terms, yet they affirm too the continuing importance of both religious <u>Vorstellung</u> and the historical actuality of the God-incarnate. But for Kierkegaard their form of immediacy results in a fantastic confusion of the divine and the human in which "the qualitative difference between God and man is pantheistically abolished . . . in a high-brow way through speculation."[71]

A primary example of this conservative Hegelianism is Hans Lassen Martensen's Christelige Dogmatik (Christian Dogmatics) (1849), which Kierkegaard often castigates as the embodiment of "the System." As Robert Horn argues, for Martensen, in contrast to Kierkegaard, Christianity is directly communicable. Furthermore, Christ, far from being God incognito, is directly recognizable.[72] As Martensen develops this in his Dogmatics, the imagination, along with reason, possesses a special function as "the organ of religious perception."[73] For Martensen (as, perhaps, for Hegel) the distinction between religious imagery as Vorstellung and religious concept as Begriff does not rule out the continuing importance of religious imagery:

> Religious cognizance of God is not knowledge in the form of abstract thought; but the idea of God assumes shape in a comprehensive view of the world, and of human life in its relation to God. . . . Piety cognizes not merely by thoughts growing out of the relations of conscience and confined to these relations, but also by means of the mental picture [Vorstellung] which springs from these same relations.[74]

Kierkegaard nowhere comments on this passage, but clearly he would consider Martensen's position to be seriously misleading, since it views the imagination's operations in so totally undialectic a fashion, as an aspect of a direct comprehension of deity. In any case, Martensen's book is the target of much of Kierkegaard's polemic from 1849. He summarizes his criticism of it in a letter to Rasmus Nielsen from 1849 or 1850; not only is a dogmatic system "a luxury item" when so few are Christians, but "a dogmatic system should not be erected on the basis of comprehending faith, but on the basis of comprehending that one cannot comprehend faith."[75]

For Martensen, corresponding to this comprehension is the interplay of the divine and human natures, first in the human being as created in the image of God, and, second and pre-eminently, in the Incarnation.[76] He maintains the important historical particularity of the Incarnation, however, and objects strenuously to the left-wing Hegelian notion that "the ideal and the real can never be reconciled or made one in actuality, but solely in thought and imagination."77 Despite Martensen's objections to the more radical Hegelians, Kierkegaard charges that Martensen's mediating theology results too in a pantheistic construal of the Incarnation that becomes fantastic by affirming direct recognition of deity. The logical outcome of Martensen's position is that the transcendence of God is lost, and the divine becomes merely the embodiment of the highest ideals of humanity.

For Kierkegaard, the peculiar difficulty the immediate imagination has in conceiving of Christ as divine is that in its enthusiasm the imagination fails to make the qualitative distinction between God and persons, but thinks of God as, for example, a lofty king. Kierkegaard does grant that one may imaginatively entertain a belief that God is in this man, but such a belief betrays a failure to grasp the conceptual distinction between God and the world. In Training in Christianity Anti-Climacus writes:

> It is not unthinkable that a man in whom imagination [Phantasi] or feeling predominates, a man who typifies childlike or childish Christianity ... might ingenuously entertain the notion that he believed this individual man to be God, and discover no offence in it. This is to be explained by the fact that such a man has no explicit conception of God, but a childlike or childish fancy [Phantasi] about something exceedingly lofty, holy, and pure, a conception of One who somehow is greater than all kings, &c., without exactly including the quality God. This means that such a man possesses no category, and hence it was possible for him to think that he believed an individual man to be God, without stumbling at the offence. But this same man will then stumble at the offence of lowliness.78

But ironically this humble, almost ignorant error lies at the bottom of the right-wing Hegelian mediation, for it too ultimately fails to recognize the infinite qualitative difference between God and persons. It uses the Incarnation as a means of supporting human confidence in the power to comprehend the divine directly in an immediately perceived Vorstellung and historical figure, revealing thereby also its confidence that divine revelation will confirm human dreams of loftiness and greatness.

The left-wing Hegelian option, represented especially by D. F. Strauss and Ludwig Feuerbach, and in Denmark by A. F. Beck, is just as fantastic.[79] For Kierkegaard, here the powers of human reason compromise even more the divine transcendence. The claim is made that Vorstellung, including not only religious imagery but also the historical nature of the Incarnation, is not necessary. The form of Vorstellung is not essential to its content; rather, Begriffe are sufficient to give the true form and true content of the religious conceptions of divine humanity. Christianity, therefore, can be understood by seeing its Vorstellung, including any historical claims about Jesus, as inessential, best understood mythically, and hence as inadequate to the idea. The realm of Vorstellung can then be left behind in grasping the concept in its purity.

In Kierkegaard's understanding of the matter, however, this simply compounds the "fantastic," for not only is the error of pantheism made, in which one loses the divine transcendence, but, furthermore, the actuality of the Incarnation is lost. Instead of simply failing to see the paradox of the God in a particular historical individual, there is also the failure to see the paradox in the fact that the God is in a particular historical individual.

The importance of the historical aspect of the Incarnation for Kierkegaard now emerges against both the right- and left-wing Hegelians. In Kierkegaard's understanding, although the historical aspect of the Incarnation is never simply brute historical fact (in this Kierkegaard agrees with Idealism), neither is it (contra Strauss) simply a myth of divine-human union nor (contra the right-wing Hegelians) the primary actual example of a general conceptual movement. The Incarnation is an historical actuality and that means, as we have noted, that it is above possibility. It cannot be confused with any myth, ideal, or human achievement: "Christianity is the absolute paradox ... precisely because it nullifies a possibility (the analogy of paganism, an eternal divine becoming) as an illusion and turns it into actuality."[80] The problem with both the right-wing Hegelians who retain Vorstellung and the left-wing Hegelians who do not is that they are caught in the aesthetic immediacy of direct recognition. Both believe that Christianity can be understood by analogy with other religious or philosophical concepts. The more conservative Hegelian thinker will

> confound Christianity with something which has indeed entered into the heart of man to believe (that is, into the heart of humanity), he will confound it with human nature's own idea and will forget the qualitative distinction which accentuates the absolutely different point of departure: what comes from God, and what comes from man.[81]

The Straussian mythicist will make a similar confusion, for he will "confound Christianity with one or another pagan analogy (analogies which lead away from factual reality)."[82] Kierkegaard is explicit that both of these errors fall into "the fantasy-medium of possibility."[83]

Kierkegaard's standpoint with regard to his theological contemporaries is thus highly dialectical. He is critical in the extreme of the notion that theological concepts can be translated into Begriffe. But on the other hand, he does not affirm simply an unmediated use of Vorstellung, of religious imagery, for that too can easily be fantastic. What is needed, rather, is an understanding, first, that Vorstellung, because it represents the actual individual God-incarnate, is not surpassed by <u>Begriffe</u>. Yet, second, <u>Vorstellung</u> by itself does not guarantee religious truth, for the form need not carry with it the content; religious imagery, even the picture of the God-incarnate, can be fantastic, that is, imaginatively misconstrued when the dialectical qualifications are ignored, and when the requirements of subjective appropriation are forgotten.

Kierkegaard therefore relentlessly directs our attention to the subjective qualifications required in encountering the God in time, and emphasizes that fallen humanity lacks the capacity to apprehend God and so find wholeness. In Religion B the negative note is sounded first, in which the God in time is the Absolute Paradox that stands in the way of the imagination's direct access to the divine.

For this reason, any access to God is possible only through God's grace. Grace is central to Kierkegaard's understanding of Christianity, despite his frequent remarks on the importance of the human will in faith.[84] It is true that, due to his fear of the dangers presented by an intellectualist distortion of Christianity, Kierkegaard often links faith with will, for it is the capacity farthest removed from aesthetic or intellectual immediacy:

> A definition of faith, that is, of the Christian conception of faith.
> What is it to believe? It is to will (what one ought and because one ought), God-fearingly and unconditionally obediently, to defend oneself against the vain thought of wanting to comprehend and against the vain imagination of being able to comprehend.[85]

But this does not mean that for Kierkegaard the will provides direct access to the divine: "faith is not an act of will, for it is always the case that all human willing is efficacious only within the condition."[86] That condition can only be given, Kierkegaard insists, by divine grace. Faith, therefore, depends on grace as the gift of God, and grace stands as the guard against any claims of the natural capacities--including the imagination--to comprehend the deity.

B. The necessity of the imagination in the Christian sphere

The limits of the imagination in the Christian sphere are, however, only half the story. Christian faith is not the death of the imagination, nor is Christ a sheer paradox that defeats imaginative apprehension. Yet Kierkegaard has often been seen as excluding the imagination from Christian faith. In our own time, W. H. Auden, a poet much influenced by Kierkegaard, expresses well this common misunderstanding:

> The Incarnation, the coming of Christ in the form of a servant who cannot be recognized by the eye of flesh and blood, but only by the eye of faith, puts an end to all claims of the imagination to be the faculty which decides what is truly sacred and what is profane. . . . The contradiction between the profane appearance and the sacred assertion is impassible to the imagination.[87]

Auden is only half right. The Incarnation is indeed open only to the eye of faith, and the imagination per se is unable to decide what is truly sacred and what is profane. But this is only one moment in the movement of faith. In the Christian sphere as well as in the ethical, the aesthetic is indeed dethroned, but not evacuated. For Kierkegaard, the new possibility opened by Christianity is so extravagant that there is ample scope for the imagination, giving "our earthly existence festivity and dignity," winning "air and vision through the relationship to the eternal. . . . Christianity at every moment procures air and vision."[88] There is a realm for imagination beyond the "fantastic," beyond the resignation of Religion A and beyond the collision with the Paradox. In the Christian sphere, the imagination is indeed redeemed, and the artistry of existence continues with new vigor. Thus while Kierkegaard uniformly criticizes the possibility that any capacity can comprehend the divine, he is willing, once the defensive measures are secure, to outline a necessary place for the imagination within Religion B, in both faith and discipleship. We may call this further dialectic an "imagination of repetition through reversal." Both aspects--repetition and reversal--are crucial.

(a) Christianity entails an imagination of repetition, for faith moves one to an even higher imaginative level on the other side of the breach of the paradox. Faith restores lost spontaneity, quickens passion, and opens up new and eternal possibility to the sinner, revealing unlimited realms for imaginative reflection. Most people live in the spiritless realms of the probable and never understand, to use Kierkegaard's parable, that God is like the king who loves the maiden, or the emperor who wishes the day-laborer for a son-in-law.[89] But the very heart of faith is that it grasps a new possibility beyond expectation.

(b) The other aspect of the dialectic is, however, that one achieves repetition as it is filtered not only through grace, but also through the imagination of reversal. The negative movement of sin-consciousness, the awareness of one's reversal by God, is not left behind in faith; the sinner continues to know his or her need for grace and the oddness of the promise that it is the suffering Christ who grants one a repetition to wholeness.[90]

The primary distinction to keep in mind in approaching this dialectic grows out of the centrality of grace: it is the distinction between Christ as atoner and Christ as prototype. While Kierkegaard stresses discipleship in imitation of Christ as prototype for the follower--directed against a misuse of the Lutheran emphasis on faith as opposed to works--he still insists that the atonement is primary:

> Although the present situation calls for stressing "imitation"
> . . . the matter must above all not be turned in such a way

that Christ now becomes only prototype [Forbillede] and not Redeemer, as if atonement were not needed, at least not for the advanced.

No, no, no--for that matter the more advanced one is, the more he will discover that he needs atonement and grace.

No, the Atonement and grace are and remain definitive.[91]

Kierkegaard further separates the atonement from the ideal by stressing how the atonement refers to the sinner's past, whereas the prototype refers to the future: "Christ is the Atoner. This is continually in relation to the past. But at the same moment he is the Atoner for the past he is 'the prototype' [Forbilledet] for the future."[92] The distinction highlights the difference between one's relation to Christ as gift and to Christ as task.[93] The shape of the Christian life reduplicates the gift-task dialectic already apparent in The Concept of Irony, and found also in the ethical sphere. As we might expect, the imagination's functions in faith are analogous to how, in the earlier stages, one accepts actuality as a gift; so too, the imagination's functions in imitation are analogous to how, in the earlier stages, one acts out the task of making a concrete self. In the Christian sphere, however, the "actuality" one accepts as gift is one's new being in Christ, and the task one engages in is imitation of Christ.

With this in mind we can describe now four major roles that the imagination, combining reversal and repetition, plays in the Christian sphere. First, there is the negative movement in which Christ presents a disanalogy to the believer. Second, the believer apprehends Christ as contemporaneous. Third, the believer understands Christian faith as a "happy passion." Fourth, Christ is the prototype for discipleship. In the first two, Christ as disanalogous and yet contemporaneous with the believer, we are primarily in the realm of the believer's relation to Christ as atoner. The third, faith as a happy passion, is a general description of faith, covering the believer's relation to Christ both as atoner and as prototype. In the fourth, Christ as prototype, we are in the subsequent moment of faith, that of obedience to Christ in faith.

(1) In the first function of the imagination in the moment of faith, the picture of Christ provides a disanalogy to the believer that curbs the imagination's claims in faith. The imagination beholds the Vorstellung of Christ, but sees it not as analogous to other religious or philosophical concepts, but rather as the disanalogous paradox, indeed, as a prototype that is an antitype in showing the sinner his or her distance from the ideal. Christ is first a prototype in bringing about full sin-consciousness, for, as Kierkegaard says in a journal entry, "'The prototype' must be presented as the requirement, and then it crushes you."[94] In the same section of the Postscript where he analyzes the misuse of analogy by both the right-wing and left-wing Hegelians, Kierkegaard also indicates a correct use of the imagination, a movement of reversal, when one employs "the analogy in order to define the paradox in contrast with it"; the believer will not "forget that this never can become his own thought (in a direct sense) without transforming faith into an illusion."[95] This use of analogy, then, is not mere "fantasy-intuition." In apprehending the God-incarnate, analogies finally fail; the Incarnation is not directly imaginable or conceivable, yet in the use of disanalogy, a kind of via negativa is envisioned that, grounded in passionate interest, allows one to apprehend if not comprehend the God-incarnate.

Thus it is that the examples Johannes Climacus gives in Philosophical Fragments to illustrate (not explain) the Absolute Paradox are appeals to the imagination to see analogies in disanalogies. The illustration of the king and the maiden, is, Climacus admits, disanalogous and inadequate: "no human situation can provide a valid analogy, even though we shall suggest one here in order to awaken the mind to an understanding of the divine."[96] The disanalogy is that while the king is incognito in order to win the maiden's love, the God's servant-form is the God's true form: "this form of a servant is not something put on like the king's plebian cloak, which just by flapping open would betray the king; . . . it is his true form."[97] Grasping at disanalogies, the imagination has a place in the apprehension of the God in time.

(2) Turning to the second role for the imagination in the moment of faith, the imagination more positively allows one to apprehend Christ as contemporaneous with the believer. The believer's new possibility is grounded in Christ; therefore, to obtain that new possibility, it is necessary to become contemporaneous with Christ. Whereas Kierkegaard earlier affirms Christ's historical actuality against those who would reduce him to a mere ideal or mythic figure, directly graspable by the imagination, Kierkegaard can now grant that the imagination may secure an "understanding" of Christ in contemporaneity. In an extended passage in Philosophical Fragments, Kierkegaard discusses how the eye of faith can apprehend the God. Such an apprehension is not dependent on direct historical contemporaneity with Christ, since most of those who saw Christ with the eye of the flesh did not discern his divinity. The condition for apprehension is given only by the grace of the God.[98]

But coming to see the divine in the human through faith involves a change in the believer's imagination, for the apprehension is not the imagination's direct achievement. Becoming contemporaneous with Christ, whatever age one lives in, means coming to perceive the God who is also the servant, and Kierkegaard thinks this reversal a miracle beyond the normal capacities of the imagination:

> Presumably it could occur to a human being to poetize himself in the likeness of the god or the god in the likeness of himself, but not to poetize that the god poetized himself in the likeness of a human being, for if the god gave no

indication, how could it occur to a man that the blessed god could need him?[99]

Our imaginations are oriented to the glorious; they associate the divine with what is best in humanity. But grace grants the condition that educates the imagination out of its usual limited expectations, allowing one to see in Christ the presence of the lowly God.

In describing contemporaneity Kierkegaard indicates the particular positive uses of the Christian imagination in the apprehension of Christ. In seeing Christ as contemporaneous, the imagination holds together the thoughts of this historical person and of God. Further, one sees the God-incarnate as "for thee" in one's own time and place.[100] As Stephen Crites says,

> faith's contemporaneousness with Christ does not mean that the believer achieves a timeless communion with Christ or that he projects himself imaginatively back into the time of Jesus. In time, in the time of his own existence, he must respond to the paradox of 'the God in time.'[101]

In contemporaneity, the imagination of repetition and of reversal are closely connected. On the one hand, the imagination of repetition is at work, for the believer who holds the contraries "divine" and "human" together is like any subjective thinker who holds contraries together in tension--the tragic and the comic, suffering and humor. On the other hand, the imagination of reversal continues here too, since the imagination achieves at most an apprehension rather than a comprehension of the God in time. The contraries compose the Absolute Paradox, and the imagination, in reversal, must be retrained to see the God in the form of this person, this person as God--in short, to see beauty where no beauty is to be found, the glory in the suffering.

(3) In faith, the imagination is integral to faith as a happy passion:

> the follower owes that teacher everything ... and this relation cannot be expressed by talking extravagantly and

trumpeting from the housetops but only in that happy
passion which we call faith, the object of which is the
paradox.[102]

The paradox and the passion of faith are a "mutual fit," and so while the

imagination of reversal persists, it nonetheless allows an imagination of

repetition that does not leave reversal behind.[103] Seeing the God's love, one

may respond happily or unhappily: the first response is faith, the second is

offense.

In faith, the believer finds that the imagination of reversal is the key to his

or her own repetition. Looking to Christ, the believer does not see the self as a

projected ideal of self-fulfillment; it is Christ who knows the self and gives one

wholeness:

And this only Christ as the sign of contradiction can do: it
draws attention to itself, and then it presents a contradiction.
There is something which makes it impossible for one to
desist from looking--and lo! while one looks, one sees as in
a mirror, one gets to see oneself, or He, the sign of
contradiction, sees into the depths of one's heart while one is
gazing into the contradiction.[104]

While one gazes at the contradiction, Christ contradicts self-reliance and yet

grants repetition, for in Christ the believer finds the goal of striving. What one

sees in Christ is not the ideal self, but one who knows the self as sinner yet as

redeemed. The imagination here becomes receptive; Christ is not a symbol of

one's own imaginative attainment of the ideal self, but is the One who knows,

judges, and yet redeems the self. The believer's passivity is not, however,

Schlegel's vegetative passivity, but a loving recognition that one is known by

this atoning ideal and in being known receives repetition. In faith the believer

relies endlessly on this figure, and is made whole, and to become whole in faith

means not lassitude but the pathos and drive toward "simultaneity" characteristic

of the lower spheres of the ethico-religious life. In faith's repetition through reversal, the imagination, thought, and will are all recruited, bringing new spontaneity.[105]

Faith as a happy passion is more than cognitive; it is a matter of character formation and training in new emotions and dispositions, including new ways of being imaginative. As Kierkegaard says in a journal entry of 1849,

> faith's conflict with the world is not a battle of thought with doubt, thought with thought. This was the confusion which finally ended in the madness of the system.
> Faith, the man of faith's conflict with the world, is a battle of character.[106]

Faith overcomes the disequilibrium of the imagination in despair by trusting the atoner, but faith also recruits the imagination in the task of learning new passions and new sources of joy.

(4) But in speaking of the dispositional aspects of faith, we are moving from faith as reliance on Christ the atoner, to faith as obedience to Christ the prototype. In speaking of faith's shaping of character, we enter now the fourth realm for the imagination within the Christian sphere, the realm of imitation (Efterfølgelse), in which repetition through reversal continues.

In imitation the same dialectic continues of (a) an opposition of faith to "the medium of imagination" and (b) a dialectical affirmation of the imagination. (a) Kierkegaard can oppose the imagination and imitation in the strongest terms:

> The existential is the characteristic that distinguishes between poetry and mythology--and Christianity. Indeed, the reason Christ proclaimed Christianity is discipleship or imitation was to prevent a merely imaginary relationship to the essentially Christian.[107]

This is expressed also in the opposition between the media of imagination and existence, an opposition that characterizes the Christian sphere as well as the lower ethico-religious spheres. Referring to the offense the apostles felt when Christ warned them of the sufferings of discipleship, Kierkegaard says:

> When I understand something in possibility, I do not become essentially changed. I remain in the old ways and make use of my imagination; when it becomes actuality, then it is I who am changed, and now the question is whether I can preserve myself. When it is a matter of understanding in possibility, I have to strain my imagination to the limit; when it is a matter of understanding the same thing in actuality, I am spared all exertion in regard to my imagination; actuality is placed very close to me, all too close; it has, as it were, swallowed me, and the question now is whether I can rescue myself from it.[108]

(b) But Kierkegaard is more subtly dialectical than these references would lead one to believe, for faith also affirms the imagination--indeed, the imagination reaches its most profound tasks in imitation. First, as a passion the imagination is the source of imitation. This is because imitation is not, in Bradley Dewey's phrase, a "facsimile imitation," rote-like and automatic, but an imitation of Christ that requires improvisation.[109] Second, even the medium of the imagination takes a place in the Christian sphere of existence, in a fashion more dialectical than any we have yet examined.

To illustrate the subtleties of this dialectic of imitation, we turn to yet another unnamed young man, found in Anti-Climacus' Training in Christianity (1850).[110] In one of the most extended discussions of the imagination in Kierkegaard's literature, Anti-Climacus continues his analysis of the imagination found in The Sickness Unto Death. Whereas in The Sickness Unto Death the concern is with the imagination as the capacity underlying despair, here the concern is with the specifically Christian functions of the imagination as it operates in the happy passion of faith.[111] Whereas The Sickness Unto Death stresses the infinitizing capacity of the imagination, Training in Christianity complements this by focussing on the movement toward the concrete involved in imitating Christ.

In this discussion, the imagination as a medium has a role in the Christian economy similar to that of the ideal self in the ethical sphere, and yet unique to the Christian sphere of existence. As in the ethical sphere, the difficulty in the Christian sphere is to live the ideal in the concrete. And as in the sphere of Religion A, the ideal is not a universal, but is highly particularized. But a further step is taken here in two ways. First, a reversal is demanded, putting one's trust in Christ as a particular individual rather than in the ethico-idealist "divine self within." Second, the oddity of the picture of Christ as the ideal is that, unlike the ethical model or the paradigms for Religion A, the reversal is embodied in the picture itself. The ideal of Christ embodies in imaginative form what is contrary to idealization: suffering throughout an entire life. To follow this ideal, one must learn the difficult lesson that the way to exaltation is only through humiliation. That is not an easy task, because even in entertaining this thought in the medium of the imagination one is still entertaining it as an idealized possibility.

Let us turn to the portrayal of the believing youth in Training in Christianity. At first the picture of Christ attracts the young man, fixing his imagination on this picture of perfection: it "becomes his more perfect (ideal) self."[112] The young man is struck by the distinctiveness of Christ, the disanalogies between Christ and other healers. In contrast to them, Christ's summons goes out to all; and unlike earthly physicians he stays with the "patient" all day long.[113] Because the picture is attractive, the young man seeks to imitate this ideal. But the problem is that this picture, like any ideal, seems easy to accomplish:

> So the imagination [Indbildningskraften] deals with this
> picture of perfection, and so even if it were with the picture
> of that perfected One whose perfection consisted precisely in
> the fact of having endured, not only frightful sufferings, but
> also what is most opposed to perfection (ideality), namely,
> daily indignity and maltreatment and vexation throughout a
> long life--as imagination presents this picture it looks so
> easy, one beholds only the perfection, even the striving
> perfection is seen only as it is completed.[114]

The difficulty with the picture is that in the medium of the imagination even the picture of the Crucified is "softened, toned-down, foreshortened."[115] The medium of imagination as "the faculty of representing perfection (idealization),"[116] presents a picture without "the reality of time and duration and of the earthly life with its difficulties and sufferings."[117] Thus, in one way, the picture is inadequate to the perfection of Christ: "the picture which imagination presents is not the picture of true perfection, there is something it lacks, namely, the suffering of reality or the reality of suffering."[118] The picture is imperfect, even when it depicts suffering.

In one sense, then, Kierkegaard's keen sense of the limitations of the imagination are stronger than ever in his understanding of the Christian sphere. Christ is the Pattern, but the Pattern cannot be understood immediately, and there is a formal difficulty in the use of this or any picture of an ideal that involves suffering, for the ideal cannot, even in portraying the sufferings, depict them adequately. The formal shortcoming of the medium of the imagination in its distance from existence is again crucial.

Yet this is only one moment of the Christian life, for Kierkegaard can also say that, taken as a whole, the Christian sphere does use the imagination, even as a medium, in its totality. Kierkegaard depicts how the young man uses the picture in a way that makes the picture adequate. The young man is enchanted by the picture and "walks like a dreamer"; he is "transformed into likeness with this picture which stamps or expresses itself upon all his thinking and upon his every utterance."[119] The ideal has a definite effect, and an important one, for it takes the young man out of himself.

The true appropriation, however, is still to come, for reality continues the young man's education. Following the ideal of Christ's love and self-denial, the young man will to his surprise meet opposition and scorn:

> To make oneself literally one with the most miserable (and this, this alone is divine compassion) is for men the 'too much', over which one weeps in the quiet hour on Sundays, and at which one bursts with laughter when one sees it in reality.[120]

Yet as a "subjective thinker," the young man possesses the factors of life in simultaneity, and so his will steps forth, refusing to let the picture go; thus he learns obedience.[121] With further sufferings, the young man still holds to the ideal, believing that the suffering cannot last forever. "In a certain sense," says Anti-Climacus,

> the youth's imagination has deceived him, but verily, if he himself will, it has not deceived him to his hurt, it has deceived him into the truth, as though by a deceit it played God into his hands; if the youth will--God in heaven waits for him, willing to help, in such ways as help can be given in an examination which yet must have the seriousness of the highest examination. Imagination has deceived the youth; by the aid of this picture of perfection it has made him forget that he is in the real world: and now he stands there--in exactly the right posture. True enough, he may experience a momentary shudder as he now contemplates the situation; but to escape from the picture--no, that he cannot persuade himself to do.[122]

And so the youth holds on to this picture of perfection, the pattern of the suffering Christ. The irony is that the imagination deceives one into the truth. The deception is not a cruel one, however, but is the deception by a gentle providence, luring a person into the realm of God's love. The reason for the deception is that the will alone is not strong enough for one voluntarily to take on suffering. Christ

> knows also that the permission to begin with the easiest . . .
> is a necessary deceit in the process of education, and that the
> fact of its becoming then harder and harder is in order that
> life may become in truth a probation and examination.[123]

Holding to the ideal, the young man has been formed in that image not only in aspiration, but in reality. The ideal has been brought to the concrete, not only in Christ, but in the imitator.

But now the medium of the imagination _serves_ the imagination as passion, for by means of that "picture of perfection" one acquires oneself in a second immediacy: "His whole inward man is reconstructed little by little."[124] Holding to the picture, the imagination too becomes passionately vivified and commitment to the picture increases: "to _will_ to be a youth, to _will_ to retain youth's enthusiasm with its spontaneity unabated, to _will_ to reacquire it by valiant effort . . . that is the task."[125]

In this way, with the help of the imaginative picture in league with enthusiasm, one discovers repetition through reversal. The young man's enthusiasm holds him to the picture and leads him to see that the only way to attain the ideal is by suffering the pains depicted. Attending more closely to the picture, he experiences reversal in "that exactly the opposite is occurring from that which he was promised by that hope."[126] Yet he does not let the picture go; in the midst of his own suffering he looks to the Pattern, without which "he could not hold out."[127] He continues, and the picture of the suffering Christ becomes to him a comfort; he discovers that reversal leads to repetition.[128] The young man learns that exaltation is humiliation and yet that there is joy in suffering. "Christianity," as Kierkegaard says elsewhere, "always puts contradictions together."[129] To have faith means to "regard everything inversely," "to remain full of hope and confidence when something happens which previously almost made [one] faint and expire with anxiety."[130]

Kierkegaard describes here a particular Christian use of the imagination in which one is able to give to the suffering of discipleship a new imaginative construal. For example, in The Gospel of Suffering, Kierkegaard discusses "How the Burden Can Be Light Though the Suffering is Heavy"; the imaginative shift in perception entails no change in the outward situation, but only in the inward: "He who bears his suffering in such a way that he believes that the yoke is profitable, he bears the yoke of Christ."[131] Kierkegaard elsewhere describes this shift in perception, when joy emerges out of suffering, as truly "seeing the Pattern." Addressing the "lowly man" who comes to perceive his lowliness in relation to that of Christ, Kierkegaard indicates how joy arises in the midst of imitative suffering when one construes that suffering in relation to the Pattern:

> True, he has not himself, with his own eyes, seen the Pattern, but he believes that He existed. There was, in a certain sense, nothing at all to see--except lowliness (for glory is something that must be believed), and of lowliness he is well able to form a conception. He has not with his own eyes seen the Pattern, nor does he make any attempt to have the senses construct such a picture. Yet he often sees the Pattern. For as often as in faith's gladness at the glory of this Pattern he completely forgets his poverty, his lowliness, the contempt in which he is held, he sees the Pattern--and he himself approximately resembles it.[132]

Yet for all the stress on the imagination of reversal as the necessary means of attaining repetition, in Training in Christianity Anti-Climacus concludes the dialectic of the imagination's place in the Christian life on a surprising note that suggests a new theme: after all is said and done, the picture of glory the medium of imagination first presented is the true picture. Discussing the connection between humiliation and exaltation in the Christian life, Anti-Climacus says that humiliation is the only way a cruel world can respond to true exaltation. Thus, the imagination correctly depicts the glory of exaltation, that of Christ and of the Christian, in its "loftiness and purity":[133]

> Such is the relationship between exaltation and lowliness. The humiliation of the true Christian is not plain humiliation, it is merely the reflected image of exaltation, but the reflection of it in this world, where exaltation must appear conversely as lowliness and humiliation.[134]

The exaltation of Christ who "being lifted up on high will draw all unto himself" in love is, reflected in this world, humiliation. So too, the Christian's discipleship is, in heaven's eyes, true exaltation, although in the world it is a suffering and humiliation that continues until death: "As soon as you eliminate the world, the turbid element which confuses the reflection, that is, as soon as the Christian dies, he is exalted on high."[135]

Kierkegaard fears, not surprisingly, to belabor this theme, yet when we remember that he is not concerned to establish a level of discourse or representation as "true" or "untrue," then it is no longer very surprising that even the medium of the imagination can partake of the truth. For Kierkegaard the question is always that of the use one makes of a picture; the same picture can be used in an untrue or a true manner. The medium of the imagination is indeed fraught with dangers. It can betray one to perdition in the aesthetic stage; its depictions of glory and exaltation can obscure the suffering of existence; and in the Christian sphere it depicts a truth that can only be achieved by one's being deceived into a suffering that is the opposite of the exaltation depicted. Yet Kierkegaard now--and only now--can hint at the counterpoint to these dangers: the exaltation and glory the medium of the imagination depicts is the first and last word. Finally, in the figure of the young man, Kierkegaard can now say: "Let us suppose that he holds out until his death--then he has passed his examination. He himself became that picture of perfection which he loved, and verily imagination has not deceived him, nor has governance."[136]

Imagination has not deceived him. The imagination is finally right in its depiction of perfection. The exaltation the imagination depicts is the goal, however severe the sufferings on the way. The dreams of youth, the imagination's yearning for blessedness, are finally fulfilled. The imagination does adequately depict eternity, on the condition that those pictures are properly used within the Christian sphere.

But this must remain for Kierkegaard a subordinate theme, for the dialectic of the imagination demands that one follow the way of pilgrimage to the goal, "and the way is the truth." Speaking in The Gospel of Suffering of the rejuvenation the idea of eternity gives, Kierkegaard adds,

> I shall not pursue it farther, for in my opinion it is so beautiful that it is almost dangerous, and may very easily become an illusion, because just at the moment when it appears in all its beauty to a man, instead of giving him headway in his striving, it deludes the imagination, as if the renewing came to pass by magic.[137]

In the end, it is faith and imitation that, by way of the cross, point to the fulfillment of the dreams of the aesthetic medium of the imagination. "Art," Vigilius Haufniensis and Johannes Climacus agree, "is an anticipation of eternal life."[138] But finally, for Kierkegaard "faith . . . is the anticipation of the eternal," because in faith the subjective thinker holds even the medium of the imagination in simultaneity with suffering in actuality.[139] Faith is "an idealizing passion" and in its grasp of the glory of the Pattern, and in suffering imitation, it anticipates and fulfills all the dreams of art.[140]

[1] Kierkegaard, EO2 356.

[2] Kierkegaard, SLW 458; part of this discourse is printed in Walter Lowrie's translation of SLW. For a discussion of this passage, see Reidar Thomte, Kierkegaard's Philosophy of Religion (Princeton: Princeton UP, 1948) 147ff.

[3] Kierkegaard, SLW 458.

[4] Kierkegaard, SLW 458.

[5] Kierkegaard, SLW 458.

[6] Kierkegaard, JP 1: 48 (V A 25), n.d., 1844; cited in Thomte, Kierkegaard's Philosophy of Religion 147.

[7] Kierkegaard, CUP 497.

[8] Kierkegaard, SLW 465.

[9] Kierkegaard, EO2 291.

[10] Kierkegaard, SUD 13.

[11] Kierkegaard, SUD (Lowrie's trans.)192-93.

[12] Kierkegaard, CUP 230; the latter is, of course, a central theme of Fear and Trembling.

[13] In a journal entry, Kierkegaard writes, "in Repetition feeling and irony are kept separate each in its representative: the young man and Constantine," JP 5: 5865 (VII[1] B 83), n.d., 1846.

[14] Søren Kierkegaard, Repetition: A Venture in Experimental Psychology, in Fear and Trembling and Repetition, ed. and trans., with introd. and notes Howard V. Hong and Edna H. Hong, Kierkegaard's Writings 6 (Princeton: Princeton UP, 1983) 154 (hereafter, R). Brita Stendahl writes of this passage that "suddenly we hear Constantine speaking about the image-forming process,

about the importance of heroes and models for the young imagination to test its empathy. We pay attention because we feel we are very near the heart of the Kierkegaardian psychology," Brita Stendahl, <u>Søren Kierkegaard</u>, Twayne's World Authors Series 392 (Boston: Twayne, 1976) 202-03.

[15] Kierkegaard, <u>R</u> 169.

[16] Kierkegaard, <u>R</u> 183.

[17] Kierkegaard, <u>R</u> 183-84.

[18] Kierkegaard, <u>R</u> 229.

[19] Kierkegaard, <u>R</u> 210.

[20] Kierkegaard, <u>R</u> 204.

[21] Kierkegaard, <u>R</u> 210.

[22] Stendahl 205; see also Kierkegaard, <u>CA</u> 18n: "If repetition is not posited, ethics becomes a binding power."

[23] Kierkegaard, <u>R</u> 226.

[24] Kierkegaard, <u>CUP</u> 235.

[25] Kierkegaard, <u>R</u> 212.

[26] Kierkegaard, <u>R</u> 220.

[27] Kierkegaard, <u>R</u> 221.

[28] Kierkegaard, <u>R</u> 228.

[29] Kierkegaard, <u>R</u> 229.

[30] Even if we grant Constantin his claim that the young man is his invention, Constantin admits that "the most I can do is to imagine a poet and to produce him by my thought. . . . I myself cannot become a poet." Nor is Constantin religious. Kierkegaard, <u>R</u> 228.

[31] Kierkegaard, <u>R</u> 228-29.

[32] Kierkegaard, <u>CUP</u> 494.

[33] Kierkegaard, <u>SLW</u> 383.

34 Kierkegaard, CUP 235.

35 The situation is, of course, more dialectical than this, since if one suffers from a "fantastic" God-relationship that infinitizes, then one needs necessity; see Kierkegaard, SUD 32: "The God-relationship is an infinitizing, but in fantasy this infinitizing can so sweep a man off his feet that his state is simply an intoxication"; so too, in CA 155f, Vigilius Haufniensis analyzes how the imagination calls up dreadful possibilities, driving one from an "excess" of possibility to seek refuge in faith. This need for necessity is, of course, compatible with the continuing search for possibility in the God-relationship, a possibility beyond the dreadful possibilities of the fantastic; cf. Frater Taciturnus in SLW 423-24.

36 Kierkegaard, SUD 38.

37 Kierkegaard, SUD 38-39.

38 Kierkegaard, CUP 235.

39 Kierkegaard, R 210; CUP 235; Adi Shmueli, Kierkegaard and Consciousness, trans. Naomi Handelman, introd. Paul L. Holmer (Princeton: Princeton UP, 1971) seriously restricts the religious significance of repetition by failing to see how it operates on the immanent levels of the religious sphere. Repetition has its own dialectic and is more than a category to be located, as Shmueli does, beyond resignation and repentance. Cf. Elrod 230 for a similar misunderstanding.

40 Kierkegaard, CUP 347ff.

41 Kierkegaard, CUP 353.

42 Kierkegaard, CA 161; cf. CUP 471ff.

43 Frater Taciturnus claims to be the creator of the suffering young man he analyzes, SLW 367.

44 Stendahl 152.

45 On "taciturnity" as a central theme in <u>SLW</u>, see Paulsen 160-61.

46 Kierkegaard, <u>SLW</u> 356.

47 Kierkegaard, <u>SLW</u> 390.

48 Kierkegaard, <u>SLW</u> 384.

49 Kierkegaard, <u>SLW</u> 334.

50 Kierkegaard, <u>SLW</u> 408.

51 Kierkegaard, <u>SLW</u> 389; Johannes Climacus confirms this in <u>CUP</u> 239.

52 Kierkegaard, <u>CUP</u> 507.

53 Kierkegaard, <u>CUP</u> 495.

54 Kierkegaard, <u>CUP</u> 493.

55 Kierkegaard, <u>SUD</u> 38-39.

56 Kierkegaard, <u>SUD</u> 80.

57 Kierkegaard, <u>SUD</u> 81.

58 Kierkegaard, <u>PF</u> 18.

59 Kierkegaard, <u>PF</u> 37.

60 Diem 70.

61 On paradox in Kierkegaard, see, for example, Cornelio Fabro, "Faith and Reason in Kierkegaard's Dialectic," <u>A Kierkegaard Critique,</u> ed. Howard A. Johnson and Niels Thulstrup (New York: Harper, 1962) 156-206; N. H. Søe, "Kierkegaard's Doctrine of the Paradox," Johnson and Thulstrup, 207-27, esp. 219f.

62 Kierkegaard, <u>CUP</u> 524.

63 Kierkegaard, <u>JP</u> 6: 6150 (IX A 39), n.d., 1848; cf. <u>JP</u> 6: 6844 (XI^2 A 283), n.d., 1853-54: "Bishop Mynster does not place Christianity into actuality, but at imagination's distance from actuality (the poetic)"; cf. <u>JP</u> 6: 6677 (X^3 A 43), n.d., 1850. See also the polemic against the established church, and on Mynster in particular, in Søren Kierkegaard, <u>Kierkegaard's Attack Upon</u>

"Christendom," 1854-1855, trans. and introd. Walter Lowrie (Princeton: Princeton UP, 1944). For Kierkegaard's critical re-evaluation of his own earlier stress on "hidden inwardness," see TC 195.

[64] Kierkegaard, CA 19.

[65] Kierkegaard, CA 20.

[66] Kierkegaard, JP 2: 1096 (I A 273), n.d., 1836.

[67] Whether Schleiermacher would associate imagination and the feeling of absolute dependence is a complex issue we need not go into here. Kierkegaard nowhere makes an explicit connection between Schleiermacher's "feeling of absolute dependence" and the imagination, but he would most certainly make the connection. Kierkegaard describes the feeling of absolute dependence as a falsification of Christianity, because Schleiermacher "has conceived it aesthetically-metaphysically merely as a condition, whereas Christianity is essentially to be conceived ethically, as striving. Schleiermacher conceives of religiousness as completely analogous to erotic love," JP 4: 3853 (X^2 A 417), n.d., 1850; cf. JP 4: 3852 (X^2 A 416), n.d., 1850. On the relation of aesthetic and religious experience in Schleiermacher, see Louis Dupré, A Dubious Heritage: Studies in the Philosophy of Religion after Kant (New York: Paulist, 1977) 24-28.

[68] The many dimensions of this distinction and the issues it raises cannot be explored here. Again, on Vorstellung and Begriff, see Fackenheim 154-55; Malcolm Clark, Logic and System: A Study of the Transition from "Vorstellung" to Thought in the Philosophy of Hegel (The Hague: Nijhoff, 1971). For the theological dimension of Vorstellung, see James Yerkes, The Christology of Hegel, American Acad. of Religion Diss. Series 23 (Missoula, MT: Scholars, 1978) 249ff. On Strauss's use of Vorstellung, see Peter C. Hodgson, "Editor's Introduction," The Life of Jesus Critically Examined, by David Friedrich

Strauss, ed. Peter C. Hodgson, trans. George Eliot, Lives of Jesus Series, ed. Leander E. Keck (Philadelphia: Fortress, 1972) xx; Hodgson translates Vorstellung as "religious imagery," but also warns against equating this too closely with Phantasie, see p. 1.

[69] Hegel, Phenomenology of Spirit sec. 765, p. 463.

[70] Mark Taylor, Journeys to Selfhood 121.

[71] Kierkegaard, SUD 117.

[72] Horn 264.

[73] Hans Lassen Martensen, Christian Dogmatics: A Compendium of the Doctrines of Christianity, trans. Rev. William Urwick (Edinburgh: T. & T. Clark, 1898) 9.

[74] Martensen, Christian Dogmatics 9. Martensen supervised the German translation; see Hans Lassen Martensen, Die Christliche Dogmatik, trans. from Danish, 2nd ed. (Kiel: Schröder, 1853) 22.

[75] Kierkegaard, LD 321 (Letter 231).

[76] Martensen, Christian Dogmatics 240.

[77] Martensen, Christian Dogmatics 246.

[78] Kierkegaard, TC 85.

[79] On Kierkegaard's knowledge of Strauss, see Thulstrup, Kierkegaard's Relation to Hegel 155-63, which treats Kierkegaard's reading in 1838 of Julius Schaller's Der historische Christus und die Philosophie, a moderate Hegelian critique of Strauss; cf. Kierkegaard, JP 3: 3260-3263 (II C 54-57), 1838; see also SUD 118, where Kierkegaard says that the doctrine of the God-incarnate has become a means of intimidating God: "It is God who devised the teaching about the God-man and now Christendom has brazenly turned it around and foists kinship on God." On Kierkegaard's knowledge of Feuerbach, see Thulstrup's note in Søren Kierkegaard, Philosophical Fragments, or A Fragment of

Philosophy, trans. David Swenson, new introd. and commentary Niels Thulstrup, trans. revised and commentary trans. Howard V. Hong (Princeton: Princeton UP, 1976) 204. On Kierkegaard's knowledge of Beck, see J. H. Schjørring, "Martensen," Thulstrup and Thulstrup, Kierkegaard's Teachers 192-93, 203.

[80] Kierkegaard, CUP 515. Not only is the bare historical actuality, the "facticity" of the God-incarnate important, but so too is the content that is united to that form: the God is revealed truly to be a servant. The humility of God in the Incarnation is vital to Kierkegaard; this is often overlooked because of Johannes Climacus' comment that it would be "more than enough" to know that the God was among us as a servant, lived, and died, PF (Hongs' translation) 104. But this does not mean that the narrative content of the story is unimportant for Kierkegaard. In Fragments Kierkegaard explores in a thought-project the contrast between historical apprehension and the apprehension of faith. In terms of this contrast, Kierkegaard does not discuss the historical detail of the story, in order to emphasize that faith, not historical understanding, grasps the story's qualitative uniqueness. Nonetheless, the full narrative of the gospels is important for Kierkegaard, precisely because it details how the servant form is the God's true form. The picture of Christ as Redeemer and as the prototype of obedience requires narrative content, and not simply "facticity"; this is clear especially in such works as Training in Christianity.

[81] Kierkegaard, CUP 514.

[82] Kierkegaard, CUP 514.

[83] Kierkegaard, CUP 514.

[84] Louis Dupré, Kierkegaard as Theologian: The Dialectic of Christian Existence (New York: Sheed, 1963) 96ff.

[85] Kierkegaard, JP 2: 1130 (X^1 A 368), n.d., 1849.

86 Kierkegaard, PF 62.

87 W. H. Auden, "Postscript: Christianity and Art," The Dyer's Hand and Other Essays (New York: Vintage-Random, 1968) 457.

88 Søren Kierkegaard, Works of Love: Some Christian Reflections in the Form of Discourses, trans. Howard and Edna Hong, pref. R. Gregor Smith, Harper Torchbooks, Cloister Library (New York: Torchbook-Harper, 1962) 231 (hereafter, WL).

89 Kierkegaard, WL 26ff; Kierkegaard, SUD 84f.

90 We therefore must wend our way between two misinterpretations of the Christian sphere that do not keep in view both the imagination of repetition and of reversal. We must disagree, first, with Eduard Geismar and Jean Wahl, who underestimate the continuing place of repetition. They argue that Kierkegaard simply abandons repetition for the sake of an imitation of Christ (Wahl, Etudes 365 and n). But on the other hand, we must disagree with writers like Wilhelm Anz who underestimate the importance of reversal. Despite his careful discussion of the role of paradox in Kierkegaard as a Gegenbegriff that puts a check on human abilities (65-66), Anz nevertheless sees Kierkegaard's understanding of the infinite as a continuing self-positing (74). This does not give enough weight to the imagination of reversal as a dialectical check on the imagination's unjustified pretensions. A more accurate account needs to see how dialectical the imagination is in the Christian sphere: it is an imagination of repetition through reversal. The infinitizing continues, but only as filtered through the imagination of reversal.

91 Kierkegaard, JP 2: 1909 (X^4 A 491), n.d., 1852.

92 Kierkegaard, JP 2: 1919 (X^5 A 44), n.d., 1852; cf. Judge for Yourselves! (hereafter, JFY), in Søren Kierkegaard, For Self-Examination and Judge for Yourselves! and Three Discourses, 1851, trans., introd., and notes

Walter Lowrie (Princeton: Princeton UP, 1941) 161. Grace, of course, gives power for future obedience as well; the point is that relying on grace requires an intention to follow Christ as prototype of that obedience; JP 2: 1918 (X[5] A 44), n.d., 1852.

[93] Kierkegaard, JP 2: 1862 (X[2] A 361), n.d., 1849.

[94] JP 1: 349 (X[2] A 170), n.d., 1849; the entry concerns Galatians 2:19: "For I through the law died to the law, that I might live to God."

[95] Kierkegaard, CUP 514.

[96] Kierkegaard, PF 26.

[97] Kierkegaard, PF 31-32; on the implications of this for poetry as an art of aesthetic analogy and comparison, and the Incarnation as the inversion of poetic striving, see Naomi Lebowitz, Kierkegaard: A Life of Allegory (Baton Rouge and London: Louisiana State UP, 1985) 174-215, esp. 190-91.

[98] Kierkegaard, PF 64.

[99] Kierkegaard, PF 36.

[100] On the errors of "picturing Christ," see Kierkegaard, TC 247-49.

[101] Crites, Twilight 65; see also Kierkegaard, CUP 499.

[102] Kierkegaard, PF 61.

[103] Kierkegaard, CUP 206.

[104] Kierkegaard, TC 126.

[105] It is important in this context to remember that from the standpoint of faith the understanding comes back too in a new, and finally successful, establishment of simultaneity: the absurd is no longer absurd. Kierkegaard, JP 1: 10 (X[6] B 79), n.d., 1850; see also Fabro 179ff.

[106] Kierkegaard, JP 2: 1129 (XI A 367), n.d., 1849.

[107] Kierkegaard, JP 3: 2805 (XI[1] A 217), n.d., 1854.

[108] Kierkegaard, JP 3: 3346 (X[2] A 202), n.d., 1849.

[109] Bradley R. Dewey, The New Obedience: Kierkegaard on Imitating Christ, fwd. Paul L. Holmer (Washington: Corpus, 1968) 105ff.

[110] Kierkegaard, TC 180ff; this passage is in Part III, Section IV, "From on High He Will Draw All Unto Himself"; cf. also The Gospel of Suffering, which is part of the Edifying Discourses in Various Spirits of 1847, published in English as Søren Kierkegaard, The Gospel of Suffering and The Lilies of the Field, trans. David F. Swenson and Lillian Marvin Swenson (Minneapolis: Augsburg, 1948) 14ff (hereafter, GS).

[111] Stendahl 186.

[112] Kierkegaard, TC 185; see Hirsch 333.

[113] Kierkegaard, TC 12, 14-15.

[114] Kierkegaard, TC 185; on a dialectically lower level Socrates illustrates the same gap between the beauty of the ideal and the indignity he suffered; see Kierkegaard, JP 1: 1054 (IX A 382), n.d., 1848.

[115] Kierkegaard, TC 186; cf. CUP 347, and JP 3: 3345 (X^2 A 114), n.d., 1849.

[116] Kierkegaard, TC 190.

[117] Kierkegaard, TC 186.

[118] Kierkegaard, TC 187.

[119] Kierkegaard, TC 187.

[120] Kierkegaard, TC 63.

[121] Kierkegaard, CUP 316.

[122] Kierkegaard, TC 188; cf. Kierkegaard's comment on Savonarola, JP 4: 3839 (X^4 A 264), n.d., 1851.

[123] Kierkegaard, TC 184, 205; cf. Kierkegaard, JP 4: 4890 (X^4 A 297), n.d., 1851, Kierkegaard's praise to God for deceiving him into the truth, this taken as evidence of God's faithfulness, "for then I would have gone on living

with an imaginary notion of your faithfulness but without ever becoming involved with you." The ability to "deceive one into the truth" is attributed to anxiety also (CA 160). Kierkegaard saw the significance of his authorship as a "pious deception" (PV 39), in the sense that an aim of the literature is to unmask the illusion that all are Christians; one begins with another's illusion (Indbildning), taking it as good money, and then unmasks it. On the psychology and ethics of maieutic deception, see Nordentoft 354ff.

124 Kierkegaard, TC 191.

125 Kierkegaard, TC 190.

126 Kierkegaard, TC 192.

127 Kierkegaard, TC 195.

128 Kierkegaard, TC 193.

129 Kierkegaard, JFY 172; this is the central theme of many of Kierkegaard's later works, such as Christian Discourses and The Gospel of Suffering, extended essays on the imagination of repetition through reversal as it applies to Christian formation. See especially "Joyful Notes in the Strife of Suffering" in CD 95-163.

130 Kierkegaard, JP 2: 1401 (X^2 A 493), n.d., 1850.

131 Kierkegaard, GS 29.

132 Kierkegaard, CD 46.

133 Kierkegaard, TC 191.

134 Kierkegaard, TC 195-96.

135 Kierkegaard, TC 196.

136 Kierkegaard, TC 190.

137 Kierkegaard, GS 62.

138 Vigilius Haufniensis' remark is found in Kierkegaard, CA 153; Kierkegaard owed this thought to Poul M. Møller, "the happy lover of Greek

culture," to whom The Concept of Anxiety is dedicated. Johannes Climacus echoes this in CUP 277 and n3.

[139] Kierkegaard, JP 2: 1347 (VII[1] A 139), n.d., 1846.

[140] Kierkegaard, CUP 277; see Lebowitz, esp. ch. 5, who investigates extensively the relation of art and faith, and how Kierkegaard's literature "works not for fulfillment and consolation but for need" (222), a need satisfiable only beyond art.

CONCLUSION

I have argued that implicit in Kierkegaard's writings is a detailed, nuanced, and consistent set of observations on the imagination, an aspect of the human spirit he thought so important that he called it "the capacity instar omnium." Although his remarks are often imbedded in the midst of other concerns, an analysis of these remarks yields, indeed, a dialectic of the imagination.

There are three strands in Kierkegaard's dialectic of the imagination: first, the opposition of the media of the imagination and existence; second, the imagination's uses in existence as artistry and a simultaneity of factors; third, the religious and especially Christological dialectic of repetition through reversal. The third strand is the culmination of the first two, and occupied Kierkegaard's reflections on the place of the imagination in Christian faith. In the Christological dialectic he returns again to the two problems that occupied him as early as the mid-1830's: first, how to exclude any undue claims of the imagination--whether in art, philosophy, or existence--to give human wholeness and transcendence; second, how to maintain the imagination's rightful place as a vital part of ethical and religious life. The Christological dialectic continues and intensifies both themes, for the Absolute Paradox defeats not only the medium of imagination, but also the imagination of existence in Religion A. Hence, Kierkegaard continually extends the critique of "fantasy," first aimed at the Romantics' "poetic imperialism," to "childish Christianity," religious intuitionism, and mediated speculation of all kinds, however orthodox or unorthodox. But the second emphasis continues too in the Christological dialectic, for in Christian discipleship the existential imagination, and even the medium of the imagination, come back in a rich and complex way in the movements of repetition through reversal.

With its ethical and religious purpose, Kierkegaard's dialectic of the imagination is strenuous and tensive; the critique of "fantasy" informs the whole dialectic, from beginning to end, and is more intense than ever in the later writings. Nonetheless, the imagination is always for Kierkegaard more than the privilege of genius; it is the birthright of every human being, a gift of creation, and the task for any person is to use this gift in a way that transcends fantasy, illusion, self-deception, and the waywardness of moods. Further, Christian repetition is a gift of grace, one that quickens the imagination, giving "air and vision" to persons even in the midst of the rigors of suffering. Thus, Kierkegaard maintains consistently that the imagination is not limited to artistic production, but is as central to life as to art; it is nothing less than the "first condition" determining what a person will turn out to be.[1] Even in 1854 Kierkegaard could write that "man too has wings, he has imagination, intended to help him actually rise aloft."[2]

The stages reflect this continuing tensiveness and yet affirmation of the imagination by dialectically distinguishing the variety of ways a person employs imagination. The stages indicate the immense breach between living in fantasy and living in existence. Renunciation is required if one is to give up dreams in order to test those very dreams in life. Yet while there are disjunctions between the stages in ways of being imaginative, there are close relations too; should a person move through the stages, one accumulates imaginative capacities. Ilham Dilman observes in another context that one sense of "imagination" is that a person works from a tradition or background and then produces unsuspected variations that open new possibilities.[3] The stages describe a cumulative earning of imaginative capacities. Some are altered in the transition between the stages--

the fantastic must yield to a healthy imagination, the imagination of repetition suffers reversal--but in general the imagination's creation of ideals and possibilities with the goal of a unified self produces new variations that are not left behind, but are incorporated in a further stage. One must have the aesthetic ability to dream of another self if one is to be ethical; an ethical person must learn devotion to an ideal if one is to acquire the God-relationship of Religion A; and a religious person must relate to God in suffering and hope if one is to approach Christ as the Absolute Paradox. It is for these reasons that Kierkegaard calls the imagination the first condition for becoming a person and the capacity instar omnium. Without imagination there is mere spiritlessness; with imagination there is life.

So too, within each stage Kierkegaard stresses the originality that the imagination gives. As Dilman says, "what is truly imaginative differs from the merely fantastic. One who makes an imaginative contribution is thus at once following a tradition and yet departing from set practices."[4] The ethical life is never mere conformity to external norms; it requires originality to envision an ideal and make it real in one's own existence. And as Bradley Dewey has argued, Christian discipleship for Kierkegaard is never a "facsimile imitation," an automatic, unreflective imitation of Christ. Rather, discipleship requires imagination to determine how one can follow Christ as Pattern in one's own time and place.[5]

This dialectical portrayal of the imagination of the stages--both tensive and affirming--results further in a rich variety of ways of describing the imagination's roles. He describes it as "the medium for the process of infinitizing" in The Sickness Unto Death and often appears to think of it, not surprisingly, as an internal event of mental picturing. I have argued, however, that his concept of the imagination includes broader, more finely nuanced accounts that, while using "imagination" as a term for this process of infinitizing, also includes other descriptions. In different contexts it is a state of soulishness prior to reflection, a medium of artistry, an organ for concreteness, a passion of the poet or the subjective thinker, and even a long-term disposition of the self. The result is that while Kierkegaard consistently thinks of the imagination as an internal event of mental picturing, the dialectic produces a nuanced, subtle exploration of this "capacity instar omnium." Kierkegaard looks beyond the surface of imagining to discover the immense differences in the contexts of being imaginative.

Taken together, Kierkegaard's dialectic of the stages, plus these varied descriptions of the term, produce a strikingly functional account of the imagination. The "imagination" is finally not adequately understood if it is seen merely as the name for a discrete internal activity or process, or for a form of consciousness. In contemporary terms, the imagination cannot be understood apart from attending to the different contexts of the imagination's uses; to understand the imagination, we must attend not only to "what" one imagines, but "how" a person imagines. For example, the ethical person's imagination differs from the aesthete's imagination in how one relates to the imagined ideal. So too, the difference between any form of aestheticized Christianity--whether in Martensen's or Strauss' versions--and ethico-religious existence is in the "how."

Kierkegaard's interest in "how" the imagination is used can be illuminated by a remark of Wittgenstein's. Speaking of what it means to believe in a Last Judgment, Wittgenstein says that

> a certain picture might play the role of constantly admonishing me, or I always think of it. Here, an enormous difference would be between those people for whom the picture is constantly in the foreground, and others who just didn't use it at all.[6]

Wittgenstein's emphasis on the role a picture plays when used in connection with self-admonishment is close to Kierkegaard's concern to point to the distinctive "how" as well as the "what"--particularly in ethical and religious matters. Romantic claims to aesthetic transcendence, "childish Christianity," and speculative philosophy and dogmatics are for him suspect because they have lost the practices and self-concern in which the "picture" had been used. Kierkegaard's massive task, as he understood it, was to reintroduce what had been forgotten: the types of abilities, including imaginative abilities, that distinguish not only artistic production but also ethical, religious, and Christian existence.

How one deploys imaginative abilities determines, by and large, nothing less than the world in which one lives, what is one's reality and truth. For Kierkegaard, the imagination, united with passion, shapes the world of the aesthetic, ethical or religious person. For example, in seeing all things in relation to an ethical ideal or to God, the world alters for that person. "Subjectivity is truth, subjectivity is reality."[7] As we have seen, because of Kierkegaard's epistemological realism and his denial of Romantic claims to imaginative transcendence, the thought is not that the imagination creates the world in a Fichtean sense. Nor, given his strong adherence to God's transcendence and to revelation, are ethics and religion simply constructive projects and certainly not (unless aesthetic) a projection of wishes. But on the other hand, Kierkegaard does not adopt the rationalist picture of "reason" correlating with "reality" and "truth" while the imagination delivers only "unreality." In fashioning possibilities for the self, the imagination creates one's world; it is the passional, existential movements of the self that allow one "truly" to relate to the reality of an ideal or of God.

From first to last Kierkegaard's concern is consistent; the <u>uses</u> of the imagination, the "how" of the imagination as well as the "what." And this makes Kierkegaard's reflections on the imagination especially relevant to contemporary portrayals of aesthetics, ethics, and religion as forms of imaginative construction; his dialectic reminds us that such portrayals are incomplete if they point only to the content of the "imagined world," ignoring the passion of existence. If the crucial distinctiveness of "how" one is imaginative is lost, such discussions can become not only descriptively inaccurate but also "fantastic."

Because his concern is with how a person is imaginative, in the end Kierkegaard's remarks on the imagination are intended not as a system or theory, but as a series of reminders, and a therapeutic. His concern is never simply with description but with the training and eliciting of an individual's imaginative capacities as they are forged in the rigors of existence. His hope is that his remarks can aid and increase the imaginative abilities of human beings, to point out the dangers of fantasy, to raise before his readers possibilities they have not entertained.

But Kierkegaard knew as well that objective means alone--even a dialectic of the imagination--cannot guarantee an adequate subjective and passionate development of one's imagination, for all this too can be entertained in the contemplative distance of the medium of the imagination alone. The gift and task of becoming truly imaginative in existence--that belongs to the individual.

NOTES TO CONCLUSION

[1] Kierkegaard, TC 185. Because Kierkegaard works to extend the place of the imagination beyond contemplative distance and its false infinite, he strives also for a theory and practice of art as indirect communication, in which art's inescapable ideality and distancing are acknowledged yet overcome. Here too there is at once a strong and continuously tensive dialectical emphasis on the negation of art's consolation, and an equally dialectical affirmation of art, aimed at the demands and suffering of existence. The tensive dialectic of indirect communication mirrors the tensive dialectic of the imagination. On indirect communication, see Kierkegaard, JP 1: 617-81; in JP 1: 651 (VIII^2 B 83), n.d., 1847, Kierkegaard discusses indirect communication in relation to the two media of imagination and actuality.

[2] Kierkegaard, JP 3: 3067 (X^2 A 210), n.d., 1854.

[3] Ilham Dilman and Hidé Ishiguro, "Imagination," The Aristotelian Society, Supplementary Volume 41 (London: Harrison, 1967) 33.

[4] Dilman and Ishiguro 34.

[5] Dewey 105ff.

[6] Ludwig Wittgenstein, Lectures and Conversations on Aesthetics, Psychology, and Religious Belief, ed. Cyril Barrett (Berkeley and Los Angeles: U of California P, 1972) 56.

[7] Kierkegaard, CUP 306.

Abrams, M. H. Natural Supernaturalism: Tradition and Revolution in Romantic Literature. New York: Norton, 1971.

Anz, Wilhelm. Kierkegaard und der deutsche Idealismus. Tübingen: Mohr, 1956.

Auden, W. H. "Postscript: Christianity and Art." The Dyer's Hand and Other Essays. New York: Vintage-Random, 1968. 456-61.

Baeumler, Alfred. Kants Kritik der Urteilskraft: ihre Geschichte und Systematik. Halle: Niemeyer, 1923.

Brown, Robert F. The Later Philosophy of Schelling: The Influence of Boehme on the Works of 1809-1815. London: Assoc. U Presses, 1977.

Burgess, Andrew J. Passion, "Knowing How," and Understanding: An Essay on the Concept of Faith. American Acad. of Religion Diss. Series 9. Ed. H. Ganse Little, Jr. Missoula, MT: Scholars, 1975.

Capel, Lee M. "Historical Introduction." The Concept of Irony, With Constant Reference to Socrates. By Søren Kierkegaard. Trans., introd. and notes Lee M. Capel. Bloomington: Indiana UP, 1968. 7-41.

Christensen, Arild. "Der junge Kierkegaard als Schriftstellerpersönlichkeit und die Persönlichkeitsauffassung in den Frühwerken." Orbis Litterarum 18 (1963): 26-47.

---. "Zwei Kierkegaardstudien." Orbis Litterarum 10 (1955): 36-49.

Clark, Malcolm. Logic and System: A Study of the Transition from "Vorstellung" to Thought in the Philosophy of Hegel. The Hague: Nijhoff, 1971.

Coleridge, Samuel Taylor. Biographia Literaria or, Biographical Sketches of My Literary Life and Opinions. Ed. and introd. George Watson. 2nd ed. 1965. London: Everyman's Library, 1971.

Connell, George. To Be One Thing: Personal Unity in Kierkegaard's Thought. Macon, GA: Mercer UP, 1985.

Crites, Stephen. In the Twilight of Christendom: Hegel vs. Kierkegaard on Faith and History. American Acad. of Religion Studies in Religion 2. Ed. Willard G. Oxtoby. Chambersburg, PA: American Acad. of Religion, 1972.

---. "Introduction," Crisis in the Life of an Actress and Other Essays in Drama. By Søren Kierkegaard. Trans., introd. and notes Stephen D. Crites. New York: Torchbook-Harper, 1967.

---. "Pseudonymous Authorship as Art and as Act." Kierkegaard: A Collection of Critical Essays. Ed. Josiah Thompson. Modern Studies in Philosophy. Ed. Amelie Oksenberg Rorty. Garden City, NY: Anchor-Doubleday, 1972. 183-229.

Dewey, Bradley R. The New Obedience: Kierkegaard on Imitating Christ. Fwd. Paul L. Holmer. Washington: Corpus, 1968.

Diem, Hermann. Kierkegaard's Dialectic of Existence. Trans. Harold Knight. Edinburgh and London: Oliver, 1959.

Dilman, Ilham, and Hidé Ishiguro. "Imagination," The Aristotelian Society, Supplementary Volume 41. London: Harrison, 1967.

Dilman, Ilham, and D. Z. Phillips. Sense and Delusion. Studies in Philosophical Psychology. Ed. R. F. Holland. London: Routledge, 1971.

Dunning, Stephen N. Kierkegaard's Dialectic of Inwardness: A Structural Analysis of the Theory of Stages. Princeton: Princeton UP, 1985.

Dupré, Louis. A Dubious Heritage: Studies in the Philosophy of Religion after Kant. New York: Paulist, 1977.

---. Kierkegaard as Theologian: The Dialectic of Christian Existence. New York: Sheed, 1963.

Eichner, Hans. Friedrich Schlegel. Twayne's World Authors Series 98. New York: Twayne, 1970.

---. "Friedrich Schlegel's Theory of Romantic Poetry." Proceedings of the MLA 71 (1959): 1018-41.

Elrod, John W. Being and Existence in Kierkegaard's Pseudonymous Works. Princeton: Princeton UP, 1975.

Engell, James. The Creative Imagination: Enlightenment to Romanticism. Cambridge: Harvard UP, 1981.

Evans, C. Stephen. Kierkegaard's "Fragments" and "Postscript": The Religious Philosophy of Johannes Climacus. Atlantic Highlands, NJ: Humanities, 1983.

Fabro, Cornelio. "Faith and Reason in Kierkegaard's Dialectic." Johnson and Thulstrup 156-206.

Fackenheim, Emil L. The Religious Dimension of Hegel's Thought. Boston: Beacon, 1967.

Fahrenbach, Helmut. Kierkegaards existenzdialektische Ethik. Frankfurt am Main: Klostermann, 1968.

Fenger, Henning. Kierkegaard, The Myths, and Their Origins: Studies in the Kierkegaardian Papers and Letters. Trans. George C. Schoolfield. New Haven: Yale UP, 1980.

Fenger, Henning, and Frederick J. Marker. The Heibergs. Twayne's World Authors Series 105. New York: Twayne, 1971.

Fichte, Johann Gottlieb. Werke. Ed. and introd. Fritz Medicus. 7 vols. Leipzig: Eckardt, 1909-25. Vol. 1.

Fingarette, Herbert. Self-Deception. Studies in Philosophical Psychology. Ed. R. F. Holland. London: Routledge, 1969.

Firchow, Peter. "Introduction." Friedrich Schlegel's Lucinde and the Fragments. By Friedrich Schlegel. Trans. and introd. Peter Firchow. Minneapolis: U of Minnesota P, 1971. 3-39.

Forstman, Jack. A Romantic Triangle: Schleiermacher and Early German Romanticism. American Acad. of Religion Studies in Religion 13. Ed. Stephen Crites. Missoula, MT: Scholars, 1977.

Glockner, Hermann. Hegel-Lexikon. 2nd ed. 2 vols. Stuttgart: Frommanns, 1957.

Grimsley, Ronald. Søren Kierkegaard and French Literature: Eight Comparative Studies. Cardiff: U of Wales P, 1966.

Hablützel, Rudolf. Dialektik und Einbildungskraft: F. W. J. Schellings Lehre von der menschlichen Erkenntnis. Basel: Verlag für Recht und Gesellschaft, 1954.

Harris, H. S. Hegel's Development Toward the Sunlight, 1770-1801. Oxford: Clarendon, 1972.

Hart, Ray L. Unfinished Man and the Imagination: Toward an Ontology and a Rhetoric of Revelation. New York: Herder, 1968.

Hegel, G. W. F. Early Theological Writings. Trans. T. M. Knox. Introd. and Fragments trans. Richard Kroner. Chicago: U of Chicago P, 1948.

---. Hegel's Logic. Trans. William Wallace. Fwd. J. N. Findlay. 3rd ed. Oxford: Clarendon, 1975.

---. Hegel's Philosophie des Subjektiven Geistes. With English trans. Trans. and ed. M. J. Petry. 3 vols. Dordrecht: Reidel, 1978. Vol. 2, Anthropology.

---. Hegel's Philosophy of Mind. Trans. and introd. William Wallace. Oxford: Clarendon, 1894.

---. Hegels Theologische Jugendschriften. Ed. Herman Nohl. Tübingen: Mohr, 1907.

---. Lectures on the History of Philosophy. Trans. E. S. Haldane and Frances H. Simson. 3 vols. London: Routledge, 1955.

---. Phenomenology of Spirit. Trans. A. V. Miller. Analysis of the text and fwd. J. N. Findlay. Oxford: Clarendon, 1977.

---. The Philosophy of Fine Art. Trans. and notes F. P. B. Osmaston. 4 vols. London: Bell, 1920.

---. The Philosophy of History. Trans. and pref. J. Sibree. Pref. Charles Hegel. Introd. C. J. Friedrich. New York: Dover, 1956.

---. Sämtliche Werke. Jubiläumsausgabe. Ed. Hermann Glockner. 20 vols. Stuttgart: Frommann, 1961-71.

Heller, Erich. "The Realistic Fallacy." The Artist's Journey into the Interior and Other Essays. New York: Vintage-Random, 1968. 87-98.

Henricksen, Aage. Methods and Results of Kierkegaard Studies in Scandinavia: A Historical and Critical Survey. Copenhagen: Munskgaard, 1951.

Himmelstrup, Jens. Søren Kierkegaard: International Bibliografi. Copenhagen: Nyt Nordisk, 1962.

Hirsch, Emanuel. Kierkegaard-Studien. 2 vols. Gütersloh: Bertelsmann, 1933.

Hodgson, Peter C. "Editor's Introduction." The Life of Jesus Critically Examined. By David Friedrich Strauss. Trans. from 4th ed. George

Eliot. Ed. and introd. Peter C. Hodgson. Lives of Jesus Series. Ed. Leander E. Keck. Philadelphia: Fortress, 1972. xv-l.

Hofe, Gerhard vom. Die Romantikkritik Sören Kierkegaards. Frankfurt am Main: Athenäum, 1972.

Hohler, T. P. Imagination and Reflection: Intersubjectivity: Fichte's Grundlage of 1794. Martinus Nijhoff Philosophy Library 8. The Hague: Nijhoff, 1982.

Holmer, Paul L. "Kierkegaard and Logic." Kierkegaardiana II (1957): 25-42.

Hong, Howard V. "Tanke-Experiment in Kierkegaard." McKinnon, Kierkegaard: Resources and Results 39-51.

Hong, Howard V., and Edna H. Hong. "Historical Introduction." Fear and Trembling and Repetition. By Søren Kierkegaard. Ed. and trans. Howard V. Hong and Edna H. Hong with introd. and notes. Kierkegaard's Writings, 6. Princeton: Princeton UP, 1983. ix-xxxix.

---. "Historical Introduction." The Sickness Unto Death. By Søren Kierkegaard. Ed. and trans. with introd. and notes Howard V. Hong and Edna H. Hong. Kierkegaard's Writings 19. Princeton: Princeton UP, 1980. ix-xxiii.

Horn, Robert L. "Positivity and Dialectic: A Study of the Theological Method of Hans Lassen Martensen." Diss. Union Theological Seminary, New York, 1969.

Hotho, H. G. Vorstudien für Leben und Kunst. Stuttgart and Tübingen, 1835.

Immerwahr, Raymond. "The Subjectivity or Objectivity of Friedrich Schlegel's Poetic Irony," Germanic Review 26 (1951): 173-91.

Johnson, Howard A., and Niels Thulstrup, eds. A Kierkegaard Critique. New York: Harper, 1962.

Johnson, Ralph Henry. The Concept of Existence in the Concluding Unscientific Postscript. The Hague: Nijhoff, 1972.

Jørgensen, Aage. Søren Kierkegaard-Litteratur 1961-1970: En Forelobig Bibliografi. Aarhus: Akademisk, 1971.

Kant, Immanuel. Critique of Judgment. Trans. and introd. J. H. Bernard. Hafner Library of Classics 14. 1951. New York: Hafner, 1972.

---. Critique of Pure Reason. Trans. Norman Kemp Smith. 1929. New York: St. Martin's, 1965.

Kierkegaard, Søren. On Authority and Revelation: The Book on Adler, or a Cycle of Ethico-Religious Essays. Trans. and ed. Walter Lowrie. Introd. Frederick Sontag. Cloister Library. New York: Torchbook-Harper, 1966.

---. Christian Discourses and The Lilies of the Field and the Birds of the Air and Three Discourses at the Communion on Fridays. Trans., introd. and notes Walter Lowrie. Princeton: Princeton UP, 1940.

---. The Concept of Anxiety. Trans. and ed. with notes Reidar Thomte, with Albert B. Anderson. Kierkegaard's Writings 8. Princeton: Princeton UP, 1980.

---. The Concept of Dread. Trans., introd. and notes Walter Lowrie. 2nd ed. Princeton: Princeton UP, 1957.

---. The Concept of Irony, With Constant Reference to Socrates. Trans., introd. and notes Lee M. Capel. Bloomington: Indiana UP, 1968.

---. Concluding Unscientific Postscript. Trans. David F. Swenson. Trans. completed, introd., and notes Walter Lowrie. Princeton: Princeton UP, 1941.

---. Crisis in the Life of an Actress and Other Essays on Drama. Trans., introd. and notes Stephen D. Crites. New York: Torchbook-Harper, 1967.

---. Edifying Discourses: A Selection. Trans. David F. and Lillian Marvin Swenson. Ed. and introd. Paul L. Holmer. New York: Torchbook-Harper, 1958.

---. Either/Or, Vol. 1. Trans. David F. Swenson and Lillian Marvin Swenson. Rev. and fwd. Howard A. Johnson. Princeton: Princeton UP, 1959.

---. Either/Or, Vol. 2. Trans. Walter Lowrie. Rev. and fwd. Howard A. Johnson. Princeton: Princeton UP, 1959.

---. Fear and Trembling and Repetition. Ed. and trans., with introd. and notes, Howard V. Hong and Edna H. Hong. Kierkegaard's Writings 6. Princeton: Princeton UP, 1983.

---. Fear and Trembling and The Sickness Unto Death. Trans., introd. and notes Walter Lowrie. Princeton: Princeton UP, 1954.

---. For Self-Examination and Judge for Yourselves! and Three Discourses, 1851. Trans., introd. and notes Walter Lowrie. Princeton: Princeton UP, 1941.

---. The Gospel of Suffering and The Lilies of the Field. Trans. David F. Swenson and Lillian Marvin Swenson. Minneapolis: Augsburg, 1948.

---. Kierkegaard's Attack Upon "Christendom," 1854-1855. Trans. and introd. Walter Lowrie. Princeton: Princeton UP, 1944.

---. Letters and Documents. Trans. Henrik Rosenmeier. Kierkegaard's Writings 25. Princeton: Princeton UP, 1978.

---. Philosophical Fragments, or A Fragment of Philosophy. Trans. and introd. David Swenson. New introd. and commentary Niels Thulstrup.

Trans. rev. and commentary trans. Howard V. Hong. Princeton: Princeton UP, 1967.

---. Philosophical Fragments and Johannes Climacus. Ed. and trans. with introd. and notes Howard V. Hong and Edna H. Hong. Kierkegaard's Writings 7. Princeton: Princeton UP, 1985.

---. The Point of View for My Work as an Author: A Report to History, and Related Writings. Trans., introd. and notes Walter Lowrie. Ed. and pref. Benjamin Nelson. Cloister Library. New York: Torchbook-Harper, 1962.

---. Purity of Heart Is To Will One Thing: Spiritual Preparation for the Office of Confession. Trans. and introd. Douglas V. Steere. Cloister Library. New York: Torchbook-Harper, 1948.

---. Samlede Vaerker. Ed. A. B. Drachmann, P. A. Heiberg, and H. O. Lange. 2nd ed. 15 vols. Copenhagen: Gyldendal, 1920-36.

---. The Sickness Unto Death. Trans. and ed. Howard V. Hong and Edna H. Hong. Kierkegaard's Writings 19. Princeton: Princeton UP, 1980.

---. Søren Kierkegaard's Journals and Papers. Trans. and ed. Howard V. Hong and Edna H. Hong. 7 vols. Bloomington: Indiana UP, 1967-78.

---. Søren Kierkegaards Papirer. Ed. P. A. Heiberg, V. Kuhr, and E. Torsting. 20 vols., I-XI^3. Copenhagen: Gyldendal, 1909-48.

---. Stages on Life's Way. Trans. Walter Lowrie. Introd. Paul Sponheim. New York: Schocken, 1967.

---. Training in Christianity and The Edifying Discourse which 'Accompanied' It. Trans., introd. and notes Walter Lowrie. Princeton: Princeton UP, 1941.

---. Works of Love: Some Christian Reflections in the Form of Discourses. Trans. Howard and Edna Hong. Pref. R. Gregor Smith. Cloister Library. New York: Torchbook-Harper, 1962.

Lebowitz, Naomi. Kierkegaard: A Life of Allegory. Baton Rouge and London: Louisiana State UP, 1985.

Lovejoy, Arthur O. "Schiller and the Genesis of German Romanticism." Essays in the History of Ideas. Baltimore: Johns Hopkins UP, 1948.

Lukes, Steven. Individualism. Key Concepts in the Social Sciences. Ed. Philip Rieff and Bryan R. Wilson. Oxford: Blackwell, 1973.

McCarthy, Vincent A. The Phenomenology of Moods in Kierkegaard. The Hague: Nijhoff, 1978.

Mackey, Louis. Kierkegaard: A Kind of Poet. Philadelphia: U of Pennsylvania P, 1971.

McKinnon, Alastair, ed. Kierkegaard: Resources and Results. Waterloo, Ontario: Wilfred Laurier UP, 1982.

---, ed. The Kierkegaard Indices to Kierkegaards Samlede Vaerker. 4 vols. Leiden: Brill, 1970-75.

Malantschuk, Gregor. Kierkegaard's Thought. Ed. and trans. Howard V. Hong and Edna H. Hong. Princeton: Princeton UP, 1971.

Martensen, Hans Lassen. Christian Dogmatics: A Compendium of the Doctrines of Christianity. Trans. Rev. William Urwick. Edinburgh: T. & T. Clark, 1898.

---. Die Christliche Dogmatik. Trans. from Danish. 2nd. ed. Kiel: Schröder, 1853.

Matenko, Percy. Tieck and Solger: The Complete Correspondence. New York: Westermann, 1933.

Mesnard, Pierre. Le Vrai Visage de Kierkegaard. Paris: Beauchesne, 1948.

Mitchell, P.M. A History of Danish Literature. With introductory ch. Mogens Haugsted. Copenhagen: Gyldendal, 1975.

Mullen, John D. "The German Romantic Background of Kierkegaard's Psychology." Southern Journal of Philosophy 16 (Spring 1978): 649-60.

Murdoch, Iris. The Sovereignty of Good. New York: Schocken, 1970.

Nordentoft, Kresten. Kierkegaard's Psychology. Trans. Bruce H. Kirmmse. Duquesne Studies: Psychological Series 7. Pittsburgh: Duquesne UP; Atlantic Highlands, NJ: distr. Humanities, 1978.

Novalis [Friedrich von Hardenberg]. Werke. Ed. with commentary Gerhard Schulz. Munich: Beck, 1969.

Paulsen, Anna. Sören Kierkegaard: Deuter unserer Existenz. Hamburg: Wittig, 1955.

Perkins, Robert L. "Comment on Hong." McKinnon, Kierkegaard: Resources and Results 52-55.

Roberts, Robert. "Kierkegaard on Becoming an 'Individual.'" Scottish Journal of Theology 31 (1978): 133-52.

Rosenkranz, Karl. Psychologie, oder die Wissenschaft vom subjectiven Geist. 2nd ed. Königsberg: Bornträger, 1843.

Ryle, Gilbert. The Concept of Mind. New York: Barnes, 1949.

Schelling, F. W. J. System of Transcendental Idealism (1800). Trans. Peter Heath. Introd. Michael Vater. Charlottesville: UP of Virginia, 1978.

Schiller, Friedrich. "Das verschleierte Bild zu Sais." Werke. Ed. Alfred Brandstetter. 6 vols. Zürich: Stauffacher, 1967. 1: 227-30.

Schjørring, J. H. "Martensen." Thulstrup and Thulstrup, Kierkegaard's Teachers 177-207.

Schlegel, Friedrich. Friedrich Schlegel's Lucinde and the Fragments. Trans. and introd. Peter Firchow. Minneapolis: U of Minnesota P, 1971.

Schleiermacher, Friedrich. <u>Vertraute Briefe über die</u> Lucinde. Stuttgart, 1835.

Shmueli, Adi. <u>Kierkegaard and Consciousness</u>. Trans. Naomi Handelman. Introd. Paul L. Holmer. Princeton: Princeton UP, 1971.

Simpson, David, ed. <u>German Aesthetic and Literary Criticism: Kant to Hegel</u>. Cambridge: Cambridge UP, 1984.

Skjoldager, E. "An Unwanted Ally: Magnus Eiriksson." Thulstrup and Thulstrup, <u>Kierkegaard as a Person</u> 102-08.

Solger, K. W. F. <u>Nachgelassene Schriften und Briefwechsel</u>. Ed. Ludwig Tieck and Friedrich von Raumer. 2 vols. Leipzig: Brockhaus, 1826.

---. <u>Vorlesungen über Aesthetik</u>. Ed. K. W. L. Heyse. Leipzig: Brockhaus, 1829.

Søe, N. H. "Kierkegaard's Doctrine of the Paradox." Johnson and Thulstrup 207-27.

Steffens, Henrik. <u>Caricaturen des Heiligsten</u>. 2 vols. Leipzig, 1819-21.

Stendahl, Brita. <u>Søren Kierkegaard</u>. Twayne's World Author Series 392. Boston: Twayne, 1976.

Swenson, David F. "The Existential Dialectic of Søren Kierkegaard." <u>Something About Kierkegaard</u>. Ed. Lillian Marvin Swenson. Minneapolis: Augsburg, 1941. 71-94.

Taylor, Charles. <u>Hegel</u>. Cambridge: Cambridge UP, 1975.

Taylor, Mark C. <u>Journeys to Selfhood: Hegel and Kierkegaard</u>. Berkeley: U of California P, 1980.

---. <u>Kierkegaard's Pseudonymous Authorship</u>. Princeton: Princeton UP, 1975.

Thompson, Josiah, ed. <u>Kierkegaard: A Collection of Critical Essays</u>. Modern Studies in Philosophy. Ed. Amelie Oksenberg Rorty. Garden City, NY: Anchor-Doubleday, 1972.

Thomte, Reidar. "Historical Introduction." The Concept of Anxiety. By Søren Kierkegaard. Trans. and ed. with introd. and notes Reidar Thomte, with Albert B. Anderson. Kierkegaard's Writings 8. Princeton: Princeton UP, 1980. vii-xviii.

---. Kierkegaard's Philosophy of Religion. Princeton: Princeton UP, 1948.

Thulstrup, Niels. Commentary on Kierkegaard's Concluding Unscientific Postscript, with a New Introduction. Trans. Robert J. Widenmann. Princeton: Princeton UP, 1984.

---. Kierkegaard's Relation to Hegel. Trans. George L. Stengren. Ltd. Paperback Editions. Princeton: Princeton UP, 1980.

Thulstrup, Niels, and Marie Mikulová Thulstrup, eds. Kierkegaard as a Person. Vol. 12 of Bibliotheca Kierkegaardiana. 12 vols. to date. Copenhagen: Reitzel, 1978- .

---, eds. Kierkegaard's Teachers. Vol. 10 of Bibliotheca Kierkegaardiana. 12 vols. to date. Copenhagen: Reitzel, 1978- .

Tieck, Ludwig. Werke. Ed. with concluding remarks and notes Marianne Thalmann. 4 vols. Munich: Winkler, 1963-66.

Tymms, Ralph. German Romantic Literature. London: Methuen, 1955.

Wahl, Jean. Etudes Kierkegaardiennes. Paris: Librairie Philosophique J. Vrin, 1949.

---. "Kierkegaard et le romantisme." Orbis Litterarum 10 (1955): 297-302.

Walzel, Oskar. German Romanticism. Trans. Alma Elise Lussky. New York: Putnam's, 1932.

Welch, Claude. Protestant Thought in the Nineteenth Century. 2 vols. New Haven: Yale UP, 1972-85. Vol. 1, 1799-1870.

Wellek, René. The Romantic Age. Vol. 2 of A History of Modern Criticism, 1750-1950. 5 vols. New Haven: Yale UP, 1955-86.

Wheeler, Kathleen M., ed. German Aesthetic and Literary Criticism: The Romantic Ironists and Goethe. Cambridge: Cambridge UP, 1984.

Widenmann, Robert J. "Sibbern." Thulstrup and Thulstrup, Kierkegaard's Teachers 70-88.

Wittgenstein, Ludwig. Lectures and Conversations on Aesthetics, Psychology, and Religious Belief. Ed. Cyril Barrett. Berkeley and Los Angeles: U of California P, 1972.

Yerkes, James. The Christology of Hegel. American Acad. of Religion Diss. Series 23. Missoula, MT: Scholars, 1978.

INDEX